THE LIBERATION OF CAPITAL

Publications:

—in German

Grundzüge einer personalistischen Wert-theorie, Jena 1924
(Dissertation)

Volkswirtschaftliche Theorie der landwirtschaftlichen Preissteigerungen in Deutschland 1895-1913, Berlin 1925.

Der Kreislauf der Wirtschaft, Jena 1928

Metamorphosen der Wirtschaft, Jena 1931

Grundwahrheiten einer organischen Wirtschaft, Zürich 1934

Selbstgestaltung der Wirtschaft, Freiburg i. Br. 1950

Befreiung der Arbeit, Freiburg i. Br. 1965

Reform des Steuerwesens, Freiburg i. Br. 1968

Das Kapital und das Geld, Schaffhausen 1981

Das Kapital und die Zukunft, Schaffhausen 1981

—in English translation

New Forms of Ownership in Industry, Rajghat 1962

The Liberation of Work, London 1969

The Liberation of Capital

FOLKERT WILKEN

Translated by DAVID GREEN

London

GEORGE ALLEN & UNWIN

Boston　　　　　Sydney

First published in 1982

GEORGE ALLEN & UNWIN LTD
40 Museum Street, London WC1A 1LU

© Original German edition DAS KAPITAL, Novalis Verlag AG, 1976

© English language edition, George Allen & Unwin Ltd., 1982

© Editorial notes and English translation, David Green, 1982

© Foreword, Daniel Jones, 1982

© Introduction, Alasdair Clayre, 1982

British Library Cataloguing in Publication Data

Wilken, Folkert
  Liberation of capital.
  1. Cooperation
  I. Title
  334'.6   HD5650   80-41848

ISBN 0-04-334005-9

Typeset by An Grianán

Printed in Great Britain by
Biddles Ltd, Guildford, Surrey

Contents

Foreword

The beginning of the 1970's saw a complete change in the economic fortunes of the world economy. Schumacher called it a watershed in the history of the western world. After a decade of prolonged recession and ever-increasing unemployment we seem to be no nearer to really understanding the fundamental reasons for this state of affairs, or any wiser as to how we might get out of it. In contrast to the 1950's and 1960's, which might be regarded as the heyday of economics, when economists appeared to have at least some of the important answers, this is evidently not so true today. This success of economics was of course during a period of unprecedentedly rapid and sustained growth. Subsequent events showed that this growth was built upon a whole series of political, social and technological props and not only on the ability of Keynesian economics to help avoid slumps and to fine-tune the economy. As soon as some of these other props which under-pinned this growth fell away, such as the breakdown of the trade and exchange rate system led and underwritten by the USA, and the end of the era of cheap oil, the inherent limitations of conventional economics became evident.

During this time of rapid growth, and perhaps false confidence, economists, driven by a desire for scientific respectability, became increasingly intrigued with modelling the economy in a highly abstract, mechanistic way, in an attempt to bring the economy back to some kind of equilibrium. When the world ceased to behave according to this way of thinking and the assumptions behind such an approach broke down economists got caught up in a bitter dispute about the virtues of Keynesianism versus monetarism. This debate was conducted with an almost ideological fervour and encouraged, or possibly initiated, an ever-increasing ideological polarisation in the political life of the west as the search for solutions became more desperate. With the benefit of hindsight this debate seems not only to have been highly damaging to the evolution of the world economy but also a distraction from the real task of looking for a new basis on which to begin to understand the needs of the contemporary world situation.

While conventional macro-economics is bogged down in these ideological disputes, the newly-fashionable economics which looks at the supply side of the economy, and at how we manage to adjust the structure of our economy to the rapidly changing international division of labour, new technologies, etc, offers the rather dismal and unpromising prospect of the survival of the fittest in a world of intensely sharper competition. Under this scenario the nation that most single-mindedly pursues the goal of industrial competitiveness will prosper at the expense of those less able or less willing to make the necessary social and political adjustments. Some fairly fundamental changes in our lifestyle and occupations are certainly necessary to reap the benefits of our technology and to accommodate the legitimate desires of the newly industrialising countries to enter the industrial system.

This kind of future is however unconvincing and humanly unpalatable in that it is too one-sided and ignores the dignity of the human being and subjects all the other human concerns to the goal of increased efficiency. Conventional economics does not tell us how to strike the right balance between these different objectives. Taken to its logical extreme such a future carries within itself the seeds of its own destruction. As the temptation to resort to nationalistic solutions grows the very system of international co-operation and interchange that is essential for the healthy functioning of a highly interdependent world is frustrated and undermined. Once begun this development quickly becomes cumulative and even more damaging. This is exactly what happened in the 1930's, after the depression of 1929-31.

Many economists would probably admit to a distinct sense of unease about the state of the discipline today. This disillusionment with economics is certainly apparent outside the profession. But where is a new perspective to come from and what are the essential ingredients? Some would look for a new Keynes, who could stand conventional wisdom on its head and lead us to a new synthesis. However one has the distinct feeling that the current situation demands a more fundamental reappraisal that takes account of the new impulses and concerns that became visible in the 1970's. In other words we need to go back to basics, to re-examine the key elements of the economic system in a new light. This is the starting point of Wilken's analysis.

In this book Wilken builds on the foundation laid by economists from both the Anglo-Saxon and German traditions. To this he adds insights into the nature of the human being and his involvement in the economic process drawn from the work of Rudolf Steiner, which will undoubtedly present a considerable challenge to those who meet them for the first time. In doing so he lays the basis for a completely new understanding of how the economy works. As a result he develops a wealth of new insights that bring us a significant step forward in understanding such things as the ownership of capital and land, and the nature and workings of competition, amongst others, which lie at the root of our contemporary troubles. Those who meet such a challenging analysis and really grapple with what is presented here will find it unlocks many doors in their thinking and leads to a new level of awareness of their own actions in social and economic life. Many will find themselves going back to read and reread this book time and time again, thereby enriching their thinking out of their experience and vice versa.

Another impulse at work in the 1970's, which took many different forms, was a search for a more holistic, alternative approach to contemporary questions. This impulse has three dimensions. Its primary concern is to rediscover the human being in its full potential, both physical and spiritual, and to reject the statistically average economic actor of the economic models. Secondly, it is looking to develop new forms of social relationships that allow the fulfilment of the true creative faculties of the human being through collective interaction. Thirdly, it has for the first time a concern for the wealth of the world as a whole. It was of course at this time also that we first saw the image of the world as seen from space.

This impulse first found dramatic expression in the student uprisings of the late 1960's and later metamorphosed into the various strands of the ecological movement and the search for spiritual liberation, new social forms and alternative lifestyles. Ernest Schumacher captured the imagination of this generation and brought this impulse to expression in his book *Small is Beautiful*, in which, and in subsequent books, he showed us how to ask the right questions. In his deeds, for instance in founding the Intermediate Technology Development Group, he went a long way towards demonstrating some of the answers. Wilken's analysis addresses the same questions, providing a comprehensive framework out of which a deeper understanding of them is possible.

In doing so he will undoubtedly add a new dimension to the experience of those involved in the diverse practical initiatives that have sprung up in recent years. Forerunners of this movement, such as Ernest Bader, who founded the Scott Bader Commonwealth, have already found much inspiration from the German original of this book; now it can reach a wider English-speaking audience.

Perhaps surprisingly for a book with such obvious contemporary relevance, the basic ideas on which Wilken draws were first outlined in considerable detail by Rudolf Steiner shortly after the first world war. Other areas of Steiner's work were the founding of a worldwide school movement and new directions in medicine, agriculture, architecture, religion, the arts and scientific research; however his economic ideas were little understood at the time and had to wait for a more receptive period, and for their further development in such a synthesis as this. His two main works on social and economic questions are *World Economy* and *Towards Social Renewal*. Steiner, a man of extraordinary vision, who lived from 1861 to 1925, laid the foundations of a new understanding of the human being and the significance of his life on earth, known as Anthroposophy, through which he showed that it was possible in a quite modern, scientific way to develop a consciousness of the world beyond our ordinary sense experiences, and thereby reach a more complete conception of the whole human being. This he elaborated in over 6000 lectures and a number of books, of which the most important are his *Philosophy of Freedom* and *Knowledge of Higher Worlds* (Rudolf Steiner Press 1970 and 1976). Out of his own experience he was able to provide guidance to those who sought to develop new impulses in various spheres of human activity, described in more detail in *Work Arising from the Life of Rudolf Steiner*, edited by John Davy (Rudolf Steiner Press 1975). These include the Waldorf schools, the communities for the mentally handicapped, and biodynamic agriculture. More recent developments are an Anthroposophical financing enterprise, the Mercury Provident Society, and the organisation development and social relations counselling work of Social Ecology Associates. Maybe for the first time, through this book, Steiner's ideas on basic economic questions will find a wider response and lead to further practical initiatives to heal the growing sickness in our economic and social body politic.

Daniel T. Jones

Science Policy Research Unit,
The University of Sussex

Introduction

This book poses three important questions:

1 Is there a better form of economic organisation than those offered by present-day capitalism or communism?
2 Can the economy be realistically studied with a radically different set of assumptions about human nature from those hitherto conventionally accepted in economics?
3 Can capital be given a new role both in economic thought and in economic thought and in economic life, and be understood as an essential link between the 'material' aspects of the world, and what Rudolf Steiner christened the *Geistesleben*—a German word, difficult to translate precisely, meaning the intellectual, spiritual, and cultural life of mankind?*

All these threads are drawn together in a major theme of the book: that co-operation—whether in the form of the industrial common ownership movement or in the parallel forms of capital-labour partnerships now being worked out in different parts of the world—is of central importance to the future of the economy and of mankind.

The third question—about the role of capital—may sound forbiddingly abstract. It can be rephrased, in a rough way, very much more simply: 'How differently would people see the world, and how differently would they want to organise it, if they took literally rather than figuratively the saying that "the real capital of a business is its ideas"?'

These are fundamental questions. No one must expect a conventional book. It is moreover a German book springing out of a different intellectual tradition from that of 'Anglo-Saxon' economics, and addressing economic questions in an original way. The role allotted to

---

* See Glossary—Ed.

to this introduction is to bridge the gap between modes of thought more familiar to the English and American reader and the tradition in which Wilken is writing, so that the two may become more mutually comprehensible.

I believe this may best be done through a short statement—translated into 'Anglo-Saxon' terms—of the central conception of capital discussed in the book followed by a brief excursion into the history of ideas, and particularly of German and British ideas of the late eighteenth and early nineteenth centuries, to explain the differences between the two traditions.

Wilken traces the whole movement of economic history, and the origin of capital itself, from the *thought* behind inventions and behind the division or organisation of labour. It is this *thought* which is both the great source of all economic improvement and the continual disruptor of all economic and social balance.

Because of it, human society is in a constant state of disequilibrium and change. Thus the 'equilibrium' models of the economy generally favoured by Anglo-Saxon economics, with their distant origins in the dominant seventeenth century science of mechanics, are less helpful for understanding it than the restlessly changing 'organic' picture of the world offered by a German tradition of thought—which includes Hegel and Marx—and for which the study of conflict, revolution and the history of man perpetually transforming himself by his own actions are more important sources of inspiration than the contemplation of equilibrium.

Men in the earliest state of society—or in any coherent economic model of that state—can be assumed to have attained only the most temporary economic 'equilibrium' after the first division of labour between families or men. So much is common ground between the traditions—that in which Wilken is writing and that of, say, Adam Smith. For a very short time the value of the work of one family, when brought to market or exchanged in other ways, may be held to be to have been roughly equivalent to that of every other family if they had started with roughly equal endowments.

Otherwise—using conventional economic assumptions—there would have been 'trading', changes of occupation or, more brutally, starvation to bring such an approximate 'equilibrium' into being. This is very broadly in line with Adam Smith's own idea that in the very earliest stage of society—though he stressed only then—some balance between the value of the labour of each person must generally have prevailed.

Wilken follows Adam Smith in pointing out that human beings are always trying to shorten and lighten their work by invention and by the further division of labour. Wilken suggests that this is because they are trying to unite themselves, or re-unite themselves with the world of *Geist*—mind or spirit—which labour separates them from.

Adam Smith argued more prosaically that it is simply because most people like 'ease, liberty and happiness'. But *why* people try to shorten and lighten their labour is not essential to the reasoning at this stage: the fact that they do, and that they think hard about how to attain this end, is the essential point in Wilken's argument.

There is always a period during which the inventor or the more efficient organiser of work has an economic advantage: he can sell more at lower cost, while still for a time charging the old prices, or at least something above 'normal' costs. It is this gain that gives rise to 'capital' in its financial sense—the accumulation of money or other forms of command over surplus resources.

The continual inventiveness of human beings is the source—and the only source—of capital. Thus in Wilken's exposition capital is not primarily to be thought of as money in a financier's hands or equipment in an existing factory; nor is it primarily to be seen as the armoury of the rich for exploiting the poor as in Marxism; it is an intellectual, cultural, even 'spiritual' force originating in continual innovation, creating both the possibility of, and the desire for, a liberation of man from physical labour, to find his 'true' place in a world of mental and cultural activity—the *Geistesleben*; the kind of activity that is not merely engaged in for the satisfaction of needs, but is valued for its own sake alone.

Capital in this sense arises not out of any single person's intellectual effort alone but out of the accumulated inventive and creative capacities of previous generations and to some extent of other men at any one time. Furthermore as 'new suppliers enter the market', or copying the innovation, or as for other reasons prices adjust downwards in response to each new invention, the whole benefit of the innovation is eventually dispersed to society as a whole. Capital is neither by origin, nor by destination, the property of any individual. The question of who should appropriate the—temporary—benefits of new inventions is thus a wide open one in this analysis.

It ought in Wilken's view to be solved by society. But who or what exactly is society, in this context, and how is society to solve this problem?

In practice, in 'capitalism', it is overwhelmingly the provider of finance for the exploitation of new ideas who both takes the subsequent commercial risks—though not the risks and costs involved in invention itself, with its failures as well as likely successes—and, when successful, tends to appropriate most of the resultant returns today. Yet the origin of the invention is not in the financial world at all. So this, it can be argued, is unjust; and tends to heap up power unreasonably in the hands of those who already have it, and who have nothing else to offer except it.

A second solution is that the benefits should immediately belong to all men through a complete absence, for example, of patents; or through local co-operatively provided finance open equally to any inventor who donates the fruits of his ideas to 'society' in some form, e.g. to the local community, the local co-operative fund, or the state. Yet if all such benefits were immediately diffused generally—that is to say dispersed in lower prices—capital to finance the next research or develop the next invention might have been dissipated and absorbed in consumption, and as technology became more complex, development would be too expensive for any individual or small group to finance. On the other solution; the dangers of control of all resources by self-perpetuating State officials loom large, though given democratic controls, particularly of the latter, they might not by insuperable.

But perhaps, as Wilken suggests, the intellectual, cultural and spiritual life of society has a special claim on the benefits of invention, since it is here that invention originates. Capital is—to sum up—in Wilken's reasoning a mental or spiritual phenomenon, and its returns belong, if anywhere, where it originated. This is a bold idea, and one whose consequences need more space that is here available to develop it. The book explores it at length.

The introduction is not the place either to recapitulate Wilken's other ideas in detail. Certain other points he makes, however, may be of interest. Wilken stresses that the arts, unlike manual labour, are not a sphere in which people generally seek to shorten and lighten their labour; they function either 'non-economically' or by a different kind of economics, where to *give* most, rather than to hoard and minimise the expenditure of effort, is the principle of activity. Secondly, following Rudolf Steiner, he argues that the different realms of society—the cultural or intellectual (the *Geistesleben*), the political and juridical (the *Rechtsleben*) and the economic (the *Wirtschaftsleben*) can be thought of separately and ought to follow their own separate principles.

Indeed the full implications of this idea include the legal separation of the different spheres of life in society: a conception involving complexities beyond the scope of this introduction.

Let us now consider briefly the difference between the tradition of economic thought in which Wilken is writing, and that which stems, roughly, from Adam Smith. 'Anglo-Saxon' economics, as has been suggested above, has a profound affinity with the science of mechanics. Adam Smith's intellectual hero was Newton, and though he did not simply apply Newtonian mechanics to the study of social life, he did look for some single unifying principle—comparable to gravity in the Newtonian universe—that would invisibly hold together the separate atoms of the social world in an orderly rather than a chaotic way. Adam Smith argues that there was a minimum unifying social force in all economic activity—individual material self-interest—and sought to show that the results in a decentralised system, provided markets were competitive and particularly provided there was minimum government interference.

When, a century later, economics were reshaped on mathematical lines, it was again from mechanics that many of the analogies—and much of the mathematics—were derived. Thus, from Adam Smith onwards, the notion of an equilibrium outcome of free competitive exchange between self-interested agents in the market, and the association between that and the potential benefit to all, have retained a favoured place in the British and American economic tradition. Indeed one might argue that this optimistic and mechanistic model has been at the centre of thinking about markets in Anglo-Saxon economics since 1776.

By contrast, the intellectual world from which Wilken comes took its decisive shape two centuries ago out of a reaction to all such thinking. When Adam Smith's *Inquiry into the Nature and Causes of the Wealth of Nations* was translated and published in Germany about 1795, it came into an intellectual world already in revolt against the Newtonian atomistic thought of the previous hundred years. The idea of mechanism as an analogy for human nature and for society was in disgrace among the most influential German thinkers of the day. Herder, Schiller and Goethe had all argued for an 'organic' conception of both man and society—one that stressed the differences between mankind and mechanism. One of the most influential works of the time—Schiller's *On the Aesthetic Education of Man in a Series of Letters* (also published in

1795)—poses the problem of 'alienation' (as it has later been called) in terms of a battle between all that is 'organic' in the world—which is good and fully human—and what is mechanistic—which is artificial, divided, atomistic, dry and lifeless. Goethe and Schiller were formative thinkers for Rudolf Steiner, who in turn had a profound influence on Wilken.

That late eighteenth century intellectual turmoil helped to create a new tradition of social thought in Marxism. Hegel, Marx's great early influence, read the *Aethestic Letters* enthusiastically when they were published, in the formative years of his intellectual development, and although he later turned against some of his youthful enthusiasm for Schiller he retained the feeling that society must be understood in terms of growth and change and movement rather than through any static model; the sense of disequilibrium, not equilibrium, is the characteristic state of society at any time; and the idea that there is no unchanging human nature underlying the variety of historical phenomena. All these ideas were part of Marx's inheritance and have played a decisive part in the world's thought and history ever since.

Wilken, entering into the same original German tradition, has created a position of his own, different from Marx's, founded on a belief in equality and also in liberty, which Marxism can be rejected for neglecting. Wilken also offers a sharp critique of the single party and the all-powerful state, which he dismisses as inefficient as well as tyrannical. At the same time, he does not accept, as would be customary in the Anglo-Saxon tradition, that he must write only 'economics' if he is writing about the economy. Like those German writers of two hundred years ago, he fuses insights from psychology and philosophy with theories about the economy and with readings from history and from sociology, in one and the same book.

Some may find it hard to follow Wilken in taking from Rudolf Steiner an analysis of the psychological effects of mass production. For instance, he writes that the worker finds the confrontation of work with a money wage to be 'the negation of his essential humanity', and that a "desire... burns in the worker's soul... to be free from the bourgeoisie and its economic and political power"—which desire is the motive force behind the world revolutionary movement associated today with Marxist communism. If certain Third World peoples were made the subjects of such sentences, however, and if the role of political elites generally in seizing power in their own interests is given greater prominence, and if the statements were transferred to the international arena where the deep passions of nationalism do genuinely seem to have brought about in several instances feelings and experiences attributed here to the worker, then these statements might more accurately depict the modern world.

Again, the author refers frequently to a 'correct' balance between the quantity of money and the quantity of goods, without specifying how it is to be judged. His references to production for 'need' rather than of unnecessary goods and to the notion of an 'adequate' number of cars are of great interest in a world where ecology has tended to be neglected by most economists. Yet in themselves they appear to beg some of the major questions of contemporary economic theory. What are human needs, and who decides them? What if one person wants a car and another person thinks there is an adequate number already, so the first person ought not to have one? These are not easy questions. The market system, which offers one kind of solution without State control, is deeply imperfect. The question is however whether and how it can be altered, without the substitution of something worse in its place.

In this context, Wilken's distinction between competition and 'emulation' is of particular interest. Emulation is the force that leads artists, craftsmen and in the right conditions potentially all workers in Wilken's view, to wish to excel, without necessarily wishing to conquer or—still less—to destroy those with whom they may compare themselves. Competition is, in Wilken's view, the malignant growth out of emulation, with aggression, egoism, insecurity and destructiveness all confusing the fundamental human impulse to excel. How can the role of competition be diminished and that of emulation be encouraged in a market system.

One possible answer is the spread of co-operation. Co-operation often tends to be studied by people who believe that man is naturally more co-operative than economists assume: and correspondingly the subject of co-operation tends to be neglected by those who think that 'economic man' is at least a reasonable first approximation to human nature in society. Paradoxically, it can be an obstacle to the study of co-operation if it is connected with the advocacy of very much more idealistic notions of what human nature is like than those customary in economic theory.

If co-operation is to 'float'—both as an intellectual topic and as a real-world form of organisation—it must float on the general ocean.

It may be best therefore to examine it with neutral pre-suppositions about human nature—indeed possibly even to start with the 'economic man' of conventional economic theory. For if co-operation and participation can be shown to work on these terms, this may be more readily accepted than the assumption that men are more co-operative than 'economic man'. To adopt this approach as a strategy does not commit one to the belief that men really *are* so greedy or selfish—indeed, this is almost certainly false. It is highly likely that if the economy were more co-operatively organised people might find greater expression for their less greedy and selfish impulses, and thus human nature might change. Even such 'realists' as John Stuart Mill, Stanley Jevons and Alfred Marshall argued the case for co-operation and for workers' participation in the form of capital-labour partnerships.

Altruistic concern for the interests of the economic system as a whole is not the only alternative to egoism and materialistic self-interest. People can escape from such behaviour by concerning themselves with the interests of groups to which they belong. The history of the family offers a counterweight to the normal assumptions of economic theory. And at work, if people did not choose things that they know to be not narrowly in their interest at any moment, working life, and indeed human society, would hardly hang together for long. Tendencies towards non-self-interested actions do exist, and are essential elements of any model of the economy that is to shed light on its real workings. However, they are generally directed towards groups, not towards society as a whole. Changes in human nature may come about through better economic arrangements, ones that do not tend to penalise thought and action designed for the interests of groups outside the individual's ego and even ultimately of the society as a whole. It seems extremely likely that such arrangements may increasingly include co-operatives and labour-capital partnerships.

In suggesting certain fresh theoretical principles, particularly to do with capital, on which the study of the present day economy may be based, without requiring the abandonment of the main assumptions of existing economic theory, and in pointing the reader in the direction of new and hopeful changes, this book is of exceptional value. It has inspired many people, including those who have been most influential in the Industrial Common Ownership Movement, and it seems likely to inspire many more.

Alasdair Clayre

All Souls College, Oxford

ACKNOWLEDGEMENT

An Grianán wish to acknowledge the help of a devoted band of people without whom this publication would never have been possible. The prime mover and donor of a generous grant covering a significant part of the costs of production was Dr Ernest Bader, Life President of the Scott Bader Commonwealth in Wellingborough, Northants, and friend of Folkert Wilken for many years. A first working translation was prepared by Gordon Baxter, and Roger Sawtell of Daily Bread Co-operative in Northampton played an invaluable role in negotiating terms and securing various necessary business arrangements.

Galway, January 1982

Preface

Fifty years ago, Werner Sombart diagnosed the capitalist economic system as being in its final stages. Reviewing world economic changes since then, the tendency for conditions to become more chaotic suggests that this system is indeed entering its final phase.

One symptom of this is the growing dislocation of the basic equilibria in economic relationships, particularly in the capital and monetary systems that determine the functioning of the economy; these have never before been so anarchic. The workers have no interest whatsoever in the capitalist system, which is losing its ability to cope with economic events. Business leaders feel obliged increasingly to turn to the government, in the expectation that the power of the state can put the capitalist economic system back on its feet, can stabilise the chaotic currency markets, can shore up the supply of capital, can end unemployment and so on.

While economists have seen their task as one of maintaining this economic system in operation, they have not been able to work out a real social solution to these problems, but have instead avoided real economic issues in a lifeless world of abstract mathematical propositions. Their many curves say little about the forces they purport to be analysing—and nothing at all about those they *ought* to be analysing.

The conventional capitalist economic system has obtained such a hold over the peoples of the West, that many think of it as continuing for ever. (Indeed, it appears in various ways to have almost a mesmeric effect on society.) Like an impregnable fortress, it commands the social organism—for that is what society is, an organism, and one which cannot be comprehended mathematically, except in a very limited way. When a living thing is dissected by mathematics, it dies. The economic system is alive; moreover, it is essentially a matter of ethics. Economics must start by understanding the laws of life.

The analysis which follows has been made in the belief that economics must be rebuilt, from the bottom up. A lone voice calling for a new start was that of Rudolf Steiner in 1922; see his lectures published under the title *World Economy*, as well as several of his other writings.

Our investigations will go into the fundamentals of capital in the economic system. The tricky substance, capital, cannot be adequately grasped by the mind in purely material terms. On the contrary, capital reveals itself, in all its capacity to shape and sustain economic relationships, as being not only an economic category but also—and essentially —an emanation of the powers of the mind.

The very nature of the life of the economy makes it imperative that the study of capital is approached in the right frame of mind. The forms of capital need to be understood in terms of their living flow. Once we look at it in this way, we will be able to cope with the fact that many questions are best studied iteratively; that is, at first it may not be possible to explain them fully, though they can be more fully developed at a later stage in the exposition. With this approach, it becomes possible to grasp the actuality of social life, and moreover to find effective and living solutions to practical problems. Economic science cannot resolve these problems in every single detail—but it can however point out the general direction in which the solution must be sought.

To some extent, the economic theory of capital developed in this book takes the form of an *instruction manual*. Perhaps the title may give the impression that it is a specialist economic study. However, while the subject may appear to be specialist it in fact reflects not only the overall economy, but also the many interrelationships between economic activities and the other two organs in the social organism, the *Rechtsleben* and the *Geistesleben*. To the extent that this is a manual, its content needs to be studied and worked through systematically, if the approach it adopts is to be fully absorbed; for the consequences of this approach need to be recognised as both real and urgent. It has been written for those who want to change the world in the right way, but yet do not have the knowledge or the conceptual equipment which will show them just how this change can be in fact achieved. It is written for those who sense the *Geist* stirring in humanity.

Those young rebels, the socialists, who stand opposed to the existing social system, declaim in their programme against the capitalist economy and against the pro-capitalist state. Not going any further than did Karl Marx, they demand in his name the socialisation of financial institutions and of the principal concerns in industry, commerce and the service sector. In addition, they want to bring about what is termed democratic planning of the economy and control of investment. What this Marxist teaching means in practice is that the widening structural faults of capitalism are to be swept away by a collective system which can only be run by the state.

Yet Marxist teaching, on top of ignoring freedom and individuality, is in fact obsolete, advocating as it does, in a rather perverse way, a revival of theocracy, of government by an as-it-were priestly caste, only the priests are the cadres of the material authoritarian state. What is needed in society, for there to be democratic participation, is undoubtedly a social system answering the needs of the times and based on the work of individuals; but such a system would be totally paralysed if the state were to run it. Really, those who want to change the world in Marx's direction have come under the spell of authoritarian ideas, so that they put the class which manages the state over the individual. To them, a democratic self-administered economy has to be centralised.

It is vitally necessary to arouse the will to act on the part of the individual. This is the only possible basis for the future development of society, so that the economy, cultural life, and the state can each be arranged according to their own needs.

The analysis set forth in this book aims to uncover the forces underlying economic events, to show how these forces can be properly organised, and to make people aware of all this. The right awareness can proceed from seeing what is necessary, to making it come true. In the economic sphere, our analysis must be directed towards making an impact upon the working of the individual will. This calls for an awareness of responsibility and a disinterested spirit—the forces that can harmonise the potential of society with its needs.

For a deeper insight into the roots of capital, a special examination of this is to be found in Appendix I.

Folkert Wilken

Freiburg, 27 February 1975

THE LIBERATION OF CAPITAL

C H A P T E R   1

Historical Origins

1   *The crucial questions about capital*

Wherever man has gone in this world, he has encountered two unresolved and persistent social problems. One is the antithesis between rich and poor. The other is the contradiction between those with power and those without.

These two antitheses have taken quite different forms in the civilised nations of the West, in the ancient cultures of the East, and in the largely undeveloped areas of Southern Asia, Africa and South America.

In the West, it was individuals developing towards self-aware personality who experienced poverty and the lack of power as being more than mere material deprivation, as being in addition a deprivation of their essential humanity, and therefore as a social injustice.

Hence they have reacted from the depths of their whole being. They revolted against the wealth of the rich and the strength of the powerful. They see these as the causes of their deprivation, and so seek to abolish them. But being self-aware persons they also want to obtain a share in the wealth and power of others.

Popular thinking may link the idea of capital with notions of wealth and power. Business definitions are however quite different; in practice, from a management point of view, capital is defined as a money sum laid out with a view to profit.

But if we look more carefully at the nature of capital, we will see that we cannot understand its true character in mere financial terms. In reality, capital has various aspects, each distinct, each of which must be considered in its movement. Capital is a dynamic complex, changing all the time as it moves from its source to its destination in the economy.

Marx tried to analyse capital mechanistically, by fixing its genesis in the social dynamic of the relationship between workers and employers.

According to the Marxist theory of exploitation, employers pay workers less than the value of their output, thus generating a profit that is the difference between the wage and the value produced—a "surplus value" that should really not belong to the employers at all, but to the workers. This rather anti-social mode of capital formattion is indeed possible, but we shall see that it is not the normal situation. In fact, by trying to treat this special form as the general case, Marx hides the real nature of capital, hindering understanding.

Nor can one come much nearer to understanding the nature of capital, if one goes to the first historical origins of capital formation, which Marx called "primitive accumulation". This did not come from the industrial economy, but from foreign trade. In the later middle ages, and towards the beginnings of modern times, there was an outsurge of commerce, expressing the development of individuality. In the period from the thirteenth to the sixteenth centuries, the merchant adventurers, as they were called, voyaged to the newly-discovered countries. There they appropriated or otherwise acquired various sought-after commodities—primary products, rare metals, and so forth, which were then sold from the trading posts they had set up. They established regular international markets through the trade fairs, such as those in Champagne, where they were able to turn the goods they had acquired into money.

As yet there was no continuous economic system, only commerce, albeit now on a large scale, being developed by sophisticated trading techniques, using both money and such instruments of credit as bills of exchange. The driving force behind this private development of trade was the assertion of the individual self and its corollary, a will to act on a positively heroic scale. A particularly important development went hand in hand with this formation of the market economy. This was the development of a fixed ownership relationship with economic objects such as commodities and money. The newly wakened awareness of self sought a material expression as a means of self-realisation, to strengthen and confirm the consciousness of individuality. This egoistic drive, focused on material things, produces, with inexorable logic, a self bound to material values. Thus it was that the private ownership of material things became the main goal in life. This urge for private ownership will be recognised as the driving force behind the subsequent market economy, dynamically shaping and propelling the modern economic system. This led to the development of something quite different from the old handicraft system, or from plain down-to-earth small trading. In the place of these came self-industrialising large scale production, with big business working out its freedom in mass markets. In place of the small household economy providing for direct consumption, there came the big business economy with its large scale production and distribution, and its corresponding monetary system, thus generating a whole new economic way of life, on a massive scale. Thus the concepts were formed which have since shaped our economic activities.

Modern economic life derives its inner structure from the *Geist* and will power of big business. Out of this will power, and through experiencing it, the entrepreneurial élite originated. The ruling motivation of this élite was self-realisation and self-advancement of their personalities by acquiring control over material things. In this way they brought into being a continually expanding world of material goods, a veritable material cosmos. In this cosmos, capital appeared, playing the part of the chief protagonist.

Both the formation of capital and its application were entangled with the egoistic workings of this economic system. Since this economic system was called the capitalist economic system, the word capital has come to have a bad name, so that even the putting to work of capital came under condemnation. This needs thinking about. A distinction in fact needs to be made between the real substance of capital and the relationships it happens to be involved in, which have given it this bad name. It is condemned precisely because of the way in which the anti-social urge for ownership has shaped modern economic life, gripping both producers and consumers.

The previously existing economic relations had had a religious atmosphere about them, but these fell away during the nineteenth century. In their place, openly anti-social trends developed.

These anti-social trends have become widespread. We find this in the commercialisation of human labour. We find this in the exploitation of the consumer. Above all, we find it in the competitive war waged by producers and traders against each other, each trying to drive the other out of the market. The anti-social tendency is canonised in its very core, in the pursuit of capital to be owned. It is thought to be a fundamental principle, that the ideal of human freedom can be realised only in economic activity. However, the true situation is that the ego-forces stirred up and set free in the process of individualisation can at first proceed in no other way, as they increasingly turn towards the realisation of separate wills. The force of freedom, manifests itself in the gratification of the egoistic drives breaking out of the centre of the personality, and cannot find realisation except in grasping the world of material values. The liberated ego, connecting itself with these values, seeks its validation and its security in power over them. Hence it wants to take such values into private ownership and so make them into a part of itself. From this root grows economic wealth, and its corollary, economic power.

To put it more precisely, when individualised economic wealth takes the form of capital, this opens the way to the establishment of economic power over the productive forces of nature, over human labour, over, indeed, the intellectual, cultural and spiritual forces which inform and serve the economic system, and, ultimately, to a significant extent over the power of the state. The coalescence of the interests of capital as economic power, and the interests of the state as political power, has developed to such an extent that neither could survive without the other.

Most importantly, the result is that the large economy works to maintain the status quo—that is the market economy and its kingpin, the profit motive. This follows from the outdated right of ownership over that which is found *un*owned; which is in turn the corollary of the individualist drives for freedom which, in their egoistic, unrestrained, original form, stimulate the processes of the large economy to action. The aim of these strivings is not to meer human needs, not to share out the fruits of economic production equitably, but to make profit as seen from the viewpoint of the enterprise. The great distortion wrought by the market economy—said to be based on capital—is to turn the true end of economic activity—namely to provide the material goods needed by society—into a *means* of serving private goals. These private purposes are to divert the money sums appearing as profit, and so defined, into the ownership of private individuals—this being legitimised by the private ownership of the means of production. The true nature of profit remains blurred and opaque when viewed in this narrowly legalistic fashion.

Taking all the foregoing into account, we come to the following key questions:

1. What exactly *is* capital—and how does it originate?
2. To whom ought capital to belong, and how can its ownership be correctly defined?

3. Who ought to make the decisions about the best way—economically
   and socially—to invest capital, and to determine its use?
These are the critical issues of the century.

2 *The origin of capital in* Geist, *and the source of capital formation*

To see just how capital originates in the mind, we should look more
closely at the circumstances of human life on this planet.

The material needs of humanity are met by means of economic
activities. At birth the human essence and spirit is incarnated upon this
earth, where it cannot help but become increasingly separated from
its physical surroundings. Deep down it finds the material environment
to be quite alien to its own nature, to be something which harasses it;
however man is obliged by his drive for self-preservation to live in it and
fashion it into something livable in.

This shows itself in the way in which his physical existence, which
he enters at birth, has to be formed, enriched, adorned and made easier.
He continually struggles to shape it, to make it more and more suitable
for and worthy of humanity. This he does by developing a material
culture. Thought, spirit and work, effort and creative ideas, are all
needed to produce material objects that make human life better
provided for.

In order to create a material culture which will enrich life, physical
work must be combined with material natural resources. Here, man is
under the elementary need to lighten his physical work in all sorts of
ways, not only simplifying it, but, if possible, eliminating it altogether.
(We have in mind here physical labour, to which, from its etymology,
the concept "labour" should strictly speaking relate.) Now there have
been epochs in history—for example in Babylon, Egypt, Greece and
Rome, when physical work, being considered brutalising, was left to
slaves.

Work first came to rise above the material, to take on a spiritual
quality, with the advent of Christ, which had the effect of starting
the process of developing self-awareness in increasingly large numbers
of people. The Christian aim was to transform the world: thus it was
that physical labour became imbued with the force of the ego of
those who were in the process of becoming individuals, and thus it
was that labour came to be performed with a deeper sense of purpose.
Work was sanctified—as realised by the medieval monks, who tried to

give an example to the people. But in spite of the personal strengthening that people experienced in concentrating on physical work, the movement nevertheless grew, to alleviate, limit and, where possible, eliminate it. So, the reduction of physical activity soon became a preoccupation of all economic activity, becoming the most important tendency in the economic system as a whole.

Now the disadvantage of this tendency is that the economic system is thereby put increasingly out of balance. In the economy, the mind is continually working towards a harmonisation of all outputs with all reciprocal inputs, so bringing about an equilibrium. However, this is continually upset and broken through by the dynamic impacts, on the one hand, of the progressive improvement of consumption goods in order to meet continually changing and growing demand, and on the other hand, of the systematic tendency already mentioned to minimise all physical work. This is realised by the continual reorganisation of the division of labour and by technical developments aimed at saving labour, particularly physical labour, to which, of course, the application of the reasoning power of the intellect contributes.

Now, what this application of intelligence deals with is only the reflection of the world of the senses and of its dynamics. On the other hand, the work which people want to do—and indeed must do—in the sphere of the sciences, art and religion, is not affected by the drive to save labour. On the contrary, intellectual work calls for continual expansion. This is because, if humanity is to progress, it must find its destiny in the powers of the mind, the development of which is the point of the universe.

The meaning of this will be grasped only if we search deeply into history. It is to the far distant past that we must look, to the events portrayed in biblical mythology as the Fall. The Fall brought about man's expulsion from Paradise—his true home—into exile upon earth. This event is depicted figuratively in man having to earn and eat his bread by the sweat of his brow. The cosmic purpose of this was that man's further development should proceed through the encounter with nature. Man had to suffer the material existence imposed on him in continuous and reiterated life in this world as the only way in which he could strengthen his abilities, and raise himself above the material world.

The descent of the human race to the material world was consolidated in a subsequent episode, mythologically remembered in the killing of Abel by Cain, symbolising the setting aside and destruction of Abel's powers, which up to then had still retained a heavenly purity.

The consequence of this was that man, abandoned by God's power, was bound to the earth and material things. He being "inconstant and fickle" must work out his life in the material world. There is world necessity in Cain's deed. The human destiny revealing itself in the archetype of Cain released an indestructible force in man to overcome this earthly destiny. Consciously or unconsciously men are activated by the wish to ascend into the realm of the spirit and of God. Symptomatic of this is the way in which men performing material work are continually at pains to evade it.

We should understand that people imprisoned in the material world and in the power of death have to find fulfilment in this inner yearning to raise themselves above it, and so achieve reunion with the world of mind. Men becoming inwardly free seek to embellish material life on earth by creating a material culture, by making the necessities of life, by enriching every aspect of existence. It is related in myth how this spiritualisation and embellishment proceeded after Cain. Jabal-Cain invented house-building and cattle-raising; Thubal-Cain established the craft of metal work; and Jubal-Cain made inert matter, into the means of artistic creation, with his invention of the violin and the flute. All of this moved in the direction of transcending the purely physical content of human work. This took on a more fundamental character when man reached the stage of applying his faculties to shaping the economic system, thus imbuing it with intellectual content.

This leads us—and this is essential for the understanding of capital—to the basis of the creation of economic value. This does not mean the utility of goods produced, but the value that originates through the physical work expended in the production of material goods. From the standpoint of those who do the work, this value is measured according to the original social logic of reciprocal performance of useful services in society, so that the worker and his family dependants should be able to live from the goods he produces, that is, from their above mentioned market counter value. This original equilibrating principle in the formation of personal/social values for economically produced goods was however radically cut across by the continual human endeavour to eliminate physical work altogether, and so counteract the destiny imposed on man on this planet.

Economically speaking, it was in this way that a major contradiction, an antithesis difficult to resolve, came to be introduced into the evolution of economic life. While work in fact constructs the economic value of a commodity, arrangements are continually being contrived to reduce the amount of physical work and hopefully eliminate it altogether. These arrangements continually reduce the economic value of goods. Once this is grasped, we will be able to see that capital arises out of the difference between the construction and erosion of economic (labour) values.

This continuing reduction of economic work is in principle achieved through the so-called division of labour. The most primitive economic situation is that of isolated hunters and fishermen fending for themselves. However the most primitive is not, historically speaking, the first in world history; in the beginning, the family and consanguineous economic unit was the natural living form, within a large theocratic tribal society. In such a system, as later on in peasant family households which still exist, the division of labour was determined by the group make-up, and was based on sex and on natural abilities. As the economic system developed, along with individualisation, the original or basic form of all economic division of labour appeared in village communities. The essence of this was the separation of the producers of goods from the consumer of goods. No longer did the head of the family apportion the fruits of the family's work among the family members, once this separation came into effect. Although every producer was, of course, also a consumer, these two functions were socially separated, and were brought back into contact with each other through exchange and money.

Exchange enabled production to be guided towards consumption. This can be called the original economic division. Through it was realised the deployment of economic labour in various trades. The abilities necessary to each particular trade were developed to the fullest extent. This had the effect of bringing the power of the intellect to bear on the arrangements of economic life. This economic division brought about a social system in which the labour of society was increasingly sub-divided. This in turn had the further consequence of reuniting the divided labour force, as individual labour activities were brought into relation with one another, with the aim of achieving the most economic arrangement—that is, that arrangement which saved the most labour in relation to given production goals.

Thus we can see in this organisation of labour how the force of the intellect takes hold of the economic system and its working processes, and how it tends to make work lighter. The organised division of labour, however, plays a twofold role. As already mentioned, it arises directly when two or more men execute a common task in such a way that they have divided it between them. In addition to this division of labour between men working together, there is also a division of a qualitatively higher kind, between man and nature, when natural processes take a part of human work. In order to make this possible, the human intellect has to bring natural materials and forces under its control and bring them to the workplace for use. This type of intellect has to develop scientific thinking to the highest degree, hence the growth of modern technology, which remoulds natural materials, and creates an enormous material cosmos, a technical world which permeates human life on an ever-increasing scale. This works in two ways—human manual and also intellectual work is replaced by natural forces, and human work is taken over by machinery.

3 The intellectualisation of the economy resulting from the division of labour

If we look closely at the working activity of a given individual, we will see that its made up of three elements, each of which can be—and increasingly is—to varying extents substituted by technology.

1 Every job develops out of a mental perception and conceptualisation of the purpose that it is to achieve. This is accomplished by planning. This purely intellectual planning of the work to be done can to some extent be handled by computers.

2 The working process itself consists of the forming or shaping of all sorts of materials—wood, metal or stone—through human activity. This activity is directly assisted by tools. It is carried out by carefully executed movements. Technology is increasingly involved in this area, and mechanisation had come to dominate the scene. As early as the eighteenth century, the engineering intelligence revealed itself in the development of machine tools able to cope with a complete working process. The ultimate goal is reached in the combination of all processes in a fully mechanised factory, in which all the sequences of production are carried on without human intervention. Mechanisation has also been applied to commercial activities.

3 Every job is helped by auxiliary energy, the use of which, in addition to human energy, has become a guiding idea in economic development. Engineering skills are continually applied to this purpose. This started

by using the elemental forces of nature, wind, water and gravity. To these were then added steam power using natural fuels. Then, as science probed further into the basis of the natural world, still more powerful forces—some dangerous—were unleashed, such as electrical energy, the internal combustion engine, and now nuclear power. Though each of these serves the purpose of helping man to eliminate work, each also involves various environmental dangers.

The particular characteristics of electricity have brought about still further reductions in the amount of physical matter needed for various kinds of production. Power equipment, machine tools and production machinery were all built out of heavy raw materials, usually formed into steel, and tended to grow to immense sizes. But recently we have the "thinking machines" in which the amount of material in use tends to be reduced, due to the development of minute electronic components, which make use of electricity to carry out "thinking" functions. This development is enabled by the construction of computers.

This kind of functionalising of production and economic relationships is continually being developed and refined, towards the point that material processes disappear. The technical apparatus in which these electronic thinking activities are carried out creates a network of machinery in which the amount of physical matter involved is greatly reduced, and in which many workers and their machines are displaced. A worldwide saving of labour thus develops. This is seen in the automation of production processes.

The effect of this intellectualisation, which increasingly depersonalises control, is that economic life is being revolutionised by an overdose of technology and therefore put out of balance. This technical revolution has grafted itself onto the economic organism, convulsing the economy. An impersonal engineering approach manages all industrial processes. The result is a progressive elimination of the material side of industrial activity, which becomes more and more a question of the operation of pure intelligence. The burden of manual work is replaced by intellectual effort—which is not burdensome. Herbert Marcuse, in his book *One-dimensional Man*, called this the "transubstantiation" of labour power into a producing object, divorced from the individual. That is to say, the indivisible productive work process is depersonalised and objectified through the effects of a technology in which science is revealed as direct productivity. This tendency has become sufficiently widespread to dominate the economic system.

The economic world is being made more and more impersonal, because of the effect of science upon production. This is seen particularly in the automation of production processes, which are managed by computer. Through this intellectualisation, work is detached from production in the strict sense and removed to the sphere of production preparations, in the form of auxiliary activities, design, compilation of plans, etc. The independence of all these intellectual activities in specially built research centres has an effect that we can only describe as the dematerialisation of human work. Herbert Gross construed this impact of science to mean that a fourth factor of production—intellectual capital—should be included along with the traditional three factors—land, labour and capital. Recruiting the forces of the intellect to plant economics—when these forces are the source of capital formation—brings in an aspect of capital we have still to examine. The social dynamic of capital—which has so stamped our times, and generated such conflict—needs to be developed. This will necessitate a more profound conceptualisation of capital processes.

Commerce fulfils a particularly important role here as the organising force in bringing the division of labour into operation on a world wide scale, which affects the whole world economy. Trading relations between merchants and producers facilitates the whole economy, through the development of the transport system, and also particularly through the monetary system. Another example of the effect of intellectual activity in this sphere is seen in modern communications.

Without doubt, the part of mankind which has advanced intellectually is quite under the spell of technology. Its charms are twofold. On the one hand, there is the enticement of increasingly comfortable living standards; on the other, there is a reduction in the amount of work which it is necessary to do, including intellectual work. The irresistible pull towards technological development, and towards its realisation in full mechanisation is caused, we should remember, by the unconscious and deep-seated desire to free ourselves from the material oppression of the material world.

All motivational drives, particularly those involved in shaping economic life, derive their innermost drive from the guiding principle of the modern economy—emulation. The motivation of emulation in economic life derives itself from the general human drive for intellectual emulation, in its turn rooted in the longing to grow stronger, to realise oneself. And this longing results from the still deeper need in the very soul, to return to paradise, to undo the Fall. This gives a vigorous impetus to activities of the whole *Geist*, which seeks to draw near to its origin; by which means its true human value will be realised.

However, egoism tends to make this need for competition take a form in which people assert themselves against others. Out of a hidden sense of inferiority, people enter into rivalry with one another and try to overtake and outdo each other. This psychological emulation can be seen in sport and similar fields, sometimes taking a rather atavistic form.

In the economic field, this kind of impulse is directed towards material enrichment, which involves the economising of labour. The technological intellect is continually working at achieving this goal and sees the development of science and technology as constituting the essence of human progress. Because of the development of nation-states, this attitude generates international rivalry between national economies, made worse by mutual fear from a military point of view.

From the outset, the part played by emulation in economic life has been morally rather negative, and increasingly so. Healthy human emulation has been distorted, in the modern economy, into the principle of competition. Competition is a commercial concept, a concept of marketing strategy; whereas emulation is concerned with putting the forces of the psyche to work at improving performance. This proper aim is undermined whenever any improvement in perform-ance is used to gain market advantage, and so commercialised. There is a great difference between wanting to develop one's own performance, and wanting to hold back that of others. The drive to improve perform-ance for its own sake, is, however, at the basis of all real human improvement; here in fact we touch on the centre of the social driving force in human life.

4 *Economic and technological thought—the source of free capital formation*

Without human consciousness in all its forms, economic life would be nothing more than self-sufficiency at the level of the family household, the head of which would both allocate work and share out the product.

Against that conceptual backcloth, we can see the money economy and exchange as creations of human thought, continually growing and developing. The various impacts of thought upon the development of modern economic life can be summarised as follows:

1 The division of the economy by which producers and consumers were universally separated out from one another, as the antithesis of family self-sufficiency.
2 The division of labour between working groups in order to develop specialised skills and thereby increase labour productivity.
3 The division of work through mechanisation, by which manual work is replaced by the use of natural forms of energy.
4 The commercial division of labour via the money system, through which all economic activities on the entire planet are brought into inter-relationship.

It is the characteristic of modern times that humanity—particularly the leadership in economic affairs—strives as far as is possible to turn the economic system into a technical universe organised by the powers of the mind, so as to reduce the amount of human labour needed as much as possible. This tendency arises from a quite irrepressible urge to cut costs. Cost savings produce large increases in profits. The over-riding drive for maximum profits is in fact the principal motivation for the further development of science. Out of the savings in labour thus achieved, together with the opening up of new productive forces, immeasurable increases in labour productivity are derived. These do not come out of labour itself, but out of the shaping force of material intellect. This has a profound effect upon the economic formation of values. The expenditure of labour is instinctively—and quite rightly —considered to be the element which constructs the economic value of goods. Because of this, the substitution of labour by organisation and technology reduces the economic values in production. We might expect that a cheapening of production brought about in this way must directly reduce the market value of goods. But this does not happen—because the reduced expenditure on labour is first set free in the form of *money*.

It is money, as the comprehensive organising force in the social organism, that the shaping power of the *Geist* finds its most impor-tant manifestation. The total quantity of money, as it circulates through the system, is in the last analysis the product of active thought at work in changing physical relationships. As this thought penetrates these relationships via the division of labour and the process of rational-isation, so the physical burdens of life are progressively reduced. The monetary system can seem so hard to understand; it is simply the most important way in which thought affects the economy. It is through money that the human *Geist* realises itself as the comprehensive controller of the material aspects of life, and that not only in the economic sphere. All money originates in this movement of thought which is aimed at improving the material circumstances of life. Only through money can this be done. If there were only labour—and no money—barter would have to be the means of trading. It is this conceptually evolving thought process which has brought about the genesis of money, right up to its present stage of development, in which money appears as the universal organiser of the economically-based social system. In the ancient Orient it was through priestly learning, through the mysteries, that thought shaped life. Then the self-developing power of the intellect began comprehensively to structure all economic and social relationships. This shaping process realised itself through money.

In all three parts of the social organism—in economic life, in cultural life, in the life of the state—there has scarcely been any development unconnected with money. The far-reaching dynamism of money is manifest in the labour saving tendency of the economy—which is intellectually conceived. This results in sums of money being set free—which setting-free we shall term the *formation of free capital*.

Commonly, *technical economic productivity* is taken to mean that more goods are produced with the same labour, or that the same amount of goods can be produced with less labour, than heretofore. The latter case provides the foundation for the genesis and formation of capital. Capital formation is realised through the managerial and economic organisation of the production process. Take for example a production plant which becomes able to save the work of a hundred workers, through a new technical process and a corresponding plant re-organisation. The wages saved, along with any other cost savings, minus the cost of the innovations, will appear as profit in the company accounts. In the long term, however, depending on the market situation, there may be a tendency for the savings in labour to be transformed into a reduction in prices. When this happens, savings out of income accrue to the purchasers of the goods which have become cheaper; they will now need to spend a smaller part of their incomes on living expenses. We can call this "consumer rent", when cost savings are passed on in price reductions; whereas to the entrepreneur the cost savings appear as additional profit. Together, these consumer rents and additional profits make up the total sum resulting from the labour saved.

Since the tendency in the economy to try to produce goods more cheaply by saving labour goes on all the time, there is a continual reduction of production costs in the plant. In turn, values are continually generated throughout the economy, making profits for manufacturing and trading companies. These amounts of value derive from the process of reduction of economic labour values, resulting in turn from the application of *Geist* in the form of economic and technological thought. They have a specific function to fulfill in the organism as a whole—namely to be the source of free capital formation—"free" because it derives from the activities of the *Geist*.

Human creative powers are free forces. If these powers make an impact on labour costs, by devising productivity improvements, this impact is spontaneously developed, hence it is correct to speak of *free capital formation*. We have here, before our eyes, the basic polarity between labour and *Geist*; in it is contained the polarity between value creation and value reduction.

Now the term "free" is used for another reason as well. Free capital comes into existence without any previously fixed use. It is available to be used for any specific purpose. Straight away, claims are made on it, from both sides of the economy, from both producers and consumers. Consumers want reductions in price. Among producers, workers want their share in the form of wage increases, while entrepreneurs and owners of the means of production are, under existing law, automatically the owners of the sums accruing as profit. These, the parties directly involved in the economic process, are not the only claimants, either. In addition, the state and the *Geistesleben* have their own further demands. The expenses of the *Geistesleben*, which today the state pays for, though it is not its proper business, can only be met out of free capital formation.

Indicative of the financial importance of free capital formation is the increasingly sharp contradiction that people want both the newly invented consumer goods and shorter working hours, together with increased incomes. The normal thing would be for those who wanted a higher standard of living to do more work than before, but today the aim is to work less in order to enjoy the additional goods. This would bring the economic system to a standstill, if it were not for free capital.

In that part of the economy controlled by big business, free capital is there for all to see. When various incidentals are excluded, most of what is shown in the accounts of the large corporations as profit, is in fact free capital. For a particularly important example, look at the report and accounts of the multinational computer firm, IBM (International Business Machines), in 1971 when it showed a profit of over two thousand million dollars. This high profit was made from unprecedented savings in labour brought about by computerisation in large companies, which led to extensive rationalisation in office and managerial work. This resulted in exceptionally high profits being realised—which were, essentially, free capital. Nearly half of the above-mentioned sum was paid over in taxes, illustrating the way in which the state appropriates free capital. Thus the state benefited to the tune of over a thousand million dollars. At the time IBM's total plant was valued at a little over five thousand million dollars.

If such enormous sums can accumulate in just one company, the question arises, how can such sums of profit be made useful, in a way which is both socially just and economically rational, rather than for the gratification of private aims? The answer is bound up with that to a more fundamental question: who can legitimately claim to own free capital? To whom, precisely, should it rightfully belong—from the point of view either of its origination or of its use?

These questions can only be answered if we are conceptually clear about the nature of free capital, and about the practical forms it takes. Now it is not correct to treat entrepreneurial profit and free capital as being completely identical. The reason why will appear when we analyse the breakdown of what is termed "profit" more precisely.

5   Seven sources of profit-generated capital

Our analysis so far has led to a dynamic concept of capital looked at from the point of view of its origin. According to this concept, capital appears as the consequence of the application of intellectual powers in shaping economic life. We have also seen that it appears as a sum of money in the profit accounts of large corporations. These facts tend to suggest that profit can in all cases be equated with the free capital secreted by the economy. That is however an assumption which cannot easily be reconciled with the reality of present-day accountancy practice, which lumps various money sums together under the heading of "profit". This makes for a confused perception of economic values —hence the obscurity of many economic concepts. In order to clear up the facts of the case concerning "free capital", we must clarify the profit concepts in use today. For the individual concern profit is an accounting sum, a neutral abstraction made up out of the difference between costs and receipts—and costs here include wages and salaries. Big business is of course guided by the drive to maximise profits. This is a drive that also, in personal terms, inspires small businesses, to some extent, regarding their revenues. In big business, however, the profit motive, following English economic theories, is seen as the basic cause of all economic activities. Indeed, profit maximisation has reached beyond economics and become the basis of power in politics as well.

That part of profit which derives from free capital formation is, however, frequently supplemented by price increases, which the big monopolies, combines, credit and financial institutions can attain by reason of their market dominance. Even the economic growth brought about by the development of the trade cycle has the tendency to raise prices in particular areas. All this generates special profits. In this way, additions are made to the free capital formation generated by improved productivity. As for price increases arising out of imbalance in the market, cyclical increases in demand, or market dominance, these constitute a kind of exploitation of consumers. This has rightly been described as forced saving; that is, surpluses accrue to entrepreneurs who use them for self-financing. The saving involved is forced upon buyers, against their will, as a result of price increases. These forced contributions appear as part of profit; this can be considered as forced formation of capital. Parallel to this additional profit extorted from consumers through price increases, there is also another form of exploitation which occurs when wages are inadequate, so that the workforce is exploited. When this happens there is a lowering of production costs, but not through any effect of intellectual activity; instead, this results from too small a share of the social product being allocated to weaker classes in the community.

Marx was convinced that *all* profit, without exception, was due to the underpayment of labour. Hence he branded profit as the surplus value derived from the exploitation of the workers; this surplus value was withheld, but rightfully belonged to them. This belief still lives today, and can be seen when, for example, German trade unions demand transfer of the control of the means of production into the hands of the workforce, by increasing taxes on profits. Such a demand can be weighed properly only when we take into account that profit in the true sense arises out of the creative forces of social intelligence and not out of labour processes at all, though these must be properly paid. Of course, labour *can* be underpaid, as was generally the case in the nineteenth century, when workers were indeed denied part of their means of existence. Karl Marx saw this, but missed the point that there is an independent and autonomous factor in the formation of surplus value, that is, in the formation of capital. While he understood the role of technological development in labour saving, he thought of this mainly in relation to the unemployment associated with it— the "industrial reserve army", as he called it.

Inflated prices and depressed incomes both add a forced capital formation to free capital formation proper. Both are mixed up in profit as seen in accounting terms.

Strictly speaking, these profits are only shown separately in the case of limited companies or corporations. This is because in such companies the incomes of the directors are treated as a cost. In the case of private businesses, the personal income of the owner is lumped together with profit. The profit of private entrepreneurs is basically entrepreneurial income. What companies show as their profit includes only the objective financial surplus that remains when all incomes, including that of the directors, has been paid. Thus the profit calculation should be separated out from all elements of personal entrepreneurial income. Once this is seen, the true substance of profit can be distinguished from all accidental or irregular accretions. The essence, which is the constituent of the concept of profit, forms itself as profit by the distillation of free capital. This is the right way to see profit, if economics is to think clearly, with the admixed irregular accretions properly separated out.

So as to summarise in their correct order the various value elements lumped together in accounting profit, it is necessary to deepen our understanding of the basic elements in profit formation. For inflated prices and inadequate allocation to incomes are not the only sources of irregular components.

An economically perverse and parasitical form of profit results from property transactions of all kinds. These transactions are of course rooted in the overpowering obsession with obtaining control over matter, and in the individualistic acquisition of material goods. They are made possible by the modern market economy, with its unhappy tendency to treat as commodities things other than goods produced by economic activity. This applies to all immaterial objects of value, for example works of art, which the business spirit turns into marketable commodities. Such "phoney goods" are also found in the economic sphere, when the resources of the earth, that have not been created by man—but simply found—are traded. The wealth of the earth can be seen in three ways: as the natural mineral resources therein, such as coal, oil, gas, metals, etc; as the living cultivable land; and as space, as areas which people occupy. However there is no general human right to take into private possession either the dead or the living resources of the earth in order to treat them as goods, and through their sale to amass money wealth, which accountants see as "profit". It is an issue of major social importance, as to how the resources of the earth should be dealt with in the circulation process of economic values, seeing that these resources are really the gift of the universe to humanity as a whole. We will discuss this later on.

The land forms the basis of this kind of formation of assets for profit. Roman law made land into a commodity. The commercialisation of these "pseudo-goods" has led to the creation of a separate property market, into which, against all economic reason, ever larger and more monstrous cash flows are diverted, quite unproductively. The money sums received from the sale of land can make big profits for the land-owners. When a corporation owns land and sells it, the proceeds of the sale are put into its profit and inflate it abnormally. Pseudo-goods and pseudo-markets—such as the labour, property and capital markets —constitute artificial and irregular sources of profit which flow into peripheral companies. These irregular profits must be distinguished and separated out from the true profit consisting of free capital.

Profit is in fact a composite formation, complex in its origins, once these are analysed. One further component which sometimes finds its way into profit is the income of the entrepreneur, which is really quite alien to the concept of profit. Leaving that on one side, the remaining sources may be summarised under the following seven headings:

1 The central essence, which results from the secretion of free capital. This can be described as rationalisation profit, which in some cases appears, due to fundamental growth, in the form of a cyclical profit.

2 The "accidental" portions, which arise from the fruits of market situations, sometimes of a monopolistic character. Profits of this kind are the market-conditioned results of superficial growth, or the consequences of unjustified commercialisation and of the false creation of money:

a) on the regular commodity markets, in times of a rising trade cycle, cyclical profits can be made, which are however accumulated through deliberate price increases, and so constitute forced saving on the part of the customer.

b) the labour markets provide the possibility of making or increasing profits out of the workers and employees, by inadequate allocation to incomes. This was the Marxist general case, but no longer has the same importance.

c) the property market provides the means of turning urban and rural land into commodities, which can be turned into a money profit.

d) raw material markets are susceptible to monopolisation, and so may generate excessive profit formation, as has recently been the case with oil.

e) in the capital market, large sums of money can be traded as if money were a commodity, to make an irregular profit.

f) finally, there is the unhealthy creation of money without reference to the needs of circulation. This puts the economic system out of balance. This empty money creation is the basis of inflationary profits, which reflect no increase in real values, only in accounting ones.

The seven sources of profit formation outlines above are often lumped together in an undiscerning way as "capital", but as we shall see* only the results of free capital formation can really be considered as real capital.

---

*See particularly Appendix I, on the nature of capital.

C H A P T E R   2

Aspects of Free Capital Formation

1 The private use of capital
Income formation and capital formation from savings

The concept of "prospective" capital—i.e. capital that is laid out in an economically productive way—includes all types of capital investment. Economic activities are impossible—given the way industry has developed—without the investment of money capital to "prime the pump".

The nineteenth century economist Hildebrandt divided economic development into three stages—the natural economy, the money economy and the credit economy. Conventional economists did not like the last concept, arguing that it was not methodologically distinct from the other stages. In order to characterise the third stage, we must really re-christen it the "capital economy". In the capital economy, credit plays only an intermediary role, in situations when loans are advanced against credit. The term "capital money" means —if we fully grasp the nature of capital—the modern economy in which the factor of the *Geist* is coming into predominance. It takes on the form of money when it is the medium of free capital formation or of prospective capital investment. In the money form of prospective productive capital, money is at work in quite a different way from its role as a medium of exchange in the simple money economy. Capital money embodies the macro-economic organic value relationship and hence a more sophisticated kind of value, compared with the purchase money used to complete individual exchange transactions. Inside the area in which prospective capital operates, money performs only the function of accounting for what was advanced. It eventually returns in the form of exchange money, at the point in which it is paid out as incomes for managers and workers.

Here our attention is drawn to the dynamics of the cycle in which the economic system normally moves. To put it at its simplest—leaving free capital aside for the moment—this cycle begins with the investment of prospective capital, assuming this to be formed from potential capital. Part of the prospective capital is used as working capital to purchase raw materials and to provide for the remuneration of employees. The latter could, by saving, transfer a portion of the money they receive back into potential productive capital.

In the course of the economic cycle, capital is changed into exchange money (as income)—which can then be reconverted back into capital money. Each of these phases has its own dynamic. There is capital formation at the beginning, and at the end, from savings. By being deployed in the economic process, the potential capital originating from savings compresses itself into the form of prospective capital—which can be generated in other ways, either through free capital formation, or through the creation of money (credit).

At this point, we need to clarify our concepts. Under existing law, the free capital—which has been formed quite spontaneously —passes over automatically into the incomes of those who possess the means of production, either to the entrepreneur who controls the capital, or in the form of interest and dividends to outside owners. This kind of transfer takes the form of income, which can be converted back into capital by savings. Through processes of this kind the real essence of the savings process is hidden, because of a lack of data about the details of the circulation of money as income.

Whatever way income is formed, all modes of income formation have not only economic consequences, but social ones as well, which latter can be of decisive importance for the arranging of economic life. The antithesis between those incomes which are related to performance and those which are unrelated (including those which are totally unearned) is of the greatest importance both economically and socially.

Incomes related to performance are all for labour or earned incomes; and are mostly formed in economic life by economic activity, whether material or immaterial. Most other incomes derive from economic incomes, and it is these economic incomes which are to be seen as primary incomes. The term "primary" is used to differentiate them from those incomes not resulting from directly economic activity, e.g. those related to non-economic services. However, it is mainly the true, economic, primary incomes, out of which in the last analysis, these other secondary incomes are paid. Thus, the incomes of civil servants are principally derived from taxation paid by economic incomes. Since such secondary incomes are in their turn taxed, there is a chain sequence of such income formation. The income of representatives of the *Geistesleben*, e.g. of teachers, doctors and clergymen, are completely secondary in character, either in the form of fixed honorariums or as voluntary donations out of primary income. However, a small portion may also come from free capital, via taxation.

To these two categories of primary and secondary incomes, a third must be added. This is because the owner of productive capital—under existing law—takes to himself the profits produced. The critique of this appropriation must depend on the type of profit involved. As has been pointed out, some kinds of profit are to be condemned. True profits arise only from free capital formation. The main problem is, who should deploy these true profits? This question can only be settled in the juridical sphere, where a modus operandi should be established, for what and to whom free capital should be made over, as property. Free capital could be considered as being held as property only in a provisional way, as being owned *in trust*. Before being transferred into such a trust, it would be without owner, in suspense as one might say.*

Under the heading of profit ownership, we must distinguish between two different types of savings—from consumer income and from profit appropriated into ownership. The latter, as a rule, serves to provide self-financed capital. At the same time, the profits shown in capital companies do not generally take the form of income, if one does not extend the concept to corporate entities, nor consider the corporate profits as income of a legal "person", i.e. "the enterprise in itself". One cannot generally include an application of free capital or of other profits in the concept of savings, which should really be limited to what is put into bank savings accounts. These circumstances will be analysed later while dealing with the ownership issue.

All savings, so long as they are unapplied, take the form of potential capital. The original idea of saving was this: people in the simple exchange economy would abstain from a part of their purchases of consumer goods, and save the money representing this abstention. Such a savings process would presuppose income formed as remuneration for work done. The money form would embody a legal claim upon

---

*See the author's *New Forms of Ownership in Industry*, Varanasi, 1962.

a portion of the general social product which could be freely chosen. This portion of the social product would then remain unsold if the saver retained this part of his income and hoarded it. The resulting imbalance in the overall economy could generally be restored if the saver gave away or lent the money saved, so that it dovetailed once more into the cycle of the economy.

What happens now, is that the saved portion of the income is routed towards the realisation of an economic idea, by setting up an enterprise which will carry on a productive process. Such an application of the saved money enable the economic organism to grow, so that the social product increases. This however raises a further problem—how, then, will the balance of the economy be restored? This will be examined in the next section.

2 The way in which the economic balance is restored at a new level, and the impetus given to economic growth by free capital formation

The following analysis should be of particular interest for students of economic equilibrium.

The problems associated with the formation of free capital vary with how it is distributed. In addition, the ambient circumstances in which it is formed can have diverse and complicated effects.

The impact of labour saving on the economy disturbs the previously stable and static arrangement, both socially and economically. Labour power is released, and those who have this labour power have no work. In these circumstances labour and wages are saved. This means that the money hitherto used to pay the redundant workers now lies, for the time being unused, thus forming a profit. In other words, free capital is accumulated.

Specific economic issues now arise. What happens to the redundant workers—and to the free capital accumulated?

In order to survey the effect of these changes upon economic relationships and the balance of the economy, the outcome can be depicted in bookkeeping terms as shown in the following profit and loss account:

PROFIT & LOSS ACCOUNT

Debit		Credit	
Wages & salaries	500,000	Revenue from sales	1,000,000
Raw materials (iron, etc)	50,000		
Auxiliary materials (coal, electricity)	50,000		
Components	100,000		
Sundry costs, interest and taxes	80,000		
Surplus	220,000		
	1,000,000		1,000,000

The details of the individual entries need not bother us; the surplus of 220,000 may be taken as the profit of a private enterprise.

Let us assume that the so-called wages account is reduced by 100,000 as the result of labour-saving measures. The question arises, where does this 100,000 now go? From a purely book-keeping point of view, the working surplus of the company has gone up by 100,000. This is free capital, which can be deployed in various directions. It can be applied as a productive investment for economic purposes as productive prospective capital; however it can also pass directly or indirectly into the consumption sphere. Everyday experience leads us to suppose that goods manufactured more cheaply may be offered at a correspondingly lower price. If free capital formation passes into this form of general distribution, then it is simply used up—which would mean that it cannot be applied as prospective capital. The dispersion of free capital in cheaper products can involve not only consumer goods but also lead to lower prices for production goods, such as raw or auxiliary materials, and particularly the means of production.

The resulting cheapening of production processes may also be passed on to the consumers in the prices of the goods. Through every price reduction, consumers directly save a portion of their incomes. This saved portion then forms what is called a "consumer dividend". To the producers, any reduction in costs which is not passed on in prices constitutes free capital formation, as a profit. For both consumers and producers, the unspent money is set free, not being needed for purchases. In a static, growthless situation, these sums of money—unless somehow kept idle—lead to an additional demand for which, however, no corresponding supply exists. However this new demand provides the inducement for an increase in

the production of goods, through which the redundant workers could
be re-employed. In this way free capital which has been passed out to
consumers as a consumer dividend, through savings in the economic
process, can be put to productive use. Thereby the balance of the
economy tends to be re-established, if the countervailing demand
harmonises with it. Generally speaking, these dynamic processes
function only as tendencies. Their effectiveness in restoring the balance
of the economy depends upon their correct "tuning" with the whole
of the economic organism.

Arguing in this way, assuming a static balance in the economy, then
one thinks of an economy in which basically a balance exists between
the value quantities of supply and demand, in terms of both money
and goods. By contrast, in a developing economy, the balance is upset
and generally even distorted by the continuous impetus given by the
Geist, which penetrates the economy, altering the underlying relationships. Unavoidably, each labour saving measure works onesidedly in
the direction of a disproportionate increase in the production of goods.
Hence, the imbalance created by the impact on demand of the reduction in the labour force is further intensified. The government policies
which are adopted to overcome unemployment work generally in the
direction of restoring balance by increases in production. In the short
run, this can usually balance the effects of labour saving, or at least
can tend to do so.

The fundamental question posed first by free capital formation
is this: how can the apparently fallow-lying free capital, in its money
capital condition, be brought back into the overall economic process?
The ways in which this can be done are various, as are the balancing
effects which result.

In the cases in which free capital flows into the sphere of consumption to disappear there, this can happen either directly on the goods
side through the cheapening of specific goods with cheaper production
costs; or it can be indirectly transformed into a formation of income,
through a raising of incomes, whether those of the entrepreneurs and
shareholders, or of the employed. The latter case occurs in a liberal
market economy as a result of collective bargaining. A major social
question of our time lies unanswered ever since in the nineteenth
century the campaign of the working class began against the entrepreneurs to obtain higher wages and shorter working hours. Incess-
antly the workers strive, by means of wage disputes which are in
their social essence class struggles, to acquire as much as they can of

free capital—which they condemn as profit. They want to raise their standard of living to the same high level as that enjoyed by the owners of the means of production. This social and political movement however expresses a distributive tendency, which points in the direction of restoring the balance of the economy by transferring the incomes saved by the development of the economy to the incomes of those remaining in employment.

This is of course a quite unpredictable and "chancy" way of balancing the economy. If, as a result of either lower prices or higher incomes, more goods are demanded, one does not know precisely which goods these will be. In particular, it is these wage increases which—once the re-employment of the redundant workers is completed—raise consumption demand disproportionately. To a certain extent, a balance in these relationships can be created if the capital sums set free are channelled into donations to the *Geistesleben* or for charitable purposes. At present such disbursements go the long way round via personal and company taxes and through the state.

Specific economic tensions arise in the case already referred to, wherein the redundant employees have to be redeployed in the economic process. Through their re-employment they increase the total volume of goods in the economy—the so-called social product. The financial presupposition for such re-employment is meaningfully created in this way, that free capital—or indeed improper profits—that are lying fallow, are made into prospective productive capital. Through such a productive application of free capital the unemployment associated with its formation can be overcome. This serves to realise the human and social necessity for full employment. In each case, however, there is the fundamental fixed point, that the economically productive application of free capital must lead to basic growth in the economy. If capital formation is applied to consumer incomes, the same tendency to stimulate the economy appears. Today, this continuous growth is cultivated. It is thought to have an eternal merit, since it is believed that growth constitutes an unbeatable and systematic means to achieve prosperity and the correct functioning of the economy. This "model" of permanent economic expansion has been christened with the biological concept of "organic growth". However this is scarcely appropriate so long as economic processes are mechanistically conceived and arranged, according to such notions as the "price mechanism", the "market mechanism" and other such inorganic perceptions of the social system. Genuine economic growth in the economy must take the pattern that is formed by social forces. These cannot unfold in the form of the forces of self-interest, which always work anti-socially, particularly in creating social arrangements which are the ensemble of isolated, individualistic, separate actions. Organic growth must be brought about in such a way that expansion is achieved in harmony thoughout the entire organism, in every single cell. Only then could one talk about organic growth. Otherwise there is a mechanistic splintering of economic life in separate and unrelated economic processes—this being the result of the individualistic system.

The basic "model", indeed the law, is that the formation of free capital is not repeated limitlessly through time. On the contrary, the underlying impulse of the *Geist* is consumed in each ensuing economic period, finally running out. Each development of production becomes generally widespread. It then becomes embodied in the entire economy, through progressive price reductions, until in the end it is completely dispersed. Thus the free capital formed as the result of any specific production improvement is in the end fully used up. The irresistible spread of all technical developments throughout the economy results from the quite proper equalising tendency of competitive behaviour. The purpose of such competition is to bring about the most economic operation. Proper market emulation brings about a progressive cheapening of products to the point at which the gains from technology are compensated in prices, and spread throughout the economy. Through such a process of adjustment, free capital formation finds its consummation. The economy is organically structured so that all its parts are in reciprocal interaction with each other; through this interaction the organic balance of demand and supply can be brought about by the producers. This balance is however repeatedly superseded by new technological advances which re-arrange the division of labour in order to save labour. Since profits fall because of the dispersion of free capital formation, there is a continual search for such new technological developments. In view of this using up of free capital, one can speak of a law that the spontaneously formed free capital will tend to disappear. In modern times the dispersal in circulation of free capital is enforced by the necessary market competition that reduces prices. On the other hand, just now the effects of increasing inflationary depreciation of money resulting from price increases brought about through market dominance, combine to overcompensate for this tendency.

In formulating such a law of the tendency for free capital to disperse, one cannot help but call to mind Karl Marx's so-called "Law of the tendency of the falling rate of profit" dealt with in volume III of *Capital*. Since it may help towards a better understanding of the law about free capital, a comparison of the two laws is given in Appendix 2.

3   Free capital as property in trust

Everything which appears in an enterprise as profit is potential capital in the sense already explained. Profits which arise irregularly, through price increases, cyclical events, property deals, inflation or credit creation, all pass into the possession of the owners of the enterprise's capital. How right this is depends on the legitimacy of such profits. Only the regular formation of profit from free capital poses the question: to whom does or should this profit rightfully belong? In its origination it is, so to speak, ownerless. It should therefore be treated as property in trust.

Now, when free capital is appropriated, it is the fruits of the creative powers of the human *Geist* which is being taken—along, indeed, with the already existing resources of the earth. There is a choice between two alternatives: either the taking into possession is arbitrary and wrong, or else it takes place on the basis of a socially recognised and legally arranged allocation. Now, between unauthorised and lawless seizure, on the one hand, and fully developed legitimate possession on the other, there is a kind of compromise position, in which appropriation is sanctioned by statute; in our case, this compromise is the annexation of free capital by the owners of the means of production, which, because it took place arbitrarily in the historical past, is for that reason legally endured.

The key question regarding the ownership of free capital is: who can claim control over free capital *by right*, whether because of its source, or because of its utilisation? We must make a distinction between those who make a claim, and those who can *justify* a claim. That is indeed a distinction! Under the first heading come not only the owners of the means of production, the entrepreneurs and capitalists, but also the workers and ultimately the state—all making claims for a share in free capital. For the second, we need to reflect on the fundamental principles involved. If we start from *Geist*, from the proposition that anything with *Geist* in it belongs primarily to its creator, then that decides the ownership of free capital: it belongs to whoever created it.

So, who is the creator, then? Outwardly it seems to be brought into view through the work of the worker, the collaboration of the staff, and under the guidance of the management, and of the company directors. However, all of these taken together are not the *originators* of the labour-saving machines that they use. The originator is the person who contrived the machine.

The arbitrary appropriation of free capital does not rest on any fundamental natural right, but is what one may call "consequential possession" resulting from a mistaken analogy with nature, with natural propagation processes. For example, farmers naturally feel it is right that he who owns the cow must own the calf.* One may be inclined to carry this right suggested by natural "productivity" over into the sphere of human labour productivity. But it is not labour, but *Geist* from which is brought about the formation of free capital. Free capital derives from the productivity of *Geist*, and is nothing to do with labour activities nor with the entrepreneurial spirit which organises them, although such activities are brought into effective use by the creative force of human intellect. Of course, values—not part of free capital—are produced by human intellect and labour with the means of production; in accordance with the social *Hauptgesetz*† and the principle of the

---

*In early Irish law, which had nothing to do with the Roman law from which —particularly in respect of the doctrine of "occupatio"—the legal basis for the appropriation of free capital derives, there was a decision about a form of intellectual property couched in precisely these terms. Columba copied the text of the gospels from a manuscript belonging to Finnian. Finnian discovered this and protested to Diarmit, the High King, who gave the judgement, "To every cow her calf, to every book its transcript. Therefore the copy you have made, O Columba, belongs to Finnian"—a judgement which Columba was loth to accept seeing that the copy belonging to Finnian was in no way diminished by the existence of the copy. It is interesting to reflect that had the Irish Brehon laws not been replaced by laws based on Roman concepts, the development of the economic system might have been different, and perhaps nearer to that desired by Wilken; if this is so, then all the more compelling is Wilken's thesis that our present concepts of company law are based on historical seizures which were subsequently invested with a legal gloss, and thus are far from reflecting the natural arrangement of economic life. This would be a highly significant matter for economic science, which has generally speaking, even in Marx's case, assumed the legal forms shaping economic life to be given, even to be immutable, when this may be far from being correct. This has some practical importance in the drafting of new forms of company documentation, for example for common ownership companies as defined under the British Industrial Common Ownership Act of 1976 —Editor, English edn.

† I.e., Steiner's main social law; see Glossary.—Editor, English edn.

division of labour, these non-free capital values justify a claim to counterpart values in the form of the supply by others of the goods necessary for life. This is organised through the medium of money which "individualises" the claims of each person to own goods in relation to the size of income; but these claims do not basically cover the values which come under the heading of free capital formation. This brings us to the point that neither the capitalists, that is the owners of the means of production, nor those who produce economic values with the aid of the means of production, should be given a "consequential possession". Neither the ownership of the productive capital, nor the legitimate claim on consumer goods could extend to this particular right. The laisser-faire principle of the market economy, being pushed to extreme limits, has opened the way to the legitimate owners of the means of production, by which they have taken free capital into their own possession, so that in their turn, the workers demanding higher wages are doing so at the expense of free capital. Though the latter are not aware of the concept of free capital, they are of course aware of profit, since this is generally understood to be the indicator of productivity. None of these situations could arise if people understood the truth about this matter.

The viewpoint that the creator of an object has an ownership relationship with it, and therefore the basis of a claim on it, leads in our case to the recognition that there must be a meaningful way in which the *Geistesleben* can take a share in the capital formation which its intellectual creativity makes possible. Moreover, this share should be direct, not roundabout via the state; still less should it come about by intellectual assets being turned into commodities and sold. All creations of the mind are linked in their origin with their creator from whom they derived. They belong to that creator, by the same concept as that of copyright. The so-called intellectual property can be transferred, once it has taken the form of material objects. However, there is a special social situation here; in that the quite unstoppable principle is at work, that the *Geist* is freely available to all. Thus, the creator is, it seems, left without any ownership claim on the material fruits of the concrete realisation of his ideas, economically speaking. The machine which the engineer makes out of the ideas of the innovator gives the latter neither ownership nor even participation. For the innovator to have any share in the practical fruits, legislation would be necessary. The idea of an innovation passes through two stages in its physical realisation. In the first it is stamped with a physical form; for example, a machine has to be built. The second stage is its realisation in circulation, via the money system, starting with the formation of the proceeds of the sale of the machine itself, and then through the sales of the goods it produces. The money thus acquired can, given the right circumstances, "precipitate" as capital sums, since autonomous amounts of profit in money form can become free capital formation. This can finance new productive investment, or it can be dispersed in consumption, say by price reductions. In the first case it becomes prospective capital, for future productive use; in the second case it is decapitalised, since it is appropriated for consumption purposes. These two possibilities decisively affect the matter of ownership. This is the whole point of the struggle between entrepreneurs wanting capital and workers wanting consumption.

It will be easier to understand the right way to look at capital ownership in the light of our analysis of *Geist* if we take an example. Eugen Diesel invented the diesel engine. The Augsburger Maschinen-fabrik did the tests needed to produce it; for this, the practical *Geist* of the company engineers was needed. To make it possible to put the engine into a power-driven vehicle the intellectual skills of designers were called in. And finally skilled craftsmen brought the thing to material completion, using the particular knowhow of each trade, and with the aid of machines which themselves in turn were the result of the inspiration of *Geist*. The forces of *Geist* were at work throughout. Now we have to ask, how did Diesel and the engine technologists and the vehicle designers and finally the craftsmen and employees all develop their skills? The fountainhead of these skills springs only and solely in the general and particular *Geistesleben*, especially from schools and from teachers. Bearing this in mind, we can arrive at the conviction that many of the *Geist*-based claims on free capital can be lumped together. Since a specific personal correlation is possible only in very few cases, claims on economic life can be vindicated only for the *Geistesleben* as a whole. That is, claims would not be made by particular individual members as countervalue for their individual intellectual contributions, but these would be raised on behalf of the *Geistesleben* as a whole, and must be transferred to it as a whole. That is the basic principle. It has to be borne in mind that today's *Geistesleben* is a fragmented social category, without power; as a mere agglomeration of scattered and disjointed individuals it has fallen apart and does not constitute a whole. No coherent social move to finance itself can come from a *Geistesleben* in such a state of disintegration. This would mean the formation of organisational means through which it could raise claims for satisfactory arrangements regarding the fruits of its creative activities. At present, the individual members and institutions of the *Geistesleben* get most of their economic wherewithal via the state. The state finances cultural bodies and schools, turning their members into civil servants. This makes possible the politicisation of cultural life. Only a small number of the members of the *Geistesleben* get their means of subsistence independently of the state, via private contracts, in which a stipulated counter-value for their services is arrived at. This is the case with lawyers, private doctors, management consultants and the like. If the services of this kind of *Geist* are made into commodities, there will always be difficulties, since what doctors, teachers, clergymen and indeed civil servants do is financially incommensurable and cannot be materially quantified.

When a doctor or lawyer is paid the stipulated honorarium, this is a *pseudo*-exchange transaction, in which economic exchange is mimicked. If seen in the correct way, the doctor—if he understands his calling and practises it ethically—gives his services, healing the patient out of altruistic motives. Naturally the patient will feel the need to make a gift in return, in the form of money—which can be exchanged for goods. This reciprocity can be undermined by materialist attitudes on the part of either doctors or patients, depersonalising the relationship between them and divert the doctor into a materialistic exploitation of his abilities. This can happen just as much in nationalised health services. It is socially essential that the activities of the *Geistesleben* should not be guided by the rules of commercial exchange. The way to settle up between the services of the *Geistesleben* and the services of the economic organism can only be in reciprocal donations. The *Geistesleben* gives its intellectual activity and exertions—that is its nature; but the nature of the economic sector is not to donate its production but to sell it, and so it must find and develop a way by which the *Geistesleben*—which from an economic view only consumes —can meet its needs for material goods.

There are two ways of doing this: either the *Geistesleben* must produce the said goods itself, which means extra work if it is to maintain its proper activities; or there is free capital, which from its formation on must be put in trust. This will be dealt with more fully later.

CHAPTER 3

Limitations of Individualised Ownership

1 *The struggle for capital*

The struggle for capital reveals itself as a special case of the liberal and Darwin-inspired proposition that human life consists of a struggle for existence. This idea was developed in the total conviction that it constituted a valid and true world view. Hence it has been "acted out" on a massive scale. It has stamped itself on the social system of the West, particularly as the guiding principle of economic life. This socio-economic system is primitive, being based on a naïve self-interest, and has, in the course of time, revealed its social weaknesses and its practical shortcomings. These shortcomings are seen above all in the sphere of capital formation and management, in three particular ways. Primarily there is the inability of investment policy, when directed only by self-interest, to take the health of the entire socio-economic set-up into account—this being quite divorced from capital management. Under the constraint of self-interest all necessary investment which is unprofitable is neglected. Now unprofitable investment includes not only various economic enterprises, but also the necessary provision for the *Geistesleben*. All those investments which the economic system neglects, but which are socially necessary, have therefore to be undertaken by the state. Secondly, when economic activities are directed by self-interest, and hence dominated by a competitive struggle, a disproportionate demand for capital, and therefore disproportionate formation of capital are the result. This has been touched on already, and will be discussed more fully later. Thirdly there is the perversion—characteristic of this type of economic system and indicative of its inner flaw—by which the economy is systematically diverted from its proper purpose of meeting the need for material goods, to pursue instead the aim of acquiring money for its own sake. Competition to maximise money profits, that is capital, leads to large amounts of capital being applied uneconomically, particularly by over-investment in an economically unnecessary expansion of production. Worse still is the totally counter-productive investment seen, for example, in fruitless property deals or in exchange speculation which upsets the economic system. Not only is it economically unproductive to use capital in such a way that money capital is put into property values and left lying idle, but in addition the living current of money is obstructed by the formation of blockages of values in the overall circulation process. This point will be worked out more precisely.

An economy, to the extent that it degenerates into a competitive struggle for capital, develops a disproportionate demand for capital, met by disproportionate formation of capital. Both these tendencies result from a diversion of the stream, motivated by the demand for capital in turn brought about by economic expansion. This has the result that in such an economic system the shortage of capital becomes endemic. Those competing for capital are urged on by the "wishful thinking" that uninterrupted growth is the *sine qua non* of this economic system. The increasing shortage of capital inevitably resulting from this compels the state to intervene more and more in economic life. In this way the state gets deeper and deeper into the capitalistic premises of this economic system, so that a growing sector of industry is taken over and run by the state.

Out of the liberalistic conception of the way in which human freedom should be realised came the private capitalistic economic system; hence this system must be understood as symptomatic of a stage in the historical development of modern society. In it, people have no alternative but to cut themselves off from each other, because their wish is to become independent individuals in their own right and strength.

This dislodged man from the traditional social groupings. Each seeks to develop his own powers, to build his own individuality free from any social constraint. With these powers, the "self-individualising" human spirit seized hold of capital, so as to develop the basis of a material civilisation. This universal contemporary drive can only work itself out through the free human *Geist* and through the accumulation of capital that it brings about. This accumulation of capital constitutes the pre-condition, without which there can be no material civilis-ation, based as it is on the force of independent individualism. That is the historical preliminary stage. It can only have a future if the world of capital created by human intelligence acquires a social dimension, in which the *Geistesleben*-induced capital formation will be pledged not in a self-interested way but disinterestedly and rationally for the development of the economy. The resistance which the contemporary economic system offers to a rational arrangement will be seen in the next section, in which are considered the various kinds of excrescences that are cultivated by the struggle for capital.

2 The capital company and the "double life" of its capital: artificial capital and finance capital

The full extent of the inadequacy of the market-economy system, with its investment shaped solely by personal considerations, is revealed in the ways in which capital for investment is enticed. A whole universe of artificial incomes and artificial capital has been created.

There is in the individualist capitalist economic system of the West a terrible misdirection of the flow of capital, of what one might call "floating capital". This misdirection is inevitable given the nature of the system. The whole basis of it lies in the financial instrument called the *share*. The share is not a loan but a "cut" in the ownership of a firm, in the form of a fraction of the ownership of the means of production. The financial essence of the capital share is that it need not be paid back. Such is the way that the ownership relationship of the shareholders with the enterprise is defined. To each individual share belongs the right to participate in the profits of the enterprise, *pro rata* to the number of shares, so that the proportion of capital owned is the proportion of profit. The total share capital represents the total ownership of the firm and its ultimate control, from which the directors and managers derive their authority. It is the majority not of the shareowners but of the share capital which appoints the board, who in turn appoint the managers. Thus the majority of the share capital controls the firm as if—within the limits of company law—it had the rights of total ownership. If therefore a single shareholder gets just over half the shares, he will control the firm. In some circumstances less than half may in practice be sufficient. This has far-reaching consequences. It provides the basis for the concentration of capital into a few hands, so that economic power develops to the point where it has a significant impact in political matters. Thus, the difference between a big shareholder and a small one is not just that the former gets a bigger share of profit—this difference is also significant for the business of *power* in society.

Because shares are irredeemable, so that the relationship between owners and firm cannot be dissolved, it was necessary to devise the institution of a capital market, wherein shares could be traded as saleable and re-saleable commodities. This is the Stock Exchange. This makes it possible to opt out of an ownership relationship if desired. This is because the shares acquire a *market value*, basically calculated from the company's profitability. People with capital money would not put it at the disposal of the firm if they could not count on the one hand on having a share in the company's free capital, and on the other hand on being able to get out of the deal. The share prices consequently fluctuate, thus offering the continual chance of speculative profit. The profit on which the share has a claim is the primary factor determining its price, the rate of profit being capitalised. Changing company profits thus give rise to changing share valuations. The resulting fluctuation is used as a basis for speculative activity which is just what has given the Stock Exchange its function, and has led to it being a specialised market for negotiable securities, particularly shares. This market has its own circulation of capital, that is, of floating capital, from which unearned and artificial capital derives. The speculative valuation of share capital on the Stock Exchange does not in any way correspond with the economic productive activity of the firm; hence it constitutes a sort of "double life" for the share capital. The central location in which the productive capital of the firm is called into this double life", in which its *alter ego* is conjured forth, is the Stock Exchange. The way in which this alter ego is born and repeatedly animated leads to gross misuse of capital.

The Stock Exchange as a market for shares, i.e. for the title-deeds of companies, was analysed in detail by Hilferding in his book on finance capital. In it he gave statistics of the business of the Stock Exchange, including not only shares but fixed-interest bearing securities. Hilferding characterised this form of capital as *fiktive* ("factitious") since it had no economic fruit. The size of finance capital can be gauged by comparing statistics for market valuation with those for nominal capital—i.e. the amount of money originally put in, broadly speaking. In Germany this was reported by the German central bank as amounting, in 1971, to 59.7 thousand million marks. However the *market value* was 120 thousand million marks—over twice as much—

and this had risen by July 1972 to 145 thousand million marks, nearly two and a half times as much as the nominal capital. The difference represents the amount of finance capital which has been attracted by the activities of the Stock Exchange. If one knew the daily turnover of share dealings, the full extent of the capital channelled away would be revealed. The sheer size of this capital diversion generates a capital inflation and an inorganic increase in the quantity of money; this becomes a burden for the economy and tends to upset equilibrium. This is both psychologically and practically unavoidable so long as free capital is made into something privately owned by the owners of the means of production, with investment being allocated primarily on considerations of personal profit and only secondarily on fundamental economic grounds. This system is of course based on the assumption* that the drive to acquire money guarantees that the proper aims of the economy will be realised.

Conventional economists have tended to ignore Hilferding's book, which was developed from volumes II and III of Marx's "Capital". His analysis probes the very roots of the system. He shows just how a share, as an entitlement to profit, is priced by capitalising its earnings, so that "a second capital appears to be present. This is purely factitious. Only industrial capital and its profit has an effective role to play. But that fact does not stop this factitious capital from being treated as an accounting entity, that is as share capital... The total of shares is not a genuine capital sum but simply sums up the sale and purchase of dividend entitlements. The fluctuations of share prices leave the processes of real industrial capital quite untouched, and do not reflect its real productivity, nor its real value..." (pp. 116-7, German edition, "Das Finanzkapital", Vienna 1910). Thus, he concludes, the total share capital, being based on capitalisations of dividend payments, is usually quite unrelated to the money capital initially invested.

The circulation of factitious capital cannot take place unless there is real productive capital paid for in money or real assets. The very act of financing an enterprise establishes its ownership. The initial subscription for shares is economically productive. But after that, the shares, as titles to ownership, begin to lead a separate life. Their highs and lows have no direct bearing on company operations, and only indirectly express its creditworthiness, or otherwise, since the share prices reflect profitability. It is worth looking at Stock Exchange statistics of turnover and

---

*The key assumption made by Adam Smith.—Editor, English edition.

of the original ("nominal") capital subscribed, so as to get an idea of the extent of this factitious speculative capital.

As the productive capital of a firm is quite separate from such a capital market, it has to take on a quite artificial existence. From the standpoint of economic reality, one can see this as *artificial* capital, and the income arising from capital market transactions as artificial incomes. No economically productive activity stands behind these incomes. Of course it must not be overlooked that these artificial capitals and incomes derive in the first place from an investment of real productive capital. The initial subscription for shares reflects this. This initial subscription capital is absorbed in the enterprise, but is "resurrected" on the Stock Exchange into an artificial life. This calls for the input of pure *finance* capital, which is formed and installed in the turnover of the Stock Exchange *after* the productive investment has been made. Finance capital is therefore quite different from the initial subscription capital; finance capital is speculative and the initial subscription capital is productive. This pure finance capital, based on materialist assumptions, is developed as an instrument for the establishment of economic *power centres* of an unprecedented size. These have spread over the earth and many nations have become economically and politically dependent on them. The inherent drive for the objective of sheer size, typical of materialism, seeks its fulfilment by using the possession of means of production as an aggressive weapon with which to get control of free capital.

These modern big business power-centres, brought about by the so-called liberal market economy, have grown to such strength that they increasingly seek to influence political affairs. This is made possible by the extensive entanglement of the state and economic life. The state manages various activities, wide-ranging in scope, wherever the private economy lacks the incentive to produce. The armaments industry also accounts for a significant sector of the economy. Thus, the economy and the state have become closely interwoven. Large-scale industry, with its multinational interests, tries to get the state to help it achieve its aims, through tariff policy, subsidies, or the award of government contracts.

The biggest concentration of economic power, with its political dimension, is brought about by the great entrepreneurial personalities and the large corporations—combines, cartels, trusts, etc—striving to dominate the market. These are the "great powers" of the economic world, pursuing with determination and subtlety their object of drawing free capital to themselves because this provides the basis for their economic and social power. Another way of doing this is to manipulate company voting rights, utilising the fact that ownership of half—or sometimes less—of the share capital gives control of the given company. It is the right to appropriate free capital and the majority control principle in share companies which account for the success of the multinationals, with the management by objectives and other sophisticated techniques they employ. The psychological drives involved have a practical motive; namely that continuous technical development promotes the formation of free capital as evidenced by cost reduction and the associated augmentation of profits—for the sake of which the business is conducted.

This is what induces the economy in continued expansion, expansion which is quite inorganic since it results from individual firms trying to keep pace with their competitors, which is quite different from having real knowledge of demand. This hinders the attainment of economic balance. Finance capital is all the time trying to increase its control of more and more production, so as to appropriate the free capital resulting therefrom. This tendency promotes the growth of immense fortunes. For example in 1970 there were over 2300 taxpayers in West Germany with incomes over one million marks—and this group as a whole had a combined income of over four and a half thousand million marks. How could anyone acquire incomes of this size? More precisely, what is the principle in the economic system which can generate such incomes?

3 How the market economy can be turned to personal ends:
   Friedrich Flick

An economic system which gives a licence to the owner of the means of production—by legally unimpeachable means—to take possession of free capital, produces extraordinary results. For example, consider the case of Friedrich Flick, recognised to be one of the last great entrepreneurial personalities, who built one of the largest of German industrial groups, with extensive subsidiaries abroad.

Flick's large and well-consolidated empire was built by the personal will of its founder. His motive was, in effect, to immortalise his personal existence through his family and their descendants. This family group egoism—an extension of individualism—aims to build up an economic power centre, to which members of the family will be permanently tied.

Every person, when first developing his personality, wants immortality; so it is easy to go a step further and seek it in the activities of one's descendants. Thus Flick sought to create a world of his own in the form of a vast family business. He tried to cement this world together by making gifts of assets to his children and to his grandchildren, thus minimising death duties. But these gifts—amounting to millions—became something of an obsession. He kept back the power of sale over the assets given. The terms of the gift left him in sole control over the business. Day-to-day management was delegated to his sons and grandsons, but under his sole control. At one time his eldest son rebelled against this and nearly wrecked the scheme, but the quarrel was made up and the system continued after Flick's death. This method also, of course, provides for the dependants, who to gain their income from it, need to manage the concern well enough not merely to maintain it in existence but to make it grow still more. This requires ever-increasing appropriation of free capital. Such is the logic of this economic system, which legally gives over into private possession the free capital which the economic system as a whole has produced. This appropriation serves both to provide a luxurious life-style and to finance still more investment, the further to maximise profit.

The economic justification for this process is claimed to be that the owner of the means of production is, through the appropriation of free capital, given the ability to promote the growth of the economy, in the mistaken belief that continual growth is a necessity of the economic system. In fact, it makes it difficult to get growth into proportion. This is only possible if the owners of the means of production are restrained from helping themselves to the free capital formation of the economy. This would make it impossible to form economic power centres. These power centres are generally formed by means of share transactions, through which large groups are built up. The way in which this is done is pretty primitive. All one needs is an instinct for the market opportunity, which Flick, for example, claimed to possess. He described his method as follows: "You must have an eye for the value of a business, and be able to see how it would fit in with other interests. I flatter myself that I have this eye." He was reputed to be able to carry every detail of his empire in his mind, down to the last figure—like a computer programmed to take all the business data. At the end of the war, he was released from prison early on condition that he sold his remaining coal interests. This done, he used the money to buy shares in Daimler-Benz, in Auto-Union, in the paper group Feldmühle and the chemical concern Dynamit-Nobel. In the end his empire was worth over two thousand million marks, controlled by his patriarchal character. That was how he sought, through his family, to achieve some kind of immortality on earth.

Then at the beginning of 1975 an event took place which revealed the instability of this type of empire. Inside a concern created by a sort of Faustian craving for a gigantic economic complex, differences of opinion will occur and power struggles break out. Something of this kind happened between three of the family. It became necessary to allow two of the grandsons to withdraw their share, and this meant selling three-quarters of the shareholdings, specifically the shares in Daimler-Benz. This involved no less than 29% of Daimler-Benz's capital, and the Deutsche Bank bought the Flick shareholding for two thousand million marks. This transaction was said to have been the biggest of its kind ever to take place in Western Germany. The whole business revealed the scale of factitious capital.

A way was found of transferring this amount free of tax, so that each grandson got one thousand million marks, of factitious capital. One has to judge this pointless enrichment of a few against the fact that there are millions starving in the world today. This is made possible by the system. This private accumulation of capital is artificial. And in place of a personal will, the form of an impersonal shareholding is substituted, which through its relationship with the person owning them, entitles that person to a contrived value, the size of which is proportionate to the size of his holding. This economic system now needs government help to keep it going, though it is based on the principle of self-help; one may well think that it finds its *reductio ad absurdum* in such developments as we have been describing. Surprisingly, people still fail to see the moral issue involved, and are content to accept all this as a matter of fact.

The ways which the rules of the market economy open lead not only to excessive and self-multiplying capital "surges", but they also support the technologically stimulated tendency to large-scale units. Indeed, large and powerful monopolies are brought into being precisely by the combination of technological development and entrepreneurial willpower. Small businesses, in manufacturing and in retail, come into being in order to serve the basic human need to support existence, which is what compels the development of the economic system. Added to this there is of course also a need to enrich life through economic activity. Contrasting with this normal human economic motive, there is large industry, run on the principle that a massive increase is called for in the supply of goods for both consumption and production; for example the industrial empire of Flick and others like him. The power political will to survive of the over-size economic units has changed the simple price-regulating competitive battle into a war, waged with great skill, for utter survival. In this war, the prize is free capital, the values produced by the productivity of the human *Geist*. Through the investment of this free capital on the share markets, control over the productive capital of other firms is gained. This forms the basis of the war for an ever-increasing share of free capital, always utilised for the technological development of productivity that produces more free capital still.

4   *The rule of the managers*

One particular tendency has developed, which can be called the *de-personalisation* of the entrepreneur's role. Contrasting with the highly idiosyncratic nature of the older economic command, the recent trend has been for the directly personal element in management to be more and more replaced by objective management structures, working solely on profit calculations. Under the pressure of a dispassionately waged competitive struggle, the activities of managing a major industrial concern have to be freed from all personal considerations. They must be made objective, depersonalised, highly sophisticated, all this being combined with rigid adherence to the profit motive—such are the qualities demanded of modern managers.

Volkswagen, the largest company in Germany, is run, not by any owner, but by manager-type directors. For a long time indeed, Volkswagen had no particular owners at all, until it was changed quite arbitrarily—and from an economic viewpoint, pointlessly—into a limited company. This created a host of artificial owners, who now have a claim on profits. However, the managerial character of the directors has not altered. The very nature of the limited company favours the impersonal, the objective approach to plant management functions.

In the 20th century, as compared with the 19th, the role of the managers has increased, and the entrepreneur's role correspondingly curtailed. Management activities call for the same type of mind as the engineer—that is, what is needed is detached consideration of the optimum course. The underlying principle now is to develop specific objective abilities, which are focused on "the facts", and which brook no attempt at deflection by any personal interests whatsoever—utterly different from the style of the entrepreneur who owns the business he runs. These required abilities have been set out in detail by the various professional bodies who specialise in management development and training. Four steps are involved:

1   Analysis of the circumstances and facts
2   Deciding what to do
3   Motivating others to carry out decisions*
4   Checking up that decisions have been carried out*

Planning and organising abilities, and leadership qualities are of course necessary, as well. All these competences are exercised in a purely pragmatic way, as if by an engineer controlling an installation, who concentrates solely on the optimum way of operating the complex. The manager carries out no ownership function and is not directly guided by any considerations of personal ownership. As manager, he may be concerned to maximise profits, but they are not *his* profits; the riddle which confronts him is how to achieve this, and he has to solve this riddle, and solve it objectively. This he does by the cold and dispassionate application of intellect.

Flick was a first-class manager, as his business achievements show, but his managerial aptitudes were entwined with his entrepreneurial autocratic nature. However, the total management approach is able to beat the entrepreneurs, whose autocratic ways are out of date. Which is why Flick was described in his obituary as the last representative of the great entrepreneurs. He applied his exceptional abilities to the realisation of purely personal aims. Never did he try to develop a humane and rational economic system, which would have as its aim simply the provision of cheap and sufficient goods for the people living on the planet.

A quite inconceivable amount of expense and trouble has been

---

* Steps 3 and 4 are often, in much management literature, lumped together as "communications". As Wilken intended his book to be read by people who would be learning to manage, I have spelt them out in full.—Editor, English edn.

applied—and wasted—in order to achieve personal control over the economic system, making use of all the financial potentialities available to wrest the largest "legitimate" share possible of both free and artificial capital, all in the name of profit maximisation. One should try to envisage how fruitful the energy involved could have been had it been applied in a correctly arranged and need-oriented economic system. Now it needs to be recognised that in order to establish such a normal economic system, large scale industry would still be retained, but its present power structure would have to be done away with. This abolition of power means that free capital would need to be released from the arbitrary control now exercised by owners and managers of the means of production, motivated as they are by profit. *The economy needs to be permeated with the correct thinking.* This would be possible with an economic constitution so structured that people could work together to find the best way to meet practical and real needs.

In recent times there are increasing signs of a change in business thinking, that the entrepreneurial function and the profit motive should be depersonalised. This is from the point of view that the enterprise has a social and economic existence of its own. The idea has been put forward, for example, of the *firm in itself*. This forward-looking idea would separate a business from its owner. Thereby the profit of the enterprise would be no longer personal; in the *firm in itself* the profit would not belong to the entrepreneur, it would not be his property. While the firm would still be guided by the profit motive, the profit would no longer constitute the personal "cut" of the entrepreneur. This idea (put forward in Germany by Werner Flume) is indicative of changing ideas about the nature of business and about the proper legal standing of profit. The economic concept of profit can only be understood in relation to free capital formation and its true role in the firm. For this we need to have a clear concept of what goes to make up the money complex at present known as "profit". The diversity of its components has already been noted.

Three forms of economic system, or better, three *styles* of company can be distinguished:

1 The individualistic drive which brought the modern economic system into being now belongs to the past. It reflected the will and skills of individual free entrepreneurial personalities. Its main spring was the elemental drive to "improve" oneself, and it found

its material fulfilment in making a money profit.

2 The present time is characterised by the change from individualist entrepreneurialism to impersonal rule by managers. This gives the whole economy—both in respect of physical things, and of people —a mechanistic stamp. The managerial *Geist* has transformed the personal striving of the entrepreneur into a depersonalised corporate goal, the profit principle. The systematic realisation of this "objectified" goal is carried out in the abstract and calculating spirit of a *duty* to get results at any price.

3 The economic future will take the form of individually promoted ethical common ownership companies, forming a *social* economy. It will develop social forms which will lead to the recognition of needs and to an economic life which manages and shapes itself in the light of this recognition. This will humanise the contemporary managerial ethos with its orientation towards objective economic accountability. This accountability would no longer be directed towards abstract profit goals. Note that this humane type of social economy and the "associative" organs forming it should on no account be confused with any nationalised economy on the eastern pattern. This point will be further developed, in due course.

In this section we have seen how individual entrepreneurial personalities have brought about the formation of private economic power centres. Let us then look at the question, in what sense may we correctly speak of "capitalists" and of the "capitalist economic system".

For this it is important to study Appendix I. What has to be seen and grasped is the *hegemony* of *Geist* in making capital, unavoidable in all socio-economic phenomena, and the way in which this finds practical realisation in the money form, in which form it is behind *all* economic development. This is explained in the Appendix. With that, one can understand that the modern economic system can indeed be correctly described as capitalistic. However this recognition will be qualified; our experience is that in this economic system control over capital is legally private. The automatic "privatisation" of capital ownership has had the effect that large scale private ownership of capital can be utilised as the basis of virtually limitless economic power. The spectacle of increasing economic and social misuse of all capital values, whether tangible or latent, has in turn had the effect that the private owners of large sums of money or production complexes are called "capitalists", derogatorily. The condemnation is not only on account of the self-seeking use of capital, but also because of the general instinctive perception that an excess of personal wealth implies drawing to oneself resources of the earth that are thereby denied to others, against all justice. Hence it is that the economic system of the West is called capitalist. Objectively, it may so be called, provided this characterisation is based on the key role in the modern economy of prospective capital. The combination of this with the concept of private capital provides the starting point for agitation against the historical personal basis of the system. Marxism holds that this system can be made social by the depersonalisation of capital ownership through political collective ownership. However, leaving aside ownership relations, the system which results from this is still capitalist in the sense that it can only operate by means of capital performing its necessary function.

5 *"Privatisation" of capital, and the faults resulting from this system*

The critique of capital finds its point ultimately in the power of disposal over the massive sums of money resulting from the formation of free capital. This ability to control this money offers, to the individuals who manage free capital, free self-realisation in the so-called free market economy with its artificial markets. Normally all capital appears, accounts-wise, in the form of profits. However, as we have seen, free capital proper is lumped together with various irregular components, so that it cannot be clearly distinguished. These accretions obviously include sums representing capital formation forced by price increases in both capital and consumer markets, or by depressing employees' incomes. There is also the restrictive type of capital formation resulting from the receipts of sales of property, etc. An augmentation of a special kind results from inflation, which currently leads to a profit explosion. These artificial profits go together with the irregular creation of money capital for speculative use. All this gives rise to an unpredictable widening of the economy.

However what we are considering now is not the creation of capital or of profit but the various applications of profit—regardless of the regularity or irregularity of their formation. Conventional economics takes the view that decisions based on self interest will in fact accord with the common good, and will have the same effect as would be brought about by rational economic objectivity. Careful study of the facts discloses whether and to what extent the individualistic system of the market economy and its artificial markets leads to misapplications of capital. Various typical forms of capital misapplication can be distinguished, that are made possible, not to say made inevitable, by the privatisation of free capital and its application in the service of private interests seeking to provide themselves with material goods. In this respect, what has already been said in the first section of this chapter should be borne in mind, about the struggle for capital and its consequences. The consequences are a disproportionate demand for capital and as a result capital formation is stepped up too much. The lack of balance between the two is seen in the shortage of capital. More broadly, there is a neglect of economically and socially needed investment, precisely because capital is hard to come by; these constitute an objective shortage of capital over and above the more "subjective" shortage resulting from the competition for capital. Because of the continually recurring shortage of capital, under present-day relationships a disproportionate creation of money and credit is caused, as it were, subliminally. This is a cause of inflation. This is a direct result of the uncontrolled increase in the money supply, occasioned by the capital requirements of the private economy. In what follows, various instances are discussed, of subjective and system-induced capital shortage resulting from waste or misapplication of capital.

i) *Capital shortage through self-financing.* Both private entrepreneurs and the managers of large corporations tend to make it an objective of management to apply part or all of profits, as they arise, to the self financing of the enterprise, for making improvements or for expansion. Flick built up his empire completely by means of self-finance, by means of the legal "occupation" of the free capital appearing in his companies. Looked at with an open mind, self-financing satisfies a private demand for capital, but is restricted to the development of the one business. This sort of thing can only be assessed, as to its necessity, from the standpoint of the overall economic process. The alternative to self-finance is to borrow. This involves paying interest. Hence it is claimed from the point of view of the firm that using one's own capital for self-finance avoids both interest and the burden of repayments. That is a cost advantage in the competitive battle, which can make possible a one-sided domination of the market. When this happens, the result tends to be progressive over-expansion. According to the ethos of the market economy a private economic "power", by the logic of the competitive battle, can legitimately make use of the collapse of those defeated to develop its own productive units. In the overall social accounting, the direct or indirect damage done would be reckoned against the super-profits realised by such monopolistic concerns.

The improper private appropriation of free capital leads, for various reasons, to economic dislocation. The chief reason is that individual private economic units expanding individually are unpredictable. Through an inorganic growth of individual cells, by means of self-finance, overall economic capital is wasted, and is lacking in places where it could usefully have been invested. It is evident that the growth of any one cell in the economy can only have the correct result if it is accomplished in harmony with other member organs of the economic organism. No single cell can know how to reach this harmony. Such knowledge can only be worked out when a sufficiently large group of people with responsibility in business life—and understanding—work together. Such people must get together if they are to gain the necessary knowledge and insight. This knowledge can serve individual firms —in their own best interests—as the basis of their decision-making.*

ii) *Shortage and wastage of capital through "sterile" investment.* Self-financing is the opposite of financing by outside capital, either in the form of a loan or of share-participation. To the extent that outside capital derives from consumers' savings, or from freely formed capital, productive capital is created, that will serve the development of economic activity. This must be clearly distinguished from the formation of *finance* capital—which is a deviation from genuine economic productiveness, and puts a burden on the economy by wasting capital. In section 2 of this chapter, we have already discussed this limitation imposed by the market economic system, which instead of using capital productively, dissipates it, by means of speculative investment in the factitious market for shares.

The factitious capital values relate only as a sort of "duplicate" to the share capital as originally subscribed and paid up. Through the subsequent dealings on the Stock Exchange, the shares came to be made into commodities, although they are really no such thing at all. Thus they are valued, bought and sold. The financing of these dealings uses existing money capital, and thereby converts it into finance

---

*This is exactly the theory of indicative planning, applied successfully in France, but unsuccessfully in England in the early 1960's.—Editor, English edn.

capital—which because of its investment on the Stock Exchange is artificial capital. The point of its formation and investment is to make speculative profit, which does not correspond to any service. Much of this unproductive capital is formed from free capital. The profit taken in such misuse of capital is, economically speaking, pointless and artificial; no incentive to produce arises out of it. On the contrary, it reflects a waste of capital, the amount of which is not easy to calculate, but which creates shortages elsewhere. In order to get a rough idea of the extent to which capital is used, the turnover of the Stock Exchange can be taken as indicative.

The statistics available do not make it particularly easy to distinguish the categories we have discussed. The following tables are from the handbook to the German Stock Exchange and economy published by Societäts-Verlag of Frankfurt, for 1972. They show only the overall size of capital movements proper in the turnover figures:

GERMAN STOCK EXCHANGE TURNOVER
(thousand million marks)

Year	German Shares	Fixed-Interest Securities	Foreign Securities	Total
1970	12.2	4.7	2.8	19.7
1971	15.7	6.3	4.2	26.2

TOTAL SHARE VALUES
(533 quoted companies: thousand million marks)

Year	Nominal Capital	Stock Exchange Price Index*	New Issues	Turnover
1971	31.2	385.1	2.5	15.7

*Nominal value = 100

Note: New issues are not included in turnover.

FIXED INTEREST SECURITIES
(thousand million marks)

Year	End Year Total	New Issues	Turnover
1971	179.5	30.8	6.3

The size of the factitious capital is illustrated by the relationship of nominal capital to quoted values, and is also suggested by the high turnover in shares compared with fixed-interest bearing securities. Compared with the nominal capital of the share companies, the fixed interest securities total nearly six times as much; but on turnover the relationship is reversed. Demand for fixed interest securities of course reflects primarily the interest obtainable, not the difference between share prices at different times. At this point it must be emphatically remarked that capital investment in the various fixed-interest securities is not the same thing as the speculative investment of money capital in share speculation. In the sphere of loan money, there is mobility; all the time one can pull out. This is the justification for the loan capital market. It is altogether different with shares. Not only is there the obvious difference in quantities, there is also a decisive difference in kind. This is caused by the effect of the sterility of this use of capital, which holds back and retards the whole economic system. This situation can only be overcome either by putting loans in the place of shares, or by reforming the whole principle of share capital as set out in Appendix 5. The financing of industry by the social principle of loan capital—once thought of instinctively as normal—will not be pursued at this point.

But the phenomena discussed so far do not fully reveal the extent of the fundamentally dislocating effects of sterile capital investment. This was demonstrated on a world scale during the currency speculation associated with the 1973 oil situation. This is dealt with more fully in Appendix 3.

iii) *Capital in the mortuary*: This works in the same way as sterile capital investment, but goes much further in disabling the circulatory system. What we are referring to here is the conversion of non-economic objects into money, so that these objects artificially re-enter the sphere of economic valuation, and are turned into commodities. These may be objects which were goods previously, and are drawn back into the economic cycle, for example houses, antiques, objets d'art, or goods which have been pledged to secure a loan and are to be auctioned; or they may be things which have never been produced but are arbitrarily made into commodities. The principal item in the latter category is land, whether used agriculturally or for business, or as building land. There are also the mineral resources in the earth, which acquire a true economic value only through and to the extent of the economic exertions necessary to bring them into effective use.

Those who receive money from the sale of such objects accumulate a money capital; the circulation of this capital interferes with the money cycle, because the function which has been performed is a dead one. Those who purchase such objects—which are not proper commodities—leaves his capital for dead in the circulation of money. This applies equally whether the capital is saved or factitious. Where does the purchaser of a piece of land get his money? Maybe he has means, probably money saved, saved out of earned income, out of free profit capital or perhaps out of speculative factitious capital. In the building industry the price of land is often financed by a bank mortgage. Now the following case must be clearly distinguished; if someone uses money saved, or some other money capital proper, in order to have a house built, that is not leaving capital for dead, and does not constitute a restrictive influence on the circulation of capital money. However, when one buys a house already built, and previously financed, perhaps to take the rent, as from a "solid" investment, then this is indeed a way of investing which straightaway leaves the capital lying dead. This retards and disables the economic circulation process. This can to some extent be corrected by the reuse of the money thus invested, but that does not alter the "deadening" nature of the original investment.

To get a picture of the extent to which capital is immobilised in this way in the contemporary economy, we may examine the following figures, published by the German Industrie-institut in 1973, for the year 1970:

GERMAN REAL AND FINANCIAL ASSETS IN 1970   (thousand million marks)

	Private	State
Dwellings:	474	14
Industrial property:	681	252
Agriculture and forestry:	265	67
Financial assets:	412	87
Government administrative assets:		632

Together these total 2.88 billion (= million million) marks. This constitutes a *latent* capital value , which at any time could be economically mobilised, that is brought into the trading process, thus leading to the diversion of money capital into a dead form of investment.

The socially unfortunate and economically dislocating effects of this diversion of the stream of capital into a stagnant application can be seen from the way in which the market economy is utilised to sell real estate in various circumstances. For example, a dying firm may be resuscitated in this way. Thus, the Hanover wool-carding firm of

Döhrenwerke, which had become economically unsound, announced in 1972 that it was to close down, since production was no longer profitable. Its share capital was 8 million marks and it was counted among the largest firms of its kind in Europe. In 1971 it had 888 workers, but by 1972 employed only 436, who all became redundant. However, the company did not wind up, although production ceased. On the contrary, it has managed to find a new and continued existence, without any productive activities being carried on. It owned 1830 acres of land and the majority of the shares of another company, the Bielefelder Weberein AG. The land was sold for 55 million marks, and Döhrenwerke's shares rose by 250%. The company which bought the land used it to put up some 3000 houses, and the cost of the land will of course add about 18,000 marks to the price of the houses.

Relating this to economic reason, to social responsibility, to the principles of justice, one is here confronted with the fact that a firm bases its life—and its after-life—on this, that it need not make any productive contribution to the economy, it need add no value to the social product. On the contrary, money capital is brought by it into stagnant investment in real estate, with a view to taking a future profit by selling it at an increased price for building on. Some of this is poured into the laps of the shareholders, and the rest is used to buy shares in other companies, if possible to the extent of obtaining control over them. This makes it possible for the company to become solely a financial trust. As a so-called holding company it absorbs the profits of the subsidiaries. By thus diverting free capital to itself it maintains its artificial existence. The holding company principle—which Flick made use of—can only exist because it is possible to appropriate free capital. That is how a holding company can pursue an artificial business, and the free market economy, with its artificial markets, and its inadequately worked out economic law, tolerates this. Holding companies are the means of diverting large quantities of capital, and hence add to capital shortage. A further example will be given later.

Of course, just one case can seem harmless enough; an isolated instance can be absorbed by the dynamic of the overall circulatory process. But when the constraints on circulation are multiplied by large numbers of instances, the situation then resembles a river made stagnant, and unable to purify itself. Such are the economic consequences of letting capital lie dead.

iv) *Shortage of capital resulting from overconsumption*: Technology has gradually come to affect every sphere of life. It has revolutionised not only production but consumption as well. It is inexhaustible in the development of new goods, and of new gadgets for use in the home. It has made it possible to transform all living; there is now a culture which is turned completely towards the material. This tendency began in the 17th and 18th centuries, and broadened out to include all the civilised countries of the West in the 19th. It should be said that, funda-mentally speaking, all this has brought about a kind of victory of mind over matter, making life on this planet easier and richer. This "*Geist-ification*" of the consumer side of life was a a gain from English economic thought and pragmatism. This has decisively stamped the shape of modern history. In the twentieth century this material culture developed to the point that it transformed home life from the bottom up, and in every way, in that it is revolutionised by an abundance of successive discoveries, including electrical appliances, cars, home heating, etc. The desire for technical perfection has degenerated to an increasing extent, as more and more people engage in a virtual epidemic of seeking more wealth, more pleasure and more relaxation of all kinds. Economic competition between the producers of objects of material culture comes to meet these psychic urges by continually offering ever more sophisticated contrivances, not only for the house-hold but also for amusements and pastimes, including radio, television and sporting equipment—the latter stimulated by the increasingly competitive nature of sport. (The urge for experience in the human psyche with its inborn aggressive instincts seeks an outlet in the artificial world of sport, and hence demands technical development in this sphere too. The peak of this urge is reached in the Olympic Games. The financial outlay for this world festival of competition indicates the degree of ostentation involved. The Munich stadium cost 1.35 thousand million marks to build.)

The impetuous forward surge of competition to bring about a technologically over-stimulated affluence is a temptation to prodigality. People are thereby urged on to outdo each other in their possessions. This social "keeping up with the Joneses" takes delight in possession as an extension of personality; it is believed that real human values and purpose in life will be found in highly mechanised comfort. From the point of view of the overall economy, this is just a waste. An example of this is the senseless squandering of electrical energy in the day and night illumination of large department stores, and in their heating and air-conditioning too. Another example of similar prodigality in consumer goods is the tyranny of fashion, in which an impersonal group instinct is at work; that is, those who wish to express their personality in their clothes nonetheless do so by appealing to the esteem of an impersonal group spirit.

It is noticeable that the urge towards overconsumption is not satisfied by increased work. This is an indication of a subconscious perception of the *Geist*-induced, and continual, development of the productivity of the economy. Instead, paradoxically as it might seem, progressive reduction in working time is wanted. Of course, without the formation of free capital, such overconsumption as we have today would simply not be possible. But the utilisation of free capital for this purpose, if it goes beyond a certain point, causes a shortage of capital. The same will result if savings fall because overconsumption is being paid for out of incomes. In both cases, whether the disproportionate consumption comes out of income or out of free capital, a shortage of capital tends to result. Since the privatisation of free capital usually takes the form of income, broadly speaking it is the higher incomes which include a share of free capital. According to Bruno Gleitze*, in the year 1965 2380 West German entrepreneurs and rentiers had a monthly average income of 190,000 marks. In 1967, German stores paid their directors on average 45,304 marks per month. Incomes of this level could never be earned by personal labour. In them is reflected primarily the appropriation of free capital, which is "borrowed" to form profit. These are the fruits, not of more intensive work, but of work-*saving*, which in big concerns come plentifully, and take the form of income. Such a prodigality with economic goods, made possible by free capital formation, and generally exercised through incomes, affects not only consumption, but extends itself further into the production of goods of the general market economy, driven as it is to continual growth by the central impulse of the acquisitive principle. This sets the scene for a compulsive tendency to overproduce. This is one of the biggest problems of the contemporary economic system.

v) *Shortage of capital through overproduction:* This arises in any economic system which sees continuous growth as as the basic premise of its operation. How does this notion arise? General social development, being the result of a combination of a materialist outlook with technological advance, has been guided more and more by the idea that

---

*In his "Sozialkapital und Sozialfonds als Mittel der Vermögenspolitik".

the further progress of technology should be an end in itself. With irresistible force, and particularly in this century, the prejudice has insinuated itself into the human psyche that an absolute value attaches to dominion over matter and to the possession of material goods. From this matter-transfiguring conception have developed particular forces which shape the development of the contemporary economic system. The more people seek security in matter, the more *Angst* they feel about their existence. It is this anxiety which, along with a need for esteem, is one of the principal causes of the competition to possess more. This competition, a matter of life-style, systematically drives the market towards the competitive battle.

In its original, quite dispassionate, form, competition performs a price-regulatory function, tending to equalise prices. Underlying this, the normal human concern with physical existence was at work. This normal price-regulating competition becomes sharpened and deepened in an economy no longer oriented towards need, and moreover, driven by a passion for a kind of competitive sport. A competitive battle of this kind degenerates continually, driven by the urge for power. When this latter drive, which continually inflates one's idea of oneself, catches hold of the economy, it pushes it into compulsive growth and towards an endless multiplication of the production of both consumer and capital goods. From this drive, quite alien to the economy, derives the feverish expansion of industrial capacity. It supports the concept, seemingly based in the facts of the market situation, that an economy not continually expanding is about to collapse. From the viewpoint of the militarised drive to expand armaments competitively, it has become intolerable even to think of an economy without growth. The cessation of growth is seen as a threat. This has become a dogma in modern economic policy.

The compulsive drive for power is two sided. On the one hand, it integrates the personality and raises self-esteem; on the other, it binds the personality fast to material things, so that it is finally completely given over to them. It focuses the will on activity in the material world and drives it to create therein, and in this creation to find fulfilment. In this way, consumption and production are stepped up in a way that, from the point of view of needs, is quite unnatural. Thus the goads of anxiety and power accelerate all economic functions. This takes the form of an incessant drive for all possible technological developments that promise any result, which inevitably results in the balance of the economy being repeatedly upset.

This is manifested in the disturbed polarity between the quantity of money and the demand for money, and in the imbalance between the amount of production and the amount of demand. The lack of balance in the commodity sphere is expressed in overproduction. The economy seeks to free itself from this through an unnatural and forced competition. In a market economy without social awareness, this competition *à l'outrance* is naturally the guiding rule. In it the normal legitimate competition for the best performance is changed into a battle to market excess production—a battle that is urged on by an enormous expenditure on stimulating demand. In the marketing campaign, a force makes itself evident, which draws people powerfully towards materialism. People with the mania to buy are obliged to pay large amounts for advertising among the contending firms. In 1972 in Germany these amounts totalled 13 thousand million marks. Perhaps a quarter of this sum is justified by necessary information. However, be that as it may, the full sum must be included in the costs of goods, that is unless it is extracted from appropriated free capital—called profit—as is clearly indicated in certain cases of excessive advertising.

Karl Marx characterised overproduction as the unavoidable result of an economic system founded on the private profit motive. Factually, overproduction has become an outstanding symptom of a market economy run by the isolated drives of individual self-made economic agents. Overproduction could normally be compensated by a reduction in production. However, this would be considered a retrogressive step in the market economy. Hence all means are used to try to raise demand. The market economy in modern times has managed to utilise the state as the safety valve by which over-production can be cleared. And the state has indeed taken up the over-production, particularly in the agricultural sphere. Total (German) government expenditure on support for agriculture came to 4.6 thousand million marks. For the maintenance of agricultural prices alone, 206 millions were spent, of which 123 millions went to build up stocks of goods which could not be sold, such as butter. Another way in which the state supports overproduction is via the purchase of armaments; in 1972 such expenditure came to 28.6 thousand million marks in West Germany, and 252.9 thousand million marks in the US. The production of armaments is carried on by private industry, in whose interest it is, therefore, that these goods should be used, so that more of them can be made.

It is easy to see that excessive production, like its twin, excessive consumption, implies and produces an excessive demand for capital.

This allows a corresponding shortage of capital to arise in the framework of the reciprocal dependence of the various factors in production.* The excess demand for capital—over that which is economically
necessary and justifiable—produces the tendency for there to be a
shortage of capital. It should be noted that this works itself out in
different ways, for each of the three normal kinds of money capital.
Capital shortages depend, directly or indirectly, upon the extent to
which capital is formed, and therefore on:
1 the amount of savings from earned income.
2 the amount of free capital formation, for the most part dispersed in
incomes.
3 the possibility of creating bank credit to meet the capital shortage.
It is the creation of money through credit which theoretically can fill
almost any gap in the supply of capital. The increase in the quantity of
money which this causes cannot easily be controlled by the central
bank, and without this control, the door is wide open to inflation. Thus
the German central bank, the Deutsche Bundesbank, reported in 1972
that it found itself unable to control the flow. Its monthly report for
February 1973 reported that credit facilities by banks to businesses
and individuals had risen from 70.1 thousand million marks in 1971 to
88.8 thousand million in 1972, an increase of 18.7 thousand million.

DEVELOPMENT OF THE VOLUME OF MONEY
(Total balances in thousand million marks)

AT YEAR END

	1 Cash	Increase	2 Current A/cs	Increase	3 Total 1+2	Increase
1970	36.9	–	71.3	–	108.2	–
1971	40.3	3.4	81.2	9.9	121.5	13.3
1972	45.8	5.5	93.5	12.3	139.3	17.8

	4 New Money Capital Formation	Increase	5 Savings Deposits	Increase
1970	35.6	–	203.5	–
1971	46.8	11.2	230.3	26.8
1972	62.6	15.8	261.7	31.4

---

*Wilken may not mean factors of production as conventionally understood.—Ed.

The formation of new money capital, importantly in the form of savings deposits and interest-bearing bonds, came to 62.6 thousand million marks, up 15.8 thousand million on 1971. Further details are shown in the table, taken from the Bundesbank's Monthly Report. The rate of inflation is evident from the dramatic increases shown for each year. The disproportionately high growth in current accounts—12.3 thousand million marks in 1972—clearly expresses the increase in credit money.

6. Bad management by the state.
Correcting the market-induced shortage of capital and
the failure to invest

Consideration of the various forms of capital misuse and shortage cannot be concluded without alluding to the expenditure and burdens put on the state, without which the free market economy, worked out by innumerable individualistic acts of freedom, could not function. It is of wide-ranging significance that the allocation of investable economic productive capital is at the free disposal of people who consider investment only from the point of view of profit. Because the progress of the economy generates an increasing demand for capital, the state is thereby obliged to remedy things by meeting the capital shortage which cannot be met by the savings process, motivated as it is by profit. Both the state and the economy are continually trying to stimulate savings by various means, all of which stress the return to be made. In particular, those who have appropriated free capital cannot be made to invest in necessary productive investment, since private entrepreneurs cannot put their capital in projects which do not bring any profit, such as road construction, certain types of house building, air transport, education and research. These expenditures are dealt with by the state. Another category which the market economy cannot cope with is the financing of energy production, particularly where this is capital-intensive, as with atomic energy. Moreover the state is involved in giving increasing sums to help firms in difficulties, in both agriculture and industry. This is bound up with the problem of unemployment, which the market economy cannot solve, so that the state has to take the responsibility. To deal with all these financial gaps, the state is in many ways obliged to take on the role of entrepreneur, and has to make extensive investments, which would not be profitable for the market economy. This is made possible by the state taking into its possession, via corporate taxation, up to half of the free capital depositing itself in capital companies. Private entrepreneurs are similarly taxed —but, as we have seen, such private appropriation of free capital is from an accounting point of view lost in income formation. However, in company balance sheets free capital can be identified, prior to its disbursement in incomes, as profit. And a proportion of free capital is transferred over into the coffers of the state, to the extent that business taxes are related to capital and to the high profits of big business.

The contemporary state, encumbered as it is with expense, has further ways of appropriating free capital—through various other taxes on wealth or property and through the profit taxes applicable to artificial capital formation. From a general economic standpoint, these taxes on free or on artificial capital are not really a sacrifice, since the levy is on something that is not really the taxpayer's property, but is fundamentally an improperly acquired appropriation. In my book on the reform of the tax system* it is explained in some detail, with statistical illustrations, to what extent the state acquires free capital, and uses it for purposes both proper and improper; and it is shown how the enormous requirements of the government take pretty well a third of the social product—and *why*. The reason is the tendency for the functionally-centralised state continually to expand. By "functionally-centralised state" is meant a system of government that does not limit itself to the discharge of its proper duties at home and abroad—which would bring about correct social relationships—but which makes an ever larger part of economic life its business. Indeed, in the circumstances, it can scarcely do anything else, since tasks are pushed on it by the market economy which cannot cope with them. The following table is taken from this book:

STRUCTURE OF GOVERNMENT EXPENDITURE
(thousand million marks)

For 1964:

For governmental and social purposes proper:	81	60%
For economic purposes:	40	29%
For cultural and educational purposes:	15	11%
Total:	136	100%

Breakdown of economic expenditures:

Food and agriculture:	5.4 (thousand million
Housing:	7.1 marks)
Commerce:	3.3
Manufacturing:	5.2
Transport:	10.5

*"Reform des Steuerwesens", Freiburg 1968.

These figures show everything the market economy cannot handle. The greatest abdication of our modern system lies in this, that it has not done anything to set up what is needed to provide for the *Geistesleben* or for cultural life. As it can't do this, the state finds itself obliged, not only to take over the neglected part of *economic* life, but also to "nationalise" virtually all of *cultural* life, particularly the creative arts and education. And since such a large part of both economic and cultural matters have become the state's preserve, the power of the state has been thereby unnaturally extended.

The increasing hubbub of governmental activities, which for the most part can only be carried on with the help of systematic taxation of profits, constitutes the characteristic of the contemporary functionally centralised state. It is out of the *immaturity* of the liberalistic economic system, and out of the weakness and hence incompetence of the *Geistesleben* to run its own affairs, that the state is overburdened with duties which are not appropriate to its proper nature. Taking on such improper functions is therefore something forced on the state; this is because economic and cultural activities lack the necessary personal initiatives out of which those social structures could be created, which could be competent to take back these activities from the state and set them free from the state's incursions. It must indeed be understood that cultural life and particularly education are the job of the *Geistesleben* and not of the state. In the *Geistesleben* social structures and institutions must be developed which can treat directly with the institutions of a self-administering economic life; in this way the *Geistesleben* can raise its claim on the free capital it has contributed. For a governmental system that was concentrating on its proper tasks, the case of a requisition of free capital would in practice only occur if some unusual situation either in cultural life or in the economy so required.

As for the excessive range of activities which have been surrendered to the state, a light is thrown on these if the financing of these activities is considered simply from a static point of view—i.e. with the economy supposed to be in balance in all its commodity and money relationships, and with no dynamic tendency at work, such as would form free capital. In such a case both the production and the movement of goods will come back to depending entirely on human labour. For the tasks —said to be extraordinary—that have been left to the state, it would be necessary, therefore, that people worked harder and longer. The circulation of free capital would put a stop to this, and they would not have to do this extra work if they were in a progressive, developing economy. In the present day it is inevitable that the state should lay claim to free capital for the performance of its extra duties. Through state appropriation, private appropriation of free capital and of various profit elements is to a considerable extent itself expropriated, in the name of the state. However this does not mean that the "primary" appropriators are prevented from further strengthening their market and power postures; this is because the present legal position legitimises the owners of the means of production as the owners of free capital formation. This legal position raises the question of reforming the ownership of free capital formation and of the physical means of production in a just and economically rational way.

The response to this question must follow the lines that the rights of control over money and physical capital must be so structured that it becomes possible to invest capital according to economic rationality and social necessity, so that the satisfaction of needs for economic goods can be met on a permanent basis and to the extent socially needed, in the sphere of the *Geistesleben* and in social life, and in governmental activities. Now this degree of control over economic processes cannot be attained by a market economy which is too free, and which consists of an aggregation of isolated transactions, in themselves independent and private; this is fundamentally not possible. However, the alternative to the individualistic market economy is not the illiberal state economy, but a constitution for economic life which does not surrender the liberal achievements which have set the individual powers of humanity free. On the contrary, these powers will be invested in the establishment of social forms which will be supra-egoistic but not suprapersonal; such forms will enable the responsibility to be taken for the shaping of economic life, and will of necessity arise out of the individual powers of people who do the work.

Such socially just socio-economic forms can only meaningfully come into existence and be effective when a way is found to arrange the ownership of capital in a manner that conforms to both the facts and the people. The ensuing enquiries will go further into this.

CHAPTER 4

Ownership of the Land

There are three value quantities for which the correct form of ownership can never mature in either the market economy nor in the economic system that is centrally run by the state. These three value complexes are of a capital-forming type for which the power of control is of decisive significance for the correct shaping of economic life. They have taken on private ownership forms under the legal relationships of the individualistic market economy. These are the following three ownership spheres:

1 The land, as territorial space and as a natural resource.
2 The socially-created means of production and their money counterpart, production capital.
3 Free capital.

Three forms of individual ownership have developed over these capital quantities, which throw up unsolved economic and social problems. The ownership of the land and its resources, which provide the natural basis of all economic activity, is of fundamental importance. The clarification of the ownership issue bound up with it will help to clear the ground for understanding the more complex ownership problems of the other two categories, which have a directly capital character, whereas the land and its resources can only be considered as taking on an indirect capital quality when conceived as and changed into a money sum.

1 The ownership of the land; ownership in substance and in function

The earth, its surface and its resources serve humanity as the basis of the spatial deployment of its physical life. Therefore, people feel themselves impelled to take possession of the land surface, to use it on the one hand for building houses and cities on, and on the other hand as the living basis of agricultural production, and to an increasing extent for industry as well. This industrial use stimulates the appropriation of the substances in the earth, particularly of inorganic minerals. Ores, coal, minerals, base and precious metals, etc, are discovered and taken into possession. They are got by men out of the earth, brought into the economic system, worked and shaped into usable goods, which are then bought and sold.

Quite different from the appropriation of land for house building or industrial use is the claiming of the land with the object of meeting human needs for feeding and clothing. Agricultural production achieves this object through the utilisation of the organic creative powers of the land, out of which plant life grows and animal life develops. What the earth creates in this way is given to mankind as a basis for its existence. Now, as regards all these creations of the biosphere, mankind exercises a quite unobjectionable expropriation. Indeed, this is linked with human labour, but the true utility of agricultural land derives from the organic productivity of the earth, which is not of human origin. The economic valuation of this other-than-human productive force is recognised in economics as a rather ticklish problem in value theory. It is apprehended by means of the concept of ground rent; this is usually seen as a *differential* rent, reflecting differential cost situations. Sometimes, however—as with Ricardo—it is considered to be the money equivalent of the indestructible powers of the land. The question of rent has always concerned both economists and students of social policy. To whom does rent properly belong? Historically the situation was that it fell to the owners of the land, the so-called proprietors. Some, like Henry George and Silvio Gesell, have demanded the social-isation of rent, but we will not go into that here.

These three categories of land values, the surface, the mineral resources and the organic "stuff" of the land, succumb to human expropriation. Not till modern times did this take the form of private or state ownership. Since their first being taken into possession, the transfer of ownership of these three land values has nearly always undergone a market-economy-type form. In particular, the property market has made land into a tradable object. The form of ownership of the land that is got through a purchase of this kind usually makes the landowner also the owner of all the resources lying under the surface. In order to arrive at legal principles regarding the ownership problems tied up with the land, which would be suitable considering the nature of land as such, some quite relevant data may in fact be gathered from a historical analysis. This should show us in what social forms the appropriation of the earth's surface, whether for agriculture or for mineral exploitation, should now be organised, in a manner appropriate both for the nature of the land and for the present stage of human development.

In ancient times, and to some extent into the early Christian era, the dedication of the land was arranged in three tiers or levels. In the Egyptian and Chaldean religions, the priests who controlled society saw the physical earth as the creation of the gods. They recognised the divine powers which had created both earth and men as the owners of the earth. It was a religious dogma that the earth was given to mankind to use as the basis of material existence by the father god, and that the land should therefore be controlled in accordance with the religion which exercised theocratic rule over society. They saw the "ab-original" heavenly ownership as an overlordship; which was entrusted to them, thus giving them the power of control over the land and over its utilisation. The land was in practice worked by kinship groups (the third level) who were tied to the land in a form of divinely sanctioned tenure. In modern terms this was a kind of licensing on the part of the overlord. Later, in the territories colonised by the Germanic tribes, this took the form of the *Lehen*, which, while it did grant the usufruct, did not establish any substantial ownership. Such ownership of the usufruct did not allow any proper disposal of the substance of the land. In looking at this situation, two antithetical concepts suggest themselves:

1 *Substantial* ownership with its universal right of disposal, *and*
2 *Functional* ownership which is limited ownership.*

With substantial ownership—one could indeed call it material ownership—the power of disposal extends into the substance of the matter; the material owner has the freedom to make such use of the land as serves his personal interest. The legal concept of this thorough-going individualistic form of ownership came from Roman law, which enshrined the principle of individualism. The extreme projection of this substantial power of disposal would carry it as far as the right to destroy the property. Substantial property, once acquired, can be sold, given away or bequeathed. In the case of sale, the owner-

---

*Others have translated this as trust ownership, a usage adopted later.—Ed.

ship of the thing sold is transferred from one person to another, against money or some other counter value. The concept of "functional" ownership excludes the destruction of the substance, or its sale, and legally allows the enjoyment only of the usufruct. By means of this concept, the ownership relationship can be socially improved, that is, through the structuring of the basic social legislation about functional ownership so that it comprises both rights of control and duties as well.* Thus the owner would not only receive the right to use the property privately; he would in addition be subject to the corresponding social duty of accountability toward the common good. This would form a social counterbalance against the rights of ownership being carried too far, to the point where they would include the right to misuse the property. Above all, a proper social system of ownership rights would inhibit land ownership being turned into a commodity saleable for profit. Land ownership when put into trust ownership drawn up according to both natural justice and the needs of the economy would still attach to the substance and make it utilisable—but would not give the right to alienate it. The different kinds of land use mean in practice that three different types of land ownership are to be developed, for agricultural cultivation of the surface, for building ground and for sources of industrial raw and auxiliary materials.

2 Individualisation and capitalisation of the land

From our brief historical survey, we can see the original situation in which land ownership was shaped. In ancient times, the system of land ownership was based on spiritual concepts emanating from the supranatural, which gave guidance for the use of the earth. About eight hundred years before Christ, however, a different outlook about these matters developed. In the principal civilisations then existing, certain people began to "individualise", and were seized by an increasingly developing awareness of self. Since the fifteenth century A.D., this process of individualisation has tended towards its peak. More and more people consciously self-actualised themselves, seeking fulfilment, with their liberated willpower, through material activities.

---

*This is very close to the concept of trust in English law.—Ed. English edn.

This concentration on individual personality weakened awareness and knowledge of the world of the *Geist* and of the divine spirit within. Separated from God, the individual grew in strength and experienced himself, so to speak, as the lord of creation. Science helped him to win power over matter, which he saw as power over the world. Finally, he perceived the planets and the stars and interpreted them as a gigantic machine. From this materialistic outlook he gained the moral conviction that his destiny was to control the earth and to make it his personal property. The original divine owner of the earth was taken to be non-existent, and dethroned by a human "decree". Into his place stepped the self-aware free personality of self-actualising egos. This built states, which gave support in law to private individual substantial ownership. The whole planet was in this way divided up into individual-ised ownership-shares, under the aegis of state power. In these con-ditions a small section of society acquired economic kingdoms, which were the expression of the egoistic self-assertion of individual person-alities.

This thorough-going process of individualising the ownership of the substance of the earth gave the owners the power to convert their land holdings into financial sums, into value. They could do this by putting their estate into the circulation process of commodities and money. This raised the land to the level of being a commodity without it ever having been produced as such. The productivity incorporated in it is there as the gift of providence, and has therefore to be recognised as such. It is the individual desire to possess and the self-centred drive for profit which have *capitalised* the everlasting substance of the earth and subjected it to speculative profit-taking. Since the price of land resulting out of its capitalisation is not the reflection of any real pro-duction of goods, it cannot but distort or debase the price relationships of the economy.

Economic logic comes inexorably into play. Throughout the econ-omy, the price of land, whether of agricultural land or of raw materials, enters into the cost calculations of goods, and thereby the ultimate price of commodities is raised by this kind of arbitrary cost. Every production or trading location requires some space on the planet—for which it has to pay. To the extent this space has then to be paid for, the logic of the market economy unavoidably exercises a price-raising effect. The time has come to make it our unshakable conviction that all commercial dealings, all financial utilisation of the fundamentally monopolistic ownership of the land must be separated from the operations of the economy's monetary system. The land as such—apart from expenditure on opening it up or improving it—is not really a priceable commodity, any more than labour is.* Labour produces commodities but is not itself a commodity. The market economy has developed both property and labour markets, with the aim of handling as commodities things which are not commodities at all. These artificial markets get in the way of the social and economic requirement that men should work for each other in reciprocity. They are indeed there, but they ought not to be.

The earth which serves agriculture, livestock and other plant cultivation constitutes the original means of production for mankind on this planet. As such, it represents productive capital of a primordial kind. Not until modern times did industrial productive capital develop alongside it. Both forms of productive capital have had the lot of being individualised as private property, as a result of which they have been made the subject of profit-prospecting by the market economy, in the form of money capital. This application by the market economy of private ownership to an estate could never have been conceptualised if land had not been regarded as if it were a money sum. Thus, it is from a prospective standpoint that its capital character arises, regarding its productive use.

It is the agricultural use of the organic forces in the soil which is the source of any direct productive effect. The use of land for building, or for the extraction of minerals can only be seen as an indirect productive land value. But it is precisely to these two non-organic types of use that the abstract concept of land as capital has been stirred up. It is only as the basis of agriculture that land takes on the role of a means of production. It does not play this role in either building or in mineral exploitation. But to that type of thinking that focuses solely on personal results, these non-organic uses of land acquire a capital value. This kind of capitalisation of the land arises from the possibility of buying it and selling it. Such commercialisation of land is analogous to that form of sterile capital investment which was considered earlier, in which an ownership valuation is made of shares already issued, and these shares then traded, on the Stock Exchange. Exactly the same thing happens if an allotted or freely occupied piece of land is transferred to another by sale, and thus treated as a commodity. If it is sold for money, it then circulates through the economic process as an

---

*See the editorial note on the question of the theory of value implied.

everlasting and virtually indestructible commodity, like an empty shadow, devaluing the proper economic value aggregates. The tendency for the price of land to increase commodity prices, and the multiplication of this throughout the economy, has already been mentioned. A recent research investigation gave an indication of the importance of this factor. Th.s research estimated the total value of all land area in the Federal Republic of Germany at about 650 thousand million marks. The pure increase in land value between 1965 and 1970 was nearly half as much as the values created by investment, that is, the industrial means of production. In any economy in which the land is converted into a factitious capital and thereby made into a saleable commodity, there is an inexorable drive towards a continuous inflationary increase in the quantity of money, needed of course to finance the purchase of land, and also to some extent occasioned by the multiplier effects of the consequent price increases. Mortage finance was devised to fund this purchase, and the financial institutions concerned skim off a part of the money capital involved, causing a drain on capital which is balanced by a creation of money. Large sums of money are involved in this. The following table is taken from the monthly reports of the German central bank:

MORTGAGE STATISTICS IN GERMANY
(thousand million marks)

Year	Current Mortgages	Redemptions	New Advances
1973	65.3	1.8	3.5
1974	69.8	2.1	4.2

Of course these figures contain the value of buildings, and also of ships. What proportion is made up of land values, it is hard to say, perhaps between 10 and 20 per cent.

Only towards the end of the Middle Ages did the privatisation, that is the individual owning, of land and its substance reach a significant scale. This process was helped by the introduction of Roman law. It has had the impact of a natural force upon modern social life; in the sphere of politics and the law, private ownership has taken the form of an unalterable principle of human rights, a basis of the state. Private ownership got the ideology for this from the philosophy of liberalism, developed in the shaping of English economic life. This philosophy proclaimed human freedom as a universal principle; this in turn provided the three points upon which classical economics is based. These three points became dogmas. They are private ownership, freedom to make any legal contract, and free competition. In the first half of the nineteenth century these were the guiding ideas of all civilised economies, incorporating three radical egoistic behavioural patterns as the driving forces of economic life. These ideas were elevated to the point of being universal absolutes. Today they are still recognised by the official representatives of economic life. People have gradually become inured to—and have compounded with—these liberal principles and to the detrimental effects ensuing from private land ownership being turned into capital. This acceptance has extended to the ensuing price inflation, put up with weakly, though not without protest. Equally passively have the artificial profits made possible by the property market system been watched. However, the rapid rise in building land prices has been a matter for increasing official concern, and some have pointed out that existing property law favours profits which relate to neither risk nor service, and brings about the accumulation of national assets in the wrong place.

3 The state as the ultimate landowner

Once man had entered into the era of individualising himself—which is synonymous with the exercise of free will—the shaping of human destiny became man's own responsibility. Moreover, the task of working out this destiny appeared to be an externally-determined necessity, any sense of contact with the world of the *Geist* having been lost, and with it any notion of the role of *Geist* in human development. With this outlook there was no longer any idea of the planet ultimately belonging to a divine creator. No longer feeling themselves to be in the hands of cosmic forces, the surface of the earth was, for mankind, there to be confronted—and taken possession of. Thus in place of the former religious concept of overlordship, political kingdoms appeared, before the beginning of the Christian era, thus developing a system of developing states, a process which culminated after the end of classical times, in the division of humanity into nation-states. These states occupied clearly defined land areas. These areas made up the so-called national territory. Hence humanity lives in the instinctive conviction that a people and its members are allotted with a tract of the earth's surface. The social system for the division of this national territory is defined through the legislation made and enforced by the power of the state.

The state is the embodiment of organised power, directly or indirectly exercising social sway over the land in the national territory. Thus, the power structures of men have taken over that ownership function once exercised over the land by a divinely-sanctioned religion, and the place of the ancient theocracies occupied by the embodiment of a people in a nation-state. The part of the earth's surface separated off as the national territory forms, as it were, an imagined overlordship appertaining to the people of the state. Individual citizens of these states grew towards self-actualisation, and created, particularly during the nineteenth century, democratic national constitutions, which—expressing the democratic ideal—make the people into the highest authority for the control of the land, and for the legal forms for its utilisation for any of the three categories of purposes we have analysed.

Land which has thus gone over into the form of an idealised state overlordship can be dealt with in one of two ways. It can be taken into full state ownership, through the power of the state, so that the substance belongs to the state which can then determine arbitrarily how it shall be used and controlled; this is what has happened in the communist universal states founded as they are on the nationalisation of the entire economy. Alternatively, the state may feel itself in the position—that it will see as a natural fact—that the land is in historically determined private ownership, perhaps because it was originally appropriated by feudal lords, so that the state has to go along with the developed free will involved in this set up; which leaves the state in the role of supporting and providing legal sanction for these individualistically created ownership relationships, particularly the private ownership of the land. Or, as in the land reforms of the nineteenth century, it regulates matters under the pressures of the times. This concept of the role of the state limits its control over the land to the development of a legal system which gives legal form to substantial ownership of the land, along with the land transactions thereby enabled, including its mortgaging or pledging as collateral—all this with the modest aim of preventing abuse so far as is possible.

German lawyers have sought (in a meeting in 1972) to find ways of restricting the profits made "without risk or service" through rising land prices, particularly for building purposes in the growing towns. These profits are extorted from the social economy and distort price relationships and the organic composition of the quantity of money. After discussing legal regulations and planning, a tax on such profits was advocated. However it was not thought appropriate to divide the land-ownership function into two, combining public ownership of the right to dispose of the land with private ownership of the usufruct. Such a separation would mean reckoning with established concepts of ownership. But a new way of thinking is needed to arrive at the right social way. The lawyers referred to were still too steeped in the traditional legal approach, which hindered them from perceiving that it is *substantial* private ownership of the land which ought not to be.

It has become an extremely tricky matter to see how the substantial ownership of the land can be modified without at the same time de-personalising the use of the land. Commercial private ownership has developed a strongly entrenched legal position against any taking hold of its rights of disposal. Expropriation requires its own statutes; so far these have only been developed for the limited case of public housing programmes, to enable land to be acquired for dwellings, streets and amenities. One of the most difficult social tasks confronting us today is to decide how we should "de-privatise"—one could well say "neutralise"—the power of substantial disposal over the land, and do this in a general and fundamental way, in the context of today's relationships. What this boils down to, is this: in what practical way can we or should we legislate, in order to alter the private use of the land? A necessary prerequisite for putting into effect such a neutral-isation of landownership would be the abolition of substantial land-ownership. First there are tricky psychic resistances to be overcome. Expropriation by force could only come through a revolutionary coup. This could be avoided by a voluntary renunciation of *substantial* ownership, resulting from an understanding of the social and economic reasons for doing this. Such a renunciation is not to be expected. However, the land could be taken out of the monetary circulation process and neutralised, if the present owners were bought out. This would constitute a financial gift to the landowners; in Germany, this would amount, as already seen, to 650 thousand million marks, or 488 thousand million excluding state holdings. This is about equal to the national income for an entire year.

Between the two extreme cases of complete state ownership and complete private ownership of the land, there is trusteeship. This would be in keeping with the spirit of the age, as compared with state, private or collective ownership. Deep consideration is necessary to arrive at the recognition that the fixed substantial tying of the land to an individual owner for the use and disposal of both surface and resources is not conducive to sound economics, nor is it really just.

The only just way would be to reshape the possession of the land into the attenuated form of functional ownership. However, this could only be done by a deed of administration, either one executed by the state, or recognised in some way by those doing the administering. In either case, a piece of land would be made over to some individual or group by a higher authority. The practical running of such a system from a legal point of view impinges, of course, upon government; it would be necessary to have law regulating the power of land allocation towards any specific use, whether for agricultural or other purposes.

4 *Corporate stewardship of the land*

If there is no private substantial land ownership, and if its utilisation is no longer the result of decisions by substantial owners, then some comprehensive system of managing land use will be needed. Land free of substantial ownership must still be managed, and the system of management will need to be legally established. Either this will result from the initiative of the state acting in the common good, or it will come from the free decisions of those who are concerned, directly or indirectly, with the utilisation of the land. This is where the democratic self-administration of the land, organised in some corporate structure, can take the place of authoritative state control. Of course, free democratic land administration does require legal form and sanction. The state has to watch over things, to ensure that the self-administering land corporations do not infringe the law, but use the land justly.

Such a freely-constituted land corporation is, in its social nature, totally unlike any state administrative authority. It forms a spontaneously created social body, whose members and organs are part of the *Geistesleben*, working together. They must work out land utilisation and usufruct policies. Such a self-administering corporation would be composed of competent and suitable interested people, able as a body to judge broadly the best use of the land for agricultural, industrial or urban purposes. Those who wanted land to use and sought usufructs would be organised according to the appropriate economic categories of land use, as farmers, builders, miners, etc; and of course the state would require land and buildings for govern-

mental and military purposes; and likewise there would be the requirements of cultural life, for buildings, institutes, schools, churches, sports
grounds and stadiums, etc. The individual land corporation would
consider the allocation of function in a way suitable to these various
interests. It is not possible to lay down dogmatic guide-lines for the
constitution of land corporations; at this stage only the general idea
can be put forward. Much depends on circumstances, but the principle
is economic rationality combined with the desire for social justice.

Objections to the abolition of substantial ownership of the land will
be seen to be insubstantial, once it is grasped that the *usufruct* rights of
those at present using the land will be scarcely touched. Doing away
with the speculative capitalisation of land will not immediately affect
the actual use of the land. There may of course be difficulties where
land is mortgaged. Legal ways of overcoming these difficulties in a
way appropriate to the nature of the land need to be found. The
economist Rodbertus* was able convincingly to separate the payment
of rent from the factitious capitalisation of land. The land corporations
would be able to work out some suitable arrangement along these lines.

The constitution of land management here depicted is an ultimate
kind. Should the members of such land corporations not yet have come
together, the government might take the initiative. The ideal ownerless
land management might be preceded by an intermediate stage, in which
the land management function could be preformed by some unit of the
political state, and in order to move towards decentralisation, this
might be the local council. This has been proposed from a socialist
point of view, it being suggested that local councils should own the
land, to decide how and by whom the land should be utilised. Such a
course would socialise the land with the danger of authoritative or
bureaucratic control. As regards these possibilities, the question arises,
what rights and duties should attach to a local authority as owner of
the land, particularly as to whether it should be allowed to sell it; if
not, then the local authority would only have a formal ownership,
limited to certain functions. If one has reached the conviction that in
the matter of land *disposal* there can be no ownership, then the local
authorities could be charged not with management by *ownership*, but
with just the rights similar to those of the eventual land corporations,
which would be endowed with the rights and duties of trustees. Its task
would be to work in such a way as to bring together those interested

---

* In his "Zur Erklärung und Abhülfe der heutigen Creditnoth des Grundbesitzes".

to form a land corporation—which it would be the local authority's
duty to see was done justly, the legal authorisation of the state being
provided through the medium of the local authority.

The following table gives information about the utilisation of land in
West Germany. The total land surface of the German Federal Republic
is about 96,000 square miles. This is divided up percentagewise as
shown in the table:

LAND UTILISATION IN GERMANY

	%
Agriculture and forestry:	55.5
Virgin forest:	29.0
Transportation:	4.6
Built-up areas:	4.3
Lakes, parks, and miscellaneous:	6.6
	100.0

Of the above about 25 per cent is in the ownership of various federal,
state or local authorities, and 65 per cent in the ownership of a million
and a half farmers or foresters, the balance being owned industrially or
privately.

The surface of the earth ought not to be split up by the constraints
of individual ownership; it is not really separate from the social totality,
to which it has to stay attached. Today, that social totality is the
political community. However, the *Geistesleben*, if it organised itself
according to nationality and language, and if it were self-governing in
relation to (as it were alongside) the state, could become that totality.
The owners of the land's usufruct would be associated with the state in
so far as they were legal bodies, and with the *Geistesleben* in their role
as a *Geist* community. Both state and *Geistesleben* have a role to play
in the management of the land. A new level of understanding is needed
to achieve such a completely free form of land management. This understanding will inform both family and other agricultural units with the
powers realisable by free people; together with or in place of family
production units, free agricultural companies will develop, structured
along the three levels more fully defined in Appendix 4, namely the
level of the working group, jointly working the land, the level of the
productivity of the earth itself, and the cosmic level which arches over
the whole—the powerful forces of the *Geist*, ultimately deriving from
heaven. A fuller assessment of this triple level structure is given in
Appendix 4, wherein the peculiarities of the agricultural use of land
are more fully gone into.

CHAPTER 5

Historical Forces behind Capital Ownership

The ownership of the means of production is quite different from the ownership of land. The earth came into existence without any human effort, though of course various improvements in both agricultural and building land may be necessary to prepare it for use, say for example by excavation or levelling. Such improvements to the original land are of course like means of production, and so justly have their price; but the original land itself has not been produced, but is, as it were, a previously existing means of production. Now produced means of production only came into being with the enlightenment of human minds; indeed, they could only attain their present world-wide importance in economic life as the money economy developed, itself under the impact of the same enlightenment. Both scientific thinking and the money economy developed together, from the beginning of modern times, in the fifteenth century. Jointly they brought about the progressive and indeed unstoppable division of labour, which was the outward material sign of the inner growth in understanding.

1. How the means of production exist both as physical and as money capital: the plant and the enterprise.

The division of labour attained its present scale over the whole economy, because it is socially and physically necessary to organise production by means of an immense number of separate plants, and therefore into separate enterprises. Thus there are countless economic units whose aim is to produce, transport or sell goods, or provide services. In each such unit, the basis of all productive activity is formed by human effort and the means of production.

Now before the means of production can be acquired for any economic unit, money capital, by means of which the means of production can be purchased, must first be introduced; and this introduction of money capital must itself be preceded by the essential creative idea, which is like the hidden mainspring of the whole industrial process, without which that process cannot "tick". The will-power behind this idea achieves its object by the introduction of the technically appropriate means of production, to which human effort must be added for production to ensue. Man thus stands in the centre of the economic system, as worker and as creative entrepreneur.

The separate units established by the division of labour, as plants, and therefore as enterprises, need a relationship with other parts of the economy, and therefore with other similar units. As units they do not produce for themselves, but for the rest of the economic organism—for the market, as people say. Now this is why plants have to take on another characteristic—they have to be organised in a way which reflects the necessary orientation towards money of any economic organisation. The productive activity of which we have spoken has—in the economic system—to take on the form of an *enterprise*. Now plant and enterprise are related in this way—you can have the plant without the enterprise, but *not* the enterprise without the plant. Plant processes, with their costs and revenues, must take the form of an enterprise in economic terms.

Now this economic form, the enterprise, in its role as plant is, as it were, autonomous as a unit. Therefore, a trading organisation will also be needed, that can see to the distribution of the goods produced. Just as with the productive unit, the trading unit has various physical installations—offices, accounting files, fittings of various kinds—by which the economic process is furthered, and these installations constitute the plant of the trading enterprise.

It is by highlighting the money-accounting role of the enterprise that we can see the hidden part of the economic unit, which depends on the money system.*

For a better understanding of the distinction between plant and enterprise, the table overleaf may help.

---

*A small part of the German text has been left out here. It concerns the semantics of the fact that the same German word can mean both "plant" and "enterprise". —Editor, English edn.

Plant	*Enterprise*
1. Embodies the technologically productive ideas in the utilisation of machinery.	1. Embodies the entrepreneurially productive ideas in the application of capital.
2. Physical capital—the means of production, with their technical or physical efficiency.	2. Money capital—value productivity, economic productivity.
3. Production of physical quantities of goods. —consumer goods. —goods for further processing. —production goods, capital goods, means of production.	3. Money revenue from the products as commodities. —covering of costs. —income formation. —indirect: free capital, in its original formation.
4. Energy utilisation.	4. Money utilisation (balance sheet).
5. Production workers.	5. Administrative staff.

Thus we have contrasted in outline the distinction between the function of the plant, which is to do with work and technology, and the function of the enterprise, which is to do with the circulation of money, and the sources from which the money capital is financed. The same distinction is indeed revealed in the very essence of the means of production. The means of production have as it were a Janus-head, they face both ways, they have a double existence, one physical and one financial. The means of production have to be produced by human effort; they then become physical commodities which are bought and sold for money in the various markets for capital goods. This is why the means of production have two aspects, one relating to physical productivity, and one shaped by money. The money spent on the acquisition of means of production, which is calculated to be self-replacing, also has the character of capital. Thus productive capital can be considered in two quite different ways—directly in regard to its physical productivity and indirectly in regard to its financial significance as a sum of capital which has been laid out. Both relate to anticipations about the future, and are closely interlinked.

Thus the money spent on acquiring means of production takes on a capital character, as against the purchase money which ultimate consumers spend on consumption goods. Money can be used, say, for buying consumer goods, or for acquiring means of production. It is in the latter use that money takes on, as it were, another and higher level of function, as capital money. This is because the purchasers of capital goods are using money in a special way, different from the way in which consumers use it. (This is why the German economist Wagner suggested calling capital money "producer's money" and the money spent by consumers "consumer's money".) Capital money takes the form of account money, that is, of book entries. The means of production bought with the capital money become the property of those who buy them. Now the capital money may be the entrepreneur's own capital, or it may belong to a "legal person"—that is, a legally constituted company. A third category is loan capital which is put at the disposal of the company in return for the payment of fixed interest.

It is by the purchase of the means of production with an appropriate sum of money that their financial existence comes to be established. Thus it is that the means of production come to lead a double life, with the financial counterpart developing a capitalistic life of its own. Over time the courses of the two diverge. The physical capital, the actual machinery and equipment, wears out during use, depreciating to the point where it has no value: in compensation for this, replacement investment is from time to time made, so that the worn-out parts of the equipment are renovated. The money capital equivalent of the means of production has an accounting existence which is independent of time, and so persists as an accounting aggregate. While it is indeed related to the economic productivity of the means of production in a general way, it does not move step by step with the process of wearing out. Under the market economy system, this accounting existence of the means of production leads a life of its own. This separate life is bound up with the very nature of money. This is because the legal arrangements for capital money in the whole capital-economic system endow it with an unlimited life; this is what gives money capital its aspect of imperishability. From this follows the convention that money capital has a sort of autonomous existence in share capital, which existence is continually reactivated on the Stock Exchange.

An idea of the extent of the "producers' money" circulating in the economy can be gained from the national income statistics. Thus, for example, in Western Germany, the gross national product amounted in 1972 to 829 thousand million marks, of which a quarter, 232 thousand million marks, was accounted for by capital goods production.

Ownership over the means of production has certain significant consequences. It results in the power to decide how the means of production shall be used. This may be productive, or it may be unproductive. An example of the means of production being used unproductively is when they are turned back into commodites and resold, after having been bought in the first instance by a money capital investment. This process of turning the means of production back into money capital—against the circulatory flow—could be called re-commercialisation. Now the whole nature of the means of production is such that they are only meant to be used in production. Of course, it can happen that the investment is unsuccessful, and a calamity ensues, the plant has to be stopped and broken up into various pieces which become commodities again, in an artificial way. This process of reversal, of re-commercialisation, when the plant has been paid for and installed, is uneconomic from the point of view of economic balance. Thus goods already put to their intended use are instead auctioned. This puts a brake on the circulation of money. This is also the case when one company is taken over by another with the purpose of effecting a merger; this means that the purchasing company acquires the plant by paying for the value of the share capital corresponding to the plant. This is equally a form of re-commercialisation. To judge this sort of thing, we need to get back to basic economic principles. Now we can only understand the correct way of financing by grasping the true nature of money, from which it will be seen that the need is to limit the life-span of money capital, in order to get a correct economic system.

2 Distortion of the economy as a result of the system of ownership

Anyone who is the legal owner of money capital can use this to buy means of production, and so becomes their owner. Even if the money capital is borrowed, he will still be the owner. The law gives him power to use it as he thinks fit. He can use it productively, as an entrepreneur. He can become a shareholder and allow another entrepreneur to manage it for him, while as principal shareholder he will still be able to exercise far-reaching control over the profits. The legal owner can however take these means of production away from their productive use, by selling them, bequeathing them, or letting them lie idle. Such alienation will not be opposed by anyone (even though its deliberate destruction might be!) The free economy allows virtually complete freedom to the legal owner as to how he uses the productive forces of the economy, whether this use is economic or not. The significance of this freedom can only be assessed if we consider the real and basic productive forces, which enable economic activities to take place. These forces are three in number—forming as it were a pyramid based on the earth—namely, natural forces, labour and mind.

These three forces are in themselves, so to speak, neutral, capable of being used or misused. Used properly, they are beneficial; misused, —as they grievously are when the means of production are, as in modern times, subject to private ownership—they distort the economy. This is because this form of ownership facilitates the gratification of the owners' private whims and desires. The yield of the economic system is subordinated to the securing of private incomes, and to the aim of endlessly maximising profit. The principle of profit maximisation has typically led to the constraint whereby the fruits of the economy are distorted by competitive forces. This can be seen in the way the three productive forces are used uneconomically and indeed improperly, both in their physical utilisation, and in their financial exploitation.

1. Natural resources have been put to financial profit particularly through the capitalisation of land. It has already been shown how this has a harmful and irrational effect. In real terms, likewise, the way in which natural resources are used, shows that the earth is often over-worked due to the effect of unrestricted private ownership, which is fundamentally unethical, over such resources as metals, fuels, minerals and water.

2. Human labour resources—which include the relationship with the means of production—are similarly utilised. Though the institution of slavery has been abolished, the modern labour market has developed out of it, whereby labour is bought and sold as if it were a kind of commodity. This method is inhuman. As one side in the labour market was the stronger, it was at first possible, due to the effect of the

competitive principle—for the owners controlled the means of production—to exploit those who had their labour-power to offer. Workers were underpaid and overworked, and this involved even children. The market strength of those who owned the means of production rested mainly on the fact that there were more than enough workers living in poverty, who had to offer themselves on the labour market out of sheer necessity. The organised trade unions have outwardly corrected this.

3. As regards the resources of the human mind, the achievements of modern culture, these are taken possession of by those who control the means of production, whenever they are of any use in the organisation of labour, or in the technology of production. Now the fruits of modern culture are worthwhile, to the extent that they serve to alleviate work. This leads to the formation of free capital, and unlimited possibilities result, so that those who appropriate this free capital can gain economic power. The drive for freedom on the part of modern, individualised man, is what facilitated this right to acquire power. The requirement of freedom produced, indeed enforced, an economic law. The merchant adventurers, and the entrepreneurs who followed them, instinctively created the market economy, the rules of which echoed the demand for freedom. This led to legal formulation of these rules. According to the legal concepts developed, the owner of the plant unconditionally acquires all income arising from its employment. If this had not been so, it would not have been possible to use the means of production to make private profits, and to develop private economic power.

These, then, are the three characteristic signs of the perversion of the fruits of the productive forces of the economy: capitalisation of the land, trading in labour, and private appropriation of capital formed by cultural forces. Three "pseudo-markets" correspond to these three marks of perversion: the property market, the labour market and the capital market in the strict sense. The creation of these three markets is artificial, and means that the market principle has been expanded into being the fundamental, the universal principle of the organisation of economic life. Indeed, this is widely believed to be the only possible method there is. But it was a wrong path to have taken, and our further progression along it is the cause of the ever-increasing difficulties which beset the modern economic system. (Against this, seen properly, the economic system in fact needs only *one* market—the market for goods, for consumer goods, for capital goods, for goods being traded, etc.)

Now the whole spirit and aim of the owners of the means of production is to make profits and this pervades all markets in the economic system, so that everywhere is felt the requirement for maximisation of all factors making for material results, and the minimising of all factors obstructing material results. This tendency takes various forms according to circumstances:

For firms, the targets are as follows:

production of goods	to be as high as possible
sales	to be as much as possible
profits	as high as possible
prices	as high as possible
wages	as low as possible

For employees, the following are the demands:

incomes (wages)	as high as possible
work	as little as possible
time off	as much as possible

And for consumers, the trend is analogous:

incomes	as high as possible
consumption	as much as possible
prices	as low as possible

It is through this drive for maximisation and for minimising that modern big business has obtained its dominating position in the economy. This continually disrupts the organic balance of the economy; obviously, the organs and cells in an organism must be in a balanced relationship with one another if they are to function correctly. They cannot do this, for fundamental reasons, if they are perpetually being forced into one-sided maximising or minimising tendencies. In fact, in the economy that is properly balanced the self-adjusting values generate *correct* aggregates, with correct prices, correct production quantities, the correct amount of capital formation, etc. The correct prices are of course neither the highest nor the lowest possible. Above all, it is a question of the right level of incomes. The proper formation of incomes is of course to be determined by the demand for social justice. Moreover, correct incomes and correct prices have to be determined in relationship to each other. No price is correct in itself, no income is correct in itself, if considered in isolation; prices and incomes must be considered in relation to the whole, that is to say, they must be in a balanced relationship with all other economic values.

*3. Disturbances in the economy caused by power centres:
emulation and competition.*

The distinction between competition and emulation may not be generally recognised. Emulation is in the mind; competition in the market-place. Emulation is a matter of evolutionary progress—the idea is to emulate a standard of performance, as established by the natural human urge to achieve. However it is possible for emulation to sharpen to the point that it becomes competitive behaviour. It is in this form that it affects the circulation of economic values, and becomes an ingredient in the sales strategy of firms.

Normal competitive behaviour is seen in the situation in which sellers seek to draw the attention of buyers to the goods on offer, and to persuade them to buy. Such normal behaviour has the straightforward aim of trying to surpass a competitor, in terms of efficiency, in terms of price, and also by more effective psychology, e.g. by better advertising. Normal competitive behaviour is not seeking to drive the competitor out of the market. It is harmless enough. The self-assertion and striving for success which is involved in normal competitive behaviour is nothing more than part of man's natural instinct for self-preservation, and does not imply aggression against competitors; hence it is quite acceptable.

But it can go too far. It can degenerate into a competitive battle in which the aggressive aim is introduced, of driving the competition off the market. Whereas normal competition can be considered as part of the market situation, this element of aggression has to be seen for what it is, as something fundamentally anti-social. (In any event, normal competitive behaviour is by its nature completely different from emulation, which as explained, is a spiritually creative force. Emulation, too, can enter into the competitive battle, and be a weapon in it.)

The continual tendency is for the market economy to shift from normal competition towards the aggressive form. What happens is that the spirit of emulation, intrinsically aggressionless, and indeed a useful and creative force in society, is distorted. The market economy becomes, as it were, absolute. Individuals find opportunities to gain personal power. Power centres develop in the market, with significant but incalculable effects. These grow into industrial empires of various kinds, perhaps in the form of single large firms, perhaps in the form of combines. These growths occur not only in the markets for commodities, but also—and particularly—in the three pseudo-markets mentioned above.

Markets become part of the big-business economy, and it is in these markets that producers become involved in marketing. This means increasingly fierce competitive battles with one another, striving to maximise their sales so as to maximise their profit. Because demand is uncertain, they have to employ all possible means to push their sales on the market, if this sales maximisation is to be achieved. The campaigns to boost sales have to be expanded all the time. Advertising has to be repeatedly stepped up. Now, of course, there are necessary and justifiable forms of advertising; factual information about the goods available is useful to the consumer, information about prices, about standards of performance, etc. This kind of information need not involve any pressure on the consumer. On the contrary, it helps him to make a free choice. Now in the competitive economy, information is still part of the means employed to advertise goods, but the element of persuasion becomes increasingly important. As new means of persuasion become available, for example television, competitors are forced to increase their advertising budgets. Competition is thus sharpened through the new means of persuasion. The whole economy is then encumbered with the burden of increased advertising costs. This would perhaps seem to be the *reductio ad absurdum* of the whole process, that this form of competition actually increases the prices of goods across the board! However, one cannot say this without further analysis. While to increase advertising cost in this way is certainly senseless, it is necessary to examine whether perhaps the advertisers are covertly using free capital for the purpose of financing the additional advertising costs. Since they can legally acquire this by appropriation, and indeed can be encouraged to do so by the taxation system, it is very easy for this to be done, but from the economic point of view it is a waste. Thus, free capital can be misused in order to build up power centres in the economy, by financing unnecessarily large volumes of advertising in this way.

Ironically, the daemonic drive of the intensified competitive struggle has brought it to the point where it abrogates itself. The regulation of prices which it is supposed to achieve then ceases, and its effect is the contrary, as intensified competition works toward the establishment of monopolistic domination of the market. A monopoly, in the sense of control by one power centre, can arise in various ways. One company may drive its competitors out of the market, as Rockefeller did with his cash-register monopoly. He boasted that this was built on the graves of no less than forty competitors. Or perhaps various firms may agree to cease competing together and so form a combine.

The power of the monopoly can cross national frontiers and form what is nowadays called a "multinational". Thus a sort of economic imperialism is formed. The markets for commodities are dominated; and by restraining production, price rises may be enforced. The role of competition had been to fix prices, but this role is now interfered with. Moreover, as mentioned before, the multinationals are in a good position to speculate on the exchange rates between currencies, thus disturbing their values. As this power is unsocially used, these multinationals become a worldwide menace. Robert Liefman's "Kartelle und Trusts" (8th edition, Stuttgart, 1930) gives a clear picture of this.

What makes this development possible, whereby big business comes into being, forming a system of economic imperialism? The answer is, the legal authorisation to the owners of the means of production, to appropriate free capital for their own purposes. That is what makes this possible. In the last analysis, this economic power appears as money power. It continually extends its spheres of influence, by acquiring further production facilities, by capital investments, by speculation on the stock exchanges, by building up reserves in foreign currencies, and by speculation in property. Each of these extensions increases the ability to appropriate still more free capital, in turn then available for still further extensions. Thus it is that the large multinational conglomerates are formed. Their guiding principle is continuous growth and thereby increasing power.

Thus in modern economic life, the tendency towards concentration is continuous and domination over enormous blocks of the means of production is accomplished. This economic power is able to influence the economic policy of national states to a significant extent. This constitutes a major international problem. This is because of the nature of modern warfare. The role of machinery and technology in war, and the extent to which it is displacing conventional military forces, is such as to determine the outcome of wars. Such is the extent of the production of war material and equipment, of weapons of destruction, of chemicals and explosives, that it is to big business that countries wishing to wage war have to come. Armament manufacture is a major source of profit for big business. Moreover, the expansionist aims of big business need the help of the state to be put into effect. Therefore there is a close interdependence between economic and political power centres. Needless to say, this is hardly beneficial for humanity.

The power of monopolistic economic imperialism seems to be irresistible. The effect upon economic life is that the fundamental balance of economic relationships is disorganised. The balancing effects of normal competitive behaviour are circumvented. Further imbalances are created in the volume of production and in capital investment. Fluctuations in demand are induced. This is carried to the extent that other parts of the economy are disabled, to the monopolies' own disadvantage. Attempts have been made to restore competition, but these attempts have not been sufficient to achieve any effect. The state has indeed enacted legislation against trusts and cartels, and against the misuse of economic power, to try to rectify these distortions. However, the state has not really got enough power to override power centres such as these.

In view of the points we have discussed, which reveal the true nature of the liberal economic system of the West, it is necessary to ask how such an economic system has come about. How is it that economic life has come to be used for personal advantage, thus producing the overpowering urge for material possessions, thus marrying individuality to the possession of material things? This marriage was to be binding forever, secured by the institution of private ownership of the means of production. Arising from our investigations so far, the deeper implications of this same institution need to be looked at. How did it become the centre-piece of the private-capitalist market economic system? A historical survey is needed, to show how much effort is required to sift the matter of the private ownership of the means of production and of free capital.

4. *The development of economic absolutism as a factor in society*

The development of the private capitalist economic system grew out of the major event in all human history—the coming of Christ, which brought cosmic forces into play. The power and creativeness of the Logos opened up for each individual the possibility of becoming a completely free and independent personality. Hegel—who had great insight—was later to recognise this as the driving force in the history of human development, the force which made man emerge into the consciousness of freedom.

Now the awakening of individuality in man is one of the chief events in human history, if not the most important of all. The over-powering urge of modern times, to acquire material possessions, cannot be understood if one has not first understood this process of *becoming* as a development of the ego into a creative force able to revolutionise all relationships. From then on, individuals experienced themselves *self-consciously*, and this birth of human individuality brought about at the same time the impetus to leave the consanguinous forms of society, with their group mentality. This dissolution started to become wide-spread at the end of the Middle Ages. Up till then, society had remained anchored in the pre-Christian group mentality, even though the decisive step had already been taken, which was to be generally followed at the end of medieval times; namely, the break away from the old bonds of consanguinity, and the attainment of independent self-consciousness. Virtually every major historical event of that period is to be understood by reference to this same break away, to this same attainment. For example, in the peasant wars, the previously subordinated class tried to break its fetters, with continual appeals to Christ. The impact of Christ upon certain sections was demonstrated also in the Crusades.

It is precisely out of the impetus given by Christ, that the liberation of the individual essence started. This same impetus determined the course of history with elemental force. Modern man, maturing towards the fully developed ego, became separate from the universe [with which he had previously identified—Editor, English edition] and by the end of the Middle Ages this process was complete. He compensated for what was lost by developing the powers of the intellect; and so started to dominate the material world, by means of mechanical devices. Losing contact with the cosmos, he on the other hand deepened his involvement with physical things, deepened his sense of their reality. Now that his ego was developed, and with the force of his free will, he apprehended the earth as his field of action. He sought to shape it, using his new-found mental abilities, which consequently became orientated towards the material and the mechanical. His will, his intelligence, both became more and more separated from the spiritual world, from grace; and turned towards the earth, plunging into the material environment with all his might, wandering through the globe, discovering, conquering, colonising, founding enterprises. This turning outward of the forces of the ego, coupled with the increasingly individualised and continually growing power of the intellect, created the economic system that we now call capitalism. Such is the source, in the mind, of this system, such its origin in human individuality.

It was given to only a few exceptionally developed individuals—such as the apostles—to perform the first acts of world historical significance that were also truly acts of individuals becoming personalities. Subsequently, the new force awakened souls which were less mature. It thus revealed its power, demonstrating that people gripped by it experienced a freeing of their entire being. Now there was only one way in which these less mature souls could live out the new force of individual freedom—and that was through a radical egotism, often violent, which stirred up the drive to self-realisation, to limitless expansion of the ego. This radical egotistical passion for freedom came into the open with the Condottieri and with the emergence of absolutism.

It then spread to the adventurers who made the explorations of the globe, to risk-taking merchants who extracted the earth's economic treasures, and who sought ratification of their appropriation of the material world, of its materials, forces, and resources. This involved the violating the political and social systems of primitive peoples, either by completely destroying them, as with the Aztecs, or by subverting their spirit, as in India. This meant more than just economic and political colonisation. The achievement of personal and political goals was sought also through the development and exploitation of the new intellectual powers and the technical possibilities associated with them. Now self-realisation of the personality through the domination of the material world leads ineluctably to private possession of the material world. The urge is to draw the world as it were into oneself, in a variety of ways, almost to make it part of one's own life, to make it a part of one's own nature. Individual consciousness, when oriented towards material ownership, cuts itself off, becomes ingrown and isolated from society—hence the development of anti-social attitudes in economic life.

In the late eighteenth century, the economic theory was developed that enlightened self-interest would bring about both economic and social well-being. Hence the great social contradiction—namely, that an economic system run by private capitalism is supposed to meet needs, and, moreover, is to satisfy these needs by the "giving" of an economic

---

*See Adam Smith's "Wealth of Nations", first published 1776.—Editor, Eng. edn.

service, not out of any concern for them as human beings, but out of the said self-interest, out of the deep-rooted interest in the reciprocal "taking" of the countervalue of these services, as offered by those demanding them. Now if an entrepreneur's interest in the satisfaction of his fellow men's demands were selfless, he would not consider other similar entrepreneurs as competitors out to thwart his work, and drive him out of the market, so as to corner the business. But of course, such a selfless attitude would have shattering effects on the social system! It could not hope to be accepted in the context of an economic system in which everyone has to look to his own advantage, and has to see competitors as the opposition.

This system, whereby the economy is founded in the drive for personal self-realisation, originated in the West. It is supposed to work if everyone is striving for his own advantage, if "taking" is made the aim of all economic activity, and "giving" is used in order to be able to take. This is the spirit which pervades the legal system, which reflects the free expression of the interests of the market economy. As has been shown, this provides the ideal conditions for big business, and has grown out of an all-embracing evolutionary process, clearly evident world-wide. From this evolutionary process ensued a setting-free of the individual will, which broke out from the depths of the sub-conscious, and gushed out over the perceptible world, experiencing it as the only reality. This way of experiencing the world is then confirmed by natural science. Thus the construction of the individual self-consciousness takes place upon the ground of matter, whereon it seeks to realise itself through ownership, and particularly through the appropriation of productive capital, both physical and financial. Such ownership gives control over the productive forces of the economy, and this brings with it, at the same time, the experience of personal freedom. However, this is not genuine freedom, but is based on illusory notions, both social and economic. (The poet Novalis left a note as follows: "Ownership is what offers the possibility of experiencing freedom in the world of the senses." Novalis's own situation was that he was able to own consumption goods, for living purposes, having in his possession landed estates. However he did not own much in the way of produced means of production; hence, he could speak in this way.)

It is necessary, now, and quite justified, for individuals to develop their personalities, to attain self-consciousness, and to experience freedom. They can and should do this with all the power of their egos. However, true freedom is only to be gained in the realm of the spirit, and by psychic exertion. To cultivate the comforting of the ego by fastening on to material things leads to an illusory kind of self-consciousness. This is intensified through the corrupting promptings to self-aggrandisement without limit, which is associated with the attachment to materialism. These promptings are "luciferian".*

Thus the basis is formed for the economic power struggle, that compulsively takes the form of maximising material activities, and overstimulates the desire to possess. Thus it has become possible for the economic life of society to be subjected to absolutism. It is only because men believe the world of matter to be the sole reality, that this economic absolutism, this making the economy into the be-all and end-all of existence, becomes possible. Men in whom the awareness of individuality has awoken, but who are wholly taken up with material existence, generate an overwhelming urge to extend their personalities into the material world, and hence foster an unlimited striving to acquire economic power.

It is money which has provided the instrument whereby these aims could be accomplished. Money is, as it were, the concentrated essence of matter, of material values; and this being so, the desire for profit has gradually become the dominating central focus of human existence. Deep down is the desire to become infinite; and this desire in its proper form is quite naturally the source of all spiritual development. Now it is in the sub-soil that the desire for profit grows. What happens is that the true form of this desire is wrongly transferred into the economic sphere of social life. Hence the illusion that economic achievements have an intrinsic value for their own sake, hence these achievements are, as it were, stamped with the desire for endless growth. The seductive notion that growth is the fundamental principle of all economic systems comes particularly from money, as the representative of all commodity values, whether real or artifical. As the alter ego of all material values, particularly those which are artificially created by capitalising the land, the means of production, etc, money made these artificial values seem to have a real independent existence, and created the illusion that there was an endless ability to grow behind them. Hence the tendency to make the economic system into the quintessence of a sort of material universe on earth. This would put materialist culture into a dominating position over the whole earth, and turn

---

*In the Steinerist concept of the psyche, "Lucifer" is an archetype betokening excessive emotion.—Editor, English edn.

human society into a gigantic money-making corporation—and there are enough signs of this happening today.

The theory of historical and dialectical materialism which Karl Marx propounded in the middle of the 19th century has in the course of three generations completely fulfilled itself, become a reality. The world outlook of today has embraced the materialist philosophy. The conviction has been rammed home into the thinking of immature people, that matter—its substance, its force—constitutes the only true reality there is. This of course makes the production relationships of the economy into the basis of civilisation, into the force shaping political and legal structures. The private capitalist system of the West, and the state capitalist system of Eastern Europe, have both taken this as their guiding principle. They have both directed the work of humanity towards turning the earth into a kind of material universe. By being thus entangled, it is inevitable that the wish has been stirred up in people everywhere for ownership of the proceeds of the economic exploitation of the earth, that this should become the chief objective of living. And of course the more material goods are owned, the greater the illusion of security and betterment in life.

In modern times individual ownership has developed in the West in opposition to collective ownership. This antithesis has worked itself out through world politics, into the East/West political struggle. The Western legal system sanctioned and legalised individual or private ownership of the means of production. This system reflects precisely the modes of behaviour established by the economic development of modern industry and commerce. Modern political and economic science, working in the spirit of liberalism, found reasons to justify this pattern of action: it was claimed to be the consequence of an irreversibly valid natural law.

The earth and its resources were seized by the pioneers of the new economic system without any check on them, and those seizures were then recognised and accepted legally as private ownership in society. Private ownership had already been foreshadowed in Roman law. There were two reasons for this. On the one hand, Roman citizens wanted such ownership as an extension of the concept of legal personality; on the other hand, it fitted in with the needs of the Roman empire in subjugating other peoples. Thus was the concept of private ownership born. It opened up the way for all values, all economic objects, to come under the control of the free individuals who seized them, and all this within the framework of the law.

In international relations, the concept of sovereignty based on force was formed in a similar way. This of course legitimised the occupation of foreign countries conquered in war. This provided the basis for the colonial policies of modern times. The conquest of territory went on for economic reasons, whether directly by the state or by semi-state bodies. [Such as the East India Company—Editor, English edn.]. Once conquered, it would then be governed as if belonging to the occupying state. This, the right for the state to subjugate under its sovereign will a foreign people, extended to its own people. The Marxists have enlarged it, to transfer the entire economic system to state ownership and control. The total state economy of the Marxists is the antithesis of the liberal concept of individual ownership; impersonal collective ownership takes a universal form, as ownership by the state. Now if there is to be a genuinely human society, both concepts of ownership, the liberal and the Marxist, must be set aside, or else transformed. Only in this way can there be a legitimate and human economic system.

To see the full significance of this we need to analyse the basis of the Marxist and liberal world views. Both can be very seductive; and both revolutionary. Both are one-sided, and transitory, but both have none the less provided a historically necessary lesson.

5 The wrong turnings on the Marxist and the liberal road to freedom.

Both liberalism and Marxism have had a historical role to play in social development. Both acted as forces making for the individualisation of human nature. Liberalism performed this function for the bourgeoisie. Marxism planted in the proletariat an urge which, while different, still reflected the desire for freedom. These two modern movements for freedom, the liberal and the Marxist, were both based on unique world historical circumstances. They operated in such a way as to set loose the drive for freedom at the centre of the human individuality, and to create the independent human personality.

Man has entered upon this central stage of the process of becoming human as a result of the spiritual impact of Christianity. (This needs to be studied further in the light of the Christology of anthroposophy.)*

---

*See Steiner's "Christ-Impulse and the Development of Ego-Consciousness".

As his ego-consciousness unfolds, modern man experiences it in three ways: intellectually, as self-awareness; emotionally, as self-respect; in his will, as the impulse to self-realisation. Now to find oneself, to find freedom, it is necessary to come up against some objective thing which is not oneself. Now the impersonal world of matter provides this other thing, provides it all around one, and each person will feel this as alien to him, and as having been so since birth. One can assert oneself against this material world, on the one hand by thought, on the other hand by working it, to master it, to subject it to one's will. However, the ego-consciousness (awareness of *self*) does not develop itself only through confrontation with the material world; its own activity develops, in addition, a world of its own making, and it confronts this as well; thus it creates the antithesis to its own being. Self respect derives from this separation of the person creating from the things created.

The deepest antithesis is in the relationships of men to men; here man confronts his fellow men. This involves the sundering of individuals in mutual opposition, and in enmity to all levels of human fellowship. The social nadir is reached when there is no relationship with any other person.

These three situations—in which freedom is experienced through matter, through personal creation, and through others—are all to do with outward freedom. Inner freedom is different. Its secret is not touched on in the above cases. Inner freedom is not produced by external sensations, but embodies pure experience of self and pure consciousness of self. In characterising liberal or Marxist forms of freedom, it can be seen that neither of them are concerned with this inner freedom. About freedom of any kind, one has to ask, "free from what?", "free for what?". Asking these questions will help us to analyse the orientation of these two major contemporary movements for "freedom".

The task of liberalism was to foster the development of the bourgeois towards becoming human. The liberal idea is that man should approach the earth and material things in such a way as to free himself from them—and so achieve personal control over them.* Thus the bourgeois, whether as a scientific thinker with natural science and technology, or as an economic entrepreneur shaping and working the world of matter, sought to appropriate the material fruits of these activities.

---

*Marxists too believe freedom is got by recognising "necessity".—Ed. Engl. edn.

Thus he attained, through his achievements, which he then confronted, a personal self-awareness, which he focused on and in himself.

As a consequence, he set himself free in various ways. Science was used to break the hold of traditional spiritual authorities; in this process the philosopher Bacon played the part of iconoclast. Further freeing himself from religious authority, he transformed religious concepts into the ethical imperative that the earth should be worked tirelessly. As entrepreneur, finally, he made himself free from the authority and tutelage of the state. The positive aims of the "free-for-what?" of liberal freedom were these: to permit and to justify the free economy, so as to experience freedom in economic activity, hence the universal extension of the market economy. Thus economic liberalism characterised itself by the assertion of the principles of freedom, and these of course are the rights already mentioned, which the entrepreneur wants, to be able to engage in economic activities without state interference, entirely for his own benefit. To this end, they require freedom to conclude contracts, and conduct business as they think fit. Now such business is not limited to commodities proper, but extends to the labour, capital and property markets. Behaviour in these markets was to be defined by a further freedom, namely to obtain the largest possible profit through competition, regardless of other considerations. The culmination of the liberal free market economy principle is reached when the gift is made whereby the entrepreneurial capitalist is allowed to appropriate the free capital that the social economy has formed.

The historic role of liberalism was marked by the beginning of the modern independence of individuals. This can be seen from the powerful personalities of individual entrepreneurs, and in the economic system they created, in which all social and political ties were cut. In this system it was the entrepreneurial impulse which created the basis for individual development. Every conceivable object, every intellectual achievement, every person capable of work, was pressed into its service. The exercise of this individual power was made possible by the private ownership of the means of production, which could be used exclusively for personal self-realisation. Taking the liberal market principle to the extreme of absolutism in order to serve such self-realisation unchained a power-seeking tendency which created economic power centres which were essentially counterproductive.

It is at this point that the liberal freedoms turn into their opposite. They have been so misused that they destroy freedom. We have already

seen how market freedom abrogates itself through the formation of
trusts, cartels and conglomerates. Another important factor is the
impact of bourgeois liberalism on the innermost being of the working
man. The wage system tied the workers to the means of production,
so that they had no choice but to work them. Now wages are looked
upon from the firm's viewpoint, as a cost to be accounted as a debit
against the firm's income. The wages system reflects the whole process
of separating those who work the means of production from the
company's takings, that is from the financial proceeds of their joint
work with the means of production. This is of course the result of the
wage system, which means that the revenue of the enterprise is
concentrated into the hands of the entrepreneur or the owners of the
capital. Now it is against these individual power centres. which are
continually augmenting their control over the economy, over the monetary system and over politics, that the world-wide social-revolutionary
opposition of the proletariat is raised. Karl Marx provided the basis for
this, and stirred up its development.

Those who operate the means of production under these circumstances experience deep within themselves a growing alienation from
the bourgeoisie who cut themselves off from the workers. The labour
contract ignores the worker as a human being. The entrepreneur who
recruits him enters into no social contact with him; he simply buys his
labour-power and uses it to make profit for himself. As a human being,
he is rejected. His social existence is reduced to nothing, to less than
nothing, in fact, since he is obliged to deliver up his labour-power to the
self-centred will of the bourgeoisie. Thus he experiences exploitation.
The proletarian finds himself chained to the bourgeoisie who give him
work. Their power to do this comes of course from their ownership of
the means of production, and of free capital. The injustice of the power
of ownership is stifling. It is in this situation that the proletarian revolt
for freedom is rooted. In the worker's soul there burns a desire to be
free from the bourgeoisie and its economic and political power. The
proletariat was made aware of the "free-tor-what?" by Marx, who set
them the task of destroying the bourgeois capitalist world, and of
dispossessing the expropriators. He aroused the strongest feelings of
hatred in the workers, to motivate them to free themselves from their
chains. The positive side of the proletarian programme for freedom is to
be the formation of a new economic and political system, to be
achieved through the political and economic dictatorship of the
proletariat. As with liberalism, but in a different way, this freedom

programme also destroys itself. The dictatorship of the proletariat involves the suppression of all outward freedoms, and because the aim is to constitute a new world-outlook, a spiritual dictatorship is also involved, over inner freedom.

Just as with the liberal form of freedom, the Marxist form tends also to abrogate itself, and turn into its opposite. However, there is a major distinction to be made. Whereas the bourgeois experiences the oppression of matter, the proletarian experiences the oppression of the bourgeoisie. The bourgeois has his centre of gravity in his thought. He wants to control matter. The proletarian has his centre of gravity in his heart. He fights against the social class which oppresses him. He wants to control or destroy that class. Karl Marx sought to develop in the mind of the worker the same intelligence that the bourgeois class possesses. The task facing the bourgeoisie is to develop the powers of the heart, which are the same thing as social powers.*

6 The background to Marxism and the Marxist critique of ownership

If a humane solution to the social problem of the twentieth century is to be found, we must probe the unconscious depths of the proletarian revolt for freedom. These depths are very important. The Marxist critique of the private capitalist economic system, of the wages system and of surplus value—which is seen as exploitation—touches on the basis, in *Geist*, of modern society. Marx could only see this in terms of the class structure. The reason for this was that what had driven the proletariat to insurrection was their experience of the deeper nature of a world force; however though they *experienced* this force, they did not *understand* it. Their will to revolt came from the awareness —which Marx gave them—that their very humanity was being *negated*.†

Thus the proletariat are guided by the force of revolutionary thinking. This thinking first appeared in Marx's *Critique of Hegel's Philosophy of Law*, in 1844—before the Communist Manifesto. In it, Marx saw the central social issue as the liberation of mankind from all authority—particularly religious. Thus, he said, "in Germany...all classes

---

*Wilken is here very close to the English Marxist Caudwell; see the latter's "Studies in a Dying Culture", London, 1947.—Editor, English edn.
†See glossary for an explanation of this important term.

lack that breadth of spirit which identifies itself, if only for a moment, with the spirit of the people, that genius which can raise material force to the level of political power, that revolutionary boldness which flings into the face of its adversary the defiant words: *I am nothing and I should be everything.*" (*Early Writings*, translated by Livingstone and Benton, Penguin, 1977, p. 254). He went on: "In Germany...no class of civil society has the need and the capacity for universal emancipation unless under the compulsion of its *immediate* situation, of *material* necessity and of its *chains themselves*." (p. 256). Hence to rise to self-awareness and become free men, the Germans would need to form "a class of civil society which is not a class of society, a class* which is the dissolution of all classes, a sphere which has a universal character because of its universal suffering and which lays claim to no *particular right* because the wrong it suffers is not a *particular wrong* but *wrong in general*; a sphere of society which can no longer lay claim to a *historical* title, but merely to a *human* one, which does not stand in one-sided opposition to the consequences but in all-sided opposition to the premises of the German political system; and finally a sphere...which is, in a word, the *total loss* of humanity and which can therefore redeem itself only through the *total redemption of humanity*. This dissolution of society as a particular class* is the *proletariat*." (p. 256).

Contemplating the many interconnected ideas in the foregoing, one can understand how the experience of suffering the injustice of the private capitalist economic system created a class consciousness which bound proletarians together, since they had all shared this experience of injustice together. Through this negative experience, hatred was stirred up against the owners and managers of the means of production, and in consequence revolutionary feelings developed against the whole bourgeois economic and political system, the inhumanity of which Marx analysed. He developed the concept of the *relations of production,* to describe the way in which the workers and the means of production were brought together and the anti-social legal forms involved. Thus the entrepreneurs and capitalists were seen as a social class, whose *rationale* was to base their power on the ownership of the means of production, and to make those who worked the means of production dependent upon them and on the wages system, by means of this power.

Marx saw the significant element in profit, quite erroneously, as

---

*The original German word is, in each of these two cases, literally "estate".—Ed.

being a surplus value derived from the exploitation of labour. Now in relating the injustice suffered by the workers to the ownership of the means of production, he however got no further than the surface of the problem. In order to understand the part played by the ownership of the means of production, we must probe deeper, beyond the surface that Marx described.

Only in human relationships can we talk about what is just or unjust. There is no injustice in the mineral world, or between animals. Only men can do or suffer injustice. This is because only men have *Geist* in them, the *Geist* in the individual being what may be called the *self*. Whenever a person acts *consciously*, rather than by unconscious instinct, it is his *self* which is at work. That is to say, some part of his human spirit is entering into play, in his working activities. He expresses something of his self, which flows out of him. It is, as it were, offered, to be used up. Rudolf Steiner called what is offered the "heavenly *Anteil*".* What we call the dignity of man depends on the human *Geist* —which is the centre of the individuality, which transcends birth and death, which is immortal. In all human work there is the outflowing of this *Geist*, which is the *content* of human dignity. This outflowing cannot be measured or quantified in any material terms, so that it cannot be equated with material goods, cannot be valued in material terms. This can only be done with the material products themselves, though through being created by work they are of course created by this outflow of *Geist*.

Now to understand what ownership means, as it relates to the means of production, we must return to the concept of exploitation—in its fundamental meaning that is, the phrase having become something of a catch-phrase since Marx's day. In volume I of *Capital*, Marx put the psychology of it this way, in typical polemical style: "He, who before was the money owner, now strides in front as capitalist; the possessor of labour-power follows as his labourer. The one with an air of importance, smirking, intent on business; the other, timid and holding back, like one who is bringing his own hide to market and has nothing to expect but—a hiding." (p. 155, Moore and Aveling translation, London 1886).† Now this vignette signifies that the worker, bringing his self to the market, finds it rejected. He therefore tends to recoil from the capitalist, and cannot empathise with him—because his self-respect

---

*See glossary for explanation of this term.

†See glossary for a discussion of the Marxist term, "labour-power".

is bruised by this treatment. So he responds to the indifference of the employer towards him, with a like indifference on his part towards the employer. He has to work to live, but unconsciously he experiences the way in which his work is used as a rejection of the part of his personality that he has offered—which is just utilised for the self-seeking aims of the employer. In this situation he can hardly make this offering willingly, although it is intrinsic in all work. Anyone working for someone else in such circumstances will find it humiliating; he is giving from his *Geist* for it to be used for purely self-seeking purposes, and will thus feel himself robbed of part of his very soul. Marx felt this, and called the whole relationship between labour and this egoistic system *exploitation*. This is not a matter of paying too little; rather, it is that the wage being a material economic quantity is simply not commensurable with the work. The whole point of exploitation is this confrontation of work with a money sum, as if this were valid. That is the wage system. Of course the worker experiences this as the *negation* of his essential humanity—and hence as the grossest possible injustice. What flows out from his *Geist* is forced—an intolerable life-long humiliation. So he compensates for this, treating the employer as the latter treats him. Obviously, the worker feels the urge to suppress the outflow of *Geist* as forcefully as he can—and this generates hatred. Hence in complete egoism he turns against his work, and against the employer. He becomes quite uninterested in production, and in the company's prosperity. Instead he seeks to get what he can out of it for himself.

Hence in the private capitalist economic system, two opposed parties confront each other, both motivated by egoism, and both self-seeking. These two parties are the employer and the employee. In this relationship, the amount of the work done is stipulated by, and limited by the wage; so that the worker will only work to the extent that the wage compels the work. The work done is adjusted to the wage paid. The struggle is to reduce the amount of work, by reducing hours, increasing holidays, etc. Now in adopting that attitude the workers are in fact at war with part of themselves. But what else can they do? Their own materialistic withdrawal, and the all-pervadingly materialistic economic system push them into this.

The workers feeling themselves thus exploited, will exploit back, will "sponge" off the general proceeds of the plant. Marx gave them what seemed to be a lever and a justification as well, when he depicted the employer's profits as coming out of surplus value; which surplus value could, in his explanation, only be accounted for by the exploitation of the workers. By taking this position, he got it into the workers' heads that they were the creators of this so-called surplus value, that this surplus value had been taken from them, and that therefore it was they who were the creators of the entrepreneur's profit, or in other words, of the free capital formed. As we have already seen, there was a modicum of truth in this assertion at the time. All misunderstandings of this kind, of course, arise when the workings of the market economy are not understood. When the worker in the wage system compares his income with the income of the entrepreneur—particularly when this is augmented out of free capital—he can hardly help but think of himself as being exploited, as being unjustly treated. Hence he will feel himself impelled to exploit the economy back, whenever he can. One may well ask whether there is any future for a labour system in which the worker becomes utterly uninterested in the prosperity of the plant in which he works; so that even if the company is unproductive or bankrupt, he continues in true trade union spirit, to demand shorter hours and increased wages.

What then is the real basis of the working class opposition to the bourgeois proponents of the private capitalist economy? This movement which started in Central Europe has grown to such an extent as to have become a worldwide problem. Out of this revolutionary drive, out of this opposition to capitalism, a political system has been constructed which tries to subject human development to the dictatorship of materialism. Under the banner of Communism, this mechanistic social system is to be forced on humanity. Now, this threat is *part* of the advance of the materialist philosophy, which seeks to deny the existence of any spirit, any inner centre, any self, in the individual human being. Yet this spirit is present in every piece of work done, and, indeed, it cannot help but flow out, selflessly, into the work. Only by recognising this fact can we establish a work system in which the working man becomes a dignified human being with his part to play in operating the means of production. Under such a system men would no longer be like abstract components in the wage system; the inner spirit of the worker would no longer be oppressed; and his natural social impulses would have free rein.

Now it was Marx who brought the workers to awareness of the oppression of the wage system, so that they began to experience it as an intolerable injustice. In doing, hatred between the classes was stirred up. Marx's message had a world-wide impact because of its timing. It reached the minds of the working classes as a time when they were only just beginning to emerge into self-consciousness, at a time when their selfs were far from fully developed, far from being capable of giving them self-reliance intellectually. Hence the ideological force of Marx's ideas was able to unleash hatred from within, there being little in them to stop it. Hence he was able to implant into the proletariat the idea that force was justified in order to break the chains that held them back. Their selfs were still, it has to be understood, relatively undeveloped, lacking as yet the full force of self-consciousness. Force, Marx claimed would set them free, and this was right, even, if necessary, to the point of freedom being over the dead bodies of a part of mankind. Being born in conditions of immature self-development, and seeming to compensate for those conditions, Marxism soon found fertile soil for growth in the Eastern part of Europe, where large masses still lived in extended family groups and in village communes.

For example, the Russians were still in this situation; the Tsar was still revered as the "Little Father". In these virtually ego-less communities Marxism penetrated. It found a vocation in leading these communities, living as they did in extended family groups, towards an undeveloped level of self-consciousness—by the force of materialism. The Indians and Japanese, on the other hand, received the same force of materialism through the impact of the English and of the Americans respectively, these two Western nations acting as representatives of bourgeois materialism.

It is important to realise that it is basically the *same* materialism that pervades both the bourgeois and the proletarian worlds. There are really two styles of materialism—the pragmatic and the ideological; liberalism representing the pragmatic materialist way of thinking and Marxism the philosophical world outlook of materialist theory.

The Marxist world outlook—the so-called historical materialist philosophy—reflects back, in abstracted theoretical form, the basic force of the bourgeois social and economic system with its all-pervading business-minded spirit, the spirit of technology, of the organisation, of the counting house—all of which Marxism represents, in a generalised philosophical form. Now this has been hammered into working class thinking over generations; so that, considering their material circumstances, they became revolutionary. The content of the bourgeois mode of living—and of its reflection in liberalistic thinking—was transformed by Marx into revolutionary ideology, aimed at *overthrowing* the very bourgeois social system which this same content had led to. The destructive ruthlessness of the revolutionaries could only result from the adoption of a philosophy that extinguishes the developing individuality.

In order to assess the materialist philosophy correctly, it needs to be said that it has now reached the highest stage in its unawareness of the totality of the human spirit and mind, of the self and individuality of man. Marx created this unawareness in the minds of the workers, by his incredible display of intellectual virtuosity, in which matter was seen as the primary philosophical source of thought—which he did in order to fire the workers with zeal for the violent overthrow of society. This made it possible, up to a point, to anaesthetise the humiliation which results from the experience of having to sell one's labour as if it were a commodity, according to the rules of the market-place.

Both liberalism and Marxism are inclined to see their understanding of the world, and therefore their priorities in life, as being absolutes, and therefore to be advanced, until the whole of humanity submits to their way of doing things, and adopts their attitude of mind. However the bourgeois capitalists, being after profit, have different reasons from those of the workers, for taking this attitude. The merchant adventurers and the capitalist entrepreneurs were not against subjecting other nations to all sorts of indignities and injustices, exploiting them economically, and, to facilitate this exploitation, subjugating them politically, turning them into colonies.

The economic, business mentality is not harmful *per se*, but when caught up with the daemonic drive for power, or when overwhelmed by greed, it becomes destructive. For example, there is the manufacture and marketing of armaments and other means of destruction which if used would threaten the end of mankind and the devastation of the earth, so that humanity has become divided between two dangerous power blocs, each of which could destroy all life on earth.

To sum up, the destructive force of the proletariat is based on the release of elemental unconscious drives, previously latent, but activated by the leading revolutionary spirits, so as to bring society under the control of state institutions conceived entirely on intellectual lines, and so as to eliminate opposition to this.

The destructive force of the bourgeoisie on the other hand, is rooted in the egotistic experience of self. In the liberated self, it is manifested in the endless exploitation of both man and nature, seeking human fulfilment in piling up wealth.

Hence the apocalyptic quality of the conflict on which the fate of man now depends. On the one hand, there is the inflamed, aggressive, newly-awakened self, feeling itself to be socially deprived, wanting to destroy all authority in order to prove itself. On the other hand, humanity is afflicted by the liberated selfs of the bourgeoisie acting out their self-validation in the world of matter, by building up their material power. Both would become totalitarian, if they achieved their aims. The proletarian revolution would establish a political world state to dominate mankind. The bourgeois capitalist imperialism would similarly create a techno-economic order controlling every aspect of life.

These are two wrong turnings; both would lead mankind into misery, and ultimately to destruction. Both Marx and the bourgeois mind conceive matter to be the be-all and end-all of the universe. In practical terms, this means that the purpose of human life is thought to be nothing more than production and consumption.

It is in this perversion of human destiny, that the question of ownership acquires its unique philosophical significance. Ownership is experienced in two ways: as the basis and prop of existence—and as the means to social power, enabling the owners of capital to exploit both workers and consumers, which is the way Marx saw it, partly as a result of his own vicissitudes. Hence he urged the proletariat to expropriate, to dispossess the owners of their capital.

Now, while the wage system may sometimes appear to be withholding part of his earnings from the worker, the real nature of exploitation however lies in the dispossession of the worker's *humanity*—in that he is treated as a piece of useful material, and that he has no real human relationship in his working role. Marx however turned the thing upside down, putting exploitation at the pole of *matter* instead of that of mind, by explaining it as a question of material deprivation. Marx saw the seizure by the workers of surplus value as filling their inner emptiness—brought about. of course, by the wages system.*

The Marxist cultivation of the impersonal spirit of socialism is of course the *antithesis* of the imbalanced bourgeois mode of cultivating the individual. Socialism does not mean that the surplus value will be given to the individual worker to own; instead it is taken by the state —as a sort of collective ownership. Now herein lies the proof that

---

*See Rudolf Steiner's "Towards Social Renewal", London 1977 (3rd edn.).

Marxism is never going to make the individual human being, or his essential personality, the basis of the social system. On the contrary, Marxism has fallen for the bourgeois scientific outlook, and considers the individual as merely a sample of the *species*—as if man were an animal: hence the individual is dealt with as belonging to the state—equally, of course! What socialism involves is this—that the state is universalised, and takes over into its own hands and administers not only the entire economy, but the entire cultural life as well. This can be seen, not only in communist countries, but also as a tendency in the bourgeois states as well.

7 *The way in which economic life is shaped,*
   as propounded by Steiner in his main social law

The bourgeoisie and the proletariat confront one another as two social groups which extend beyond national frontiers. One is socially conservative and passive: the other revolutionary and active. Whoever looks into the depths of this antithesis will recognise the dominating principles shaping each side—both principles being one-sided and yet both in their way worthy—namely, being, for the bourgeoisie the development of individuality, and for the proletariat the development of social "togetherness". Man's future depends on these two forces being reconciled.

This social détente can only be established if a really human social system can be discovered. Now such a system would have to be based on Rudolf Steiner's main social law, which has already been referred to. Let us here quote his own formulation of this principle from his *Geisteswissenschaft und soziale Frage*, Dornach 1960:*

"The prosperity of a group of people working together will be the greater, the less any one member keeps for himself what he has made: that is, the more that each individual delivers over to other workers out of what he has made, and the more his own needs are met, not out of his own output, but out of the output of others. All arrangements within a group which run counter to this principle must in the end produce distress and want somewhere...

"This general principle holds good for social life as inexorably as a natural law. However, one should not suppose it to be sufficient if one

---

*Not yet available in English.

restricts the significance of this principle to a mere generalised moral precept, or perhaps tries to re-compose it as meaning that everyone should work in the service of their fellow men. On the contrary, the principle is true only if it is made to come alive, if a group of people succeed in creating arrangements such that no one can claim the fruits of his own labour for himself, but that they go, as far as possible without deduction to the group as a whole, and so that he himself must therefore be reciprocally supported by the labour of his fellows. Thus it follows that, for the group members, working, and the obtaining of a secure income, are quite separate transactions."

The economy is of course subject to the workings of this law, which propounds the ineluctable necessity that each individual has to work for others, and in so doing behaves socially. In a properly conceived social system, each would freely give of his best, each would live by being useful, because their *interest* would be in mankind, in maintaining and developing it. Now for this to be possible, work would need to be properly organised, so that it was orientated towards the common interest. This cannot be done with either state or private capitalism. The law of social development, and the business spirit which motivates present economic behaviour, are mutually incompatible.

Now the social nature of the economy, based on the division of labour, is such as to oblige men to work together with each other and with the means of production. Socially speaking, the involvement of people in economic activity draws them into production groups, towards social production—and this tendency is rather hurriedly institutionalised—hence there are as yet only caricatures of what is needed. In Eastern Europe, man has been organised into a political corporate production system, organised by the impersonal force of the state, rather than on a human level. In the West, people wanting work have to go to someone or other who owns means of production, or to the owner's manager, to encounter a total lack of interest in them, except in their willingness and ability to do some job. It is just the same when the state is the employer. All that the private owner of the means of production really cares about is the obtaining of supplies and the operation of the plant; only of course human help is needed for these functions to be carried out. To obtain this help, a labour contract is agreed, under which the performance of work is compensated by allowing the worker the means of subsistence, which are handed over in the form of a fixed sum of money, in a cold and impersonal way.

This is the arrangement that Marx stigmatised as gross injustice, as the degradation of human labour by making it into a commodity.

Only by understanding the *spirit* of work can forms of working together be developed, suitable for enabling workers to give each other of their best because they *want* to. This would of course constitute the norm, in a properly conceived social system: but would require a complete change in the system of taking on workers as prevailing at present. The attitude which the private capitalist market economy and the Marxist state economy both propagate, is the elemental egoistic one—to look after oneself. This may be acceptable in the matter of consumption, but when introduced into production relationships —which must, of their nature, be social—then the effect is destructive. As Rudolf Steiner asked in his "The Challenge of the Times" (New York, 1941): "What are you doing, then, when you perform no labour but you have money that other people must work to get? The human being then has to bring to market what constitutes his inner self and you give him only what is earthly, the purely ahrimanic. You see, this is the spiritual aspect of the matter. Wherever Ahriman is at work only destruction can come about."*

Both the market economy and the state planned economy ignore the matter of understanding what the real spirit of work is. According to the materialist philosophy, the worker offers his physical labour power; but in reality what he offers is the substance of his spirit, of his individuality. For, following the awakening of the consciousness of self in modern man, this is what his being focuses on. Hegel knew this, that work involved an externalisation of the self, a movement out and away from the self; he recognised that the basic motive for work lay in the desire to take this to the point of making an act of giving the self.

Now a man can make such an act for other men, if he goes into a social working group with them—and in so doing, *assents to it.* Now such a social working group is quite a different thing from legally contracted reciprocal services; such contracts go no deeper than the material outward surface of social relations. If the working relationship is based on such a group then there is something different or new in it, for that reason. In such a group, the man giving the work and the man receiving the work—as both must be described in abstract terms—will relate, as a matter of course, in such a way that the one receiving the

---

*Ahriman is the Mephistophelian archetype in the Steinerist view of the psyche.

work will—if he is really to experience the humanity of the fellow human working for him—recognise the thing out of the other's personality which is being offered to him, and do this with a feeling of being thereby honoured. If someone proffers his work, and is not then spiritually rejected, then he will want to join others in building such a social group: because in it, he can work without any inner resistance for the interests of others—since he will feel these interests to be the same as his own.

Now in the middle ages there could indeed be found such a normal group relationship—sanctioned as customary by the Church—between workers and the owners of such production facilities as then existed. Modern man came however to surrender himself to the domination of material things, and became imbued with desire for material values. This desire took the place of the spirit of working together in a comprehensive social group. Thus the business spirit came into working relationships, making it impossible for anyone to go on regarding his work with any interest. The business spirit stifles the spirit of common interest and hinders the working of Steiner's main social law*, according to which working relationships need to have a social dimension. In the next chapter we will see how this law can be realised, in three practical examples.

---

* See glossary.—editor, English edition.

C H A P T E R   6

New-Style Companies

1 Possession relationships, ownership, responsibility.
Political and economic democracy.

Every man who works is endowed, willy nilly, with ties binding him to the equipment with which he works and to his fellow-workers. He is drawn towards the natural working community. Should this be hampered, by the wage system, in particular, then he will form what are called informal groups with others outside the place of work, but these are really a substitute for the work-place community that is lacking. It is normal for the workers to like to develop harmonious relationships—with the machinery, with fellow workers, with supervisors, with the boss. These relationships are of a personal and subjective kind. If one goes to the roots of the matter, one finds a primordial tie between the worker and the means of production with which he works. This we will christen the *possession sentiment*; this establishes itself *alongside* the actual working activity, and, as it were, envelops it. Such a psychic attachment is based on a principle of the *Geist*. A man who relates his whole being to the tools he uses attaches and up to a point unites himself and his heavenly *Anteil** therewith. He infuses them, even though it may be unconsciously, with a part of his essence —even when the work is boring and uninteresting. The tools enter a little into his psychic possession, whether or not they actually belong to him. Now, *possession* became, as it were, *overblown* during the evolution towards personal *ownership*, which guarantees personal rights of disposal over the thing possessed, and which is made into a legal category, given the endorsement of society, by the legislation of the state.

---

*See glossary.

In complete contrast, the *possession sentiment* referred to appears as a purely human matter, and carries with it no legal rights of disposal at all. The capitalistic, private-ownership-based economic system still contains this *possession sentiment* in it, but as it is only there to control the actual working of the means of production, it is not really connected at all with the desire to *own* their substance. What the capitalist wants, on the other hand, is to take this thing that he has bought with money and make its very substance a part of himself. For this, he has to be the sole controller of it—which is how the "monarchical" principle gets into the capitalist economic system, and into its heart, the acquisition of, and outlook towards, capital. The social synthesis of these two things, the possession sentiment and the relationship of ownership will be achieved by a constitution for industry which will draw its strength from the living principle of the common possession sentiment of all those who work with the means of production.

The tendency is for each individual personal possession sentiment to extend itself over the whole of the plant, that is, of the enterprise. A common possession sentiment arises if all those working in the company feel themselves united in this spirit; and this can carry with it the basis of a socially correct unity within the plant—or of a common enterprise—in which all those working the means of production, both those doing the leading and those putting plans into effect, are inspired by the the same aim—of *using* the means of production. The concept of *utilisation* reveals itself to have two aspects. At the *personal* level the question arises of the specific rights to be given to those authorised to use the means of production. At the collective level, there is the duty to use them mutually with other users.

Practical realisation of such a community of use comes up against the problem of the division of labour activities. It is necessary that the means of production be used according to some general guiding plan. In the execution of such a plan there will be various levels of activity, classified according to the size of the *area of responsibility* involved, whether in the plant or in the offices. The kind of ownership relationship necessitated by applying the concept of *use* is explained in my "New Forms of Ownership in Industry".* In it, I counterposed two different tendencies—the tendency for ownership to devolve upon a responsible management controlling the overall enterprise, and the development of use-ownership out of labour activities. Overall responsibility is exercised over all the

---

* Published in India in 1962.

partial responsibilities in individual spheres of work, and incorporates the highest stage of use, which is both qualitatively and quantitatively different from the individual acts of use. It can therefore be considered correct if the person carrying the highest responsibility is given a special position. Historically speaking, the form in which the overall responsibility for the operation of the enterprise first developed was that of the free entrepreneur who was at one and the same time the actual owner of the means of production and the sole determiner of its functions. In recent times, this obtrusive leadership of the entrepreneurial personality has been more and more depersonalised, made objective. Through the concentration of the economy, the effective directoral function no longer is exercised by the owners of the means of production but by a hired management team. This means that the principle of ownership as the justification of the capitalistic mode of production is being substituted by the principle of management. The conclusion reached, for example by Otto Brenner, chairman of IG Metall, shortly before his death in 1972, is that worker participation in the management function is urgently needed.

The transfer of responsible management from the capital-owning entrepreneurs to the ownershipless managers has put the latter in the position of having overall responsibility for the utilisation of the means of production on behalf of the owners. The owners thus become the mere beneficiaries of the profit that the managers realise. That is in legal fact what the shareholders in a share company are. The depersonalisation of human relationships in big business has been examined by the English writer Graham Bannock, who concluded that large corporations are no longer the creation of a single entrepreneur, but are run by impersonal technology. The workers become alienated and bored, and find life meaningless. The spirit of technology is a-human and socially disruptive if elevated to a controlling position, to dominate men when it should serve them.

These facts are bringing about the recognition that private ownership over the means of production is, economically speaking, beginning to look meaningless—which indeed it is. Volkswagen showed this.† Its subquent conversion into a share company had no economic point. The most charitable construction is that this was done out of some instinct that the free capital accumulating in Volkswagen ought to be shared out in some way, to benefit the *Geistesleben* and social life.

---

* For many years after the war, the Volkswagen concern existed without any shareholders—due to the peculiar circumstances of its original foundation.—Ed.

The attempts made from the workers' side to gain worker participation focus on joint responsibility for the management of the enterprise, in order to free the application of capital from private power
interests, thereby advancing the interests of the workers. This policy
does give some indirect help to the development of a social constitution
for enterprises, the necessary precondition of which is that the
company should no longer be subject to a central authoritarian will,
whether that of the entrepreneur or that of the state, but should be
democratically—so to speak—controlled by the wills of many if not all
of the parties concerned. This has meanwhile taken the form that the
unions seek to share management of the enterprise with the entrepreneurs. However, this way of doing it distorts the responsible shaping
of the economy into a battle, in which the policy of the unions remains
focused on wage increases and shorter hours, and correspondingly, the
countervailing authoritative self-assertion of the entrepreneurial will
persists. In this situation, as desired today, worker participation remains
a mere social theory. Nevertheless, these endeavours do contain an
element of movement towards unity within the company, albeit in a
confused way. On the other hand, on the employers' side, there is
definitely a change of attitude about a more socially dignified company
constitution, so that the gulf between employer and employee is
narrowing, and the worker more and more seen as a collaborator, and
this change of attitude meets the developing self-awareness of the
workers along the way. In this situation a true participation can be
achieved, which would find its practical base in the ownership of the
usufruct. This development is coming, as is shown by various examples
of common usufruct ownership or of common responsibility starting
to occur.

The various attempts to reform the company have all had these
objects: humanising working relationships, freeing them from authoritarian control, making the distribution of incomes fairer and above
all bringing justice into the matter of the control and application of
company profits. All this adds up to a thoroughgoing reshaping of
the ownership relationship. Recovering a genuine spirit of unity in
the company is the central idea in all these attempts to develop new
and socially correct forms of ownership.

Every reform of the company has to start from the recognition that
every enterprise rests on three bases, which have to be brought into
effective collaboration. These three bases are the physical one—which
consists of the raw materials and the means of production—secondly,

the activities of human labour, and thirdly the *Geist*-imbued management of the whole. Now this triple-tiered form can be conceptually attributed to *every* organism; but when it is externally *organised*, then the principle of authoritative hierarchical command has so far been in vogue. This goes back to the ancient theocracies, in which a central will permeated and ordered all of life. It created a hierarchical structure by which all work was controlled, under the rigid direction of the *Geist* that the priests and kings embodied. This same *Geist* found its contemporary imitation in the system of private entrepreneurial control by the central will of the individual entrepreneur, which also worked out in a hierarchical way. The governing will organised the working process into higher and lower levels, utilising intellectual skills in doing this. Thus a predominantly mechanical style of organisation has resulted. The company reforms of today seek to put an *organic* social co-operation in the place of one authoritatively organised. Furthermore, they attempt to replace the central authoritative management of the plant with something more "collegial".

All these new endeavours aim at realising human work with the three productivity factors in their social essence, thereby increasing economic productivity. This social power is the opposite of the authoritative central controlling will, and it can only arise—in the present stage of human development—out of the initiatives of people working together economically, as a creation of their free will. In the political field one calls this kind of co-operation democracy, in which the common will is formed mainly by majority decisions, rather less often by reaching a consensus. Carried over into economic life this can, in principle, only be done by agreement and by reciprocal arrangements; to force through a majority decision generates conflict. Political democracy and economic co-operation should in fact be clearly distinguished from one another, as they have quite different social functions. However, both acknowledge the role of leadership. A collegial leadership may still contain the authoritative development of decisions due to the outstanding *Geist* of a particular individual; in democratic co-operation there is not only the possibility but indeed the necessity of this happening. Individual intellects vary greatly in capacity; hence, there has to be a gradation of positions, in which a natural system must establish itself, that need not be oppressive if it is restricted to the intellectual sphere and does not upset the correct social way of working together, or seek to adjust the legal claims of the workers upon the enterprise's takings. There has to be a democratic agreement about this. That would express the principle of an organic constitution of the enterprise, in contrast with the authoritatively formed organisation. This constitution could possibly be legally drawn up. This is the great alternative way that economic life today confronts. Is the economy to be conceived as a fixed hierarchical structure, or shall it be formed on the basis of an organic co-operation, in which every individual part reflects and is in harmony with the whole? The whole exists only to the extent that the individual parts continue to associate with one another, giving to the whole and taking from it; whereas a mere organisation is lifeless, like a tree without leaves.

Both the struggle to secure worker participation and the radical rejection by the workers of all authority in social life has tended to obscure the fact that there are necessary and justified authorities and social hierarchies. Such gradations of authority in fact depend on a universal principle concerning the differential development of individual intellects. The etymological meaning of the word "hierarchy" is "sacred command"—the basis of the pre-Christian theocracies. The ability of these theocracies to organise derived from the superiority of *Geist* over matter, which was quite objective, and which created the hierarchical system of tribes and peoples. They arranged the various kinship groups under the control of higher and lower overseers whose job it was to transmit the governing will. The priests and priest-kings maintained their position on account of their having the most developed *Geist*. Essentially, the social system ranged people so that the less-developed intellects had the smaller spheres of competence. Thus the whole hierarchical system was based on the gradations of *Geist*.

Through the development of human individualisation which has since taken place, each individual has developed particular powers in which he is superior to others—perhaps to all others; these can be intellectual, spiritual, social or physical (as in sport).

There are basically two kinds of true hierarchy, the one in the sphere of *Geist*, the other in the politico-social field. The first arises, as already mentioned, by the ranking of different degrees of intellectual development; and its essential nature is revealed in the voluntary submission of the lower to the higher. As Goethe observed, there is only one response to the encounter with someone with higher spiritual power, and that is *respect*. Thereby the hierarchy of *Geist* establishes itself without any external compulsion.

Politico-social hierarchies are established only in the sphere of social life, and contain no ranking by *Geist* but only by *will*. There are two main forms of such hierarchies, the administrative hierarchy and the command hierarchy. The first operates through the *instructions* of higher to lower positions; the second through orders to subordinates. Both instructions and orders express various wills whose power, for example the power of the state, makes them effective. The difference between instructions and orders lies in this, that in an administrative hierarchy, the lower positions, because of the attitude of mind of the functionaries, *agree* with the principles of the instruction. By contrast, in a command hierarchy, the will of the superiors pushes through regardless of the agreement of subordinates, and if necessary uses obvious compulsion.

If we look at hierarchy in the three organs of the social organism, we find:

—in the *Geistesleben*, there is a tendency for a *Geist*-based hierarchy to establish itself voluntarily.

—in the *Rechtsleben* not only is an administrative hierarchy necessary, but there is also a command hierarchy in the police and in the army.

—economic life, arranged as it is on reciprocal services, resists the whole idea of a hierarchical system.

The economy needs a social way of doing things, symbolised by the relationship between an organ and the whole organism. The organ is neither superior nor inferior to the organism. Its nature is to serve the whole organism, which in turn supports its various individual member organs. In this reciprocity, superior and inferior are continually changing places. The world-wide economic system, which includes all mankind, demonstrates that it is subject to the necessity of the division of labour, the social principle of which is reciprocal activity; and according to Steiner's law of social development,* each is called to offer his work to another, who will do the same for him. Now the market economy's competitive battle, being fought solely for profit, contravenes the organic principle of Steiner's law, in that this battle is, from the standpoint of a social system suitable for economic life, totally perverse, and a constraint. Any social entity that is run out of egoism and without interest in others, is perverse in this sense.

However, there are two places in economic life wherein the hierarchical principle is apposite. One is in the plant, in so far as a tech-

---

*See page 105.

nical production process is being carried out there, and the other is in company organisation, in which the movement of values has to be controlled. In the plant the hierarchy of works manager, foreman and worker has been long established. This is compelled by technical necessity. In human terms this is practically realised through a hierarchy of command. This is an extreme case of the hierarchical principle because what is at stake is the compulsion of the laws of nature. This situation necessitates a style of management graded according to personal ability.

However, the modern system of plant management has now to face a situation which previously had not been encountered by the capitalistic economic system—namely the progressive individualisation and self-actualisation drive of the dependent workers. This expresses itself in the form of working to undermine the hierarchical system in all its aspects, and to develop social equality through *participation*. The outward motive of this inner revolt against the authority of the capitalistic economy is the experience that this system is continually trying to increase its profits at the expense of the workers' incomes and if possible at the expense of the consumer, as well.

The revolutionary aim is now to abolish all human subordination and to eliminate the power of one man over another. This aim is in sharp conflict with the need for hierarchy in the plant. In the forefront is the ever-growing movement for workers to participate in the running of the company. The opposition to this aim comes from capital—the centre of the social power complex. However this exercise of power is bound up with the ownership of capital by profit-seeking private groups, whether individual or corporate. Therefore most attempts at reform focus on the private ownership of capital. The unexpected difficulties bound up with the abolition of the private ownership of capital are illustrated by the recent cases of new-type companies. On closer examination it will be seen what opposition there is to a social reshaping of economic life.

2 *The Karl Backhaus Foundation: the Ahrensburg example*

From the viewpoint of the previously mentioned triple division of the economic plant and enterprise, it is the middle division which first of all forms the relationships of the workers to the means of production; this middle division contains the possession relationship and the legal constitution of the relation of the workers to the means of production. In the case of the Ahrensburg example, we have a plant in the iron and steel industry with about 500 employees acting upon the means of production. In order to form a democratic plant community in the outward framework of private capitalistic possession relationships, it was thought necessary to adopt the legal form of an OHG* in which four company directors supervise all the employees. Legally speaking, the latter are reduced to sleeping partners in the company, however with the unusual rights and duties of equal collaborators in the plant management. They are thereby raised to the rank of partners. They should thereby be so deeply involved in the working of the plant that they should rise from the position of employees to become joint entrepreneurs, thus departing from the normal concept of entrepreneurship. The entrepreneurial function exercised by the partners is democratised through the leadership function of the company being equalised in the partnership form. The attainment of partnership rank does not come automatically, but depends on age and experience of the members. Admission follows only on the personal request of those seeking to become partners. The consent of all partners is necessary.

That it is practical is due to the fact that it was built according to the social ideas of Karl Backhaus. Backhaus recognised that a democratic plant community could only be realised if its members learnt to think independently not only to produce together but also to the point that they developed so as to take on responsibility and to play a personal part in company affairs. In order to develop these capabilities in the partners, Karl Backhaus did something decisive in this direction. He established a foundation, the task of which was to develop the understanding of the partners; this meant developing a system of education which would bring out the ability to think and express clearly. When these abilities are developed and when there is the flow of necessary information about the company coming to the partners, then they can work responsibly together in the company organs with the aim of democratising decision-making.

In the Ahrensburg example organs were created through which the directors holding the company could work with the partners and manage it together; these organs thus dealt with the economic utilisation of the company capital and with the relationship of members to

---

*A form of German company.

the means of production—the relations that Marx was concerned about. The formation of these organs reflected a deeply rooted social concern. Three of them were formed, catering on the one hand for the development of the members and on the other hand for the operation of the business.

1   The *Gesellschafter-Versammlung*: the assembly of the members; all the sleeping partners belong to this. This forms the overall directing body of the business, from which the four directors of the OHG derive their authority, so that it controls all the affairs and decisions of the company, thus embodying the concept of democratic self-management.

2   The *Beirat*: the council; this body is there to decide about any physical modifications of the plant, for all property matters, for the construction of new branches of production, and also if an individual resident director is to be deprived of office. The *Beirat* is an organ that takes an objective view of the whole direction of the company, which it has to supervise; this is how it is constituted. It has five members, two nominated by the company directors, and two by the partners. One of the members chosen by each side must not belong to the company; this is to ensure the objectivity of the decision-making.

3   The *Schlichtungsausschuss*: the board of the Foundation; this body is there to resolve conflicts impartially, and hence is "supra-company". Its five members consist of four people from outside the company and a chairman chosen by the president of the county court. Such a body guarantees the highest possible objectivity.

The view has been put forward* that partnership constitutes an associative ownership of the company's means of production and profits. In the Ahrensburg example, this form of partnership extends to include an individual personal share in the capital. This is calculated in the threefold basis of the partners' salaries. The money share of a partner is limited in such a way that the company could never become the property of one partner. This possibility is prevented in an intelligent way. The sleeping partners have no claim, under the articles, upon the company property. For the company directors and their larger stakes, the same applies. The withdrawal of either sleeping partners or directors, or the liquidation of the company, would yield only a settlement credit to the extent of their stake. This could be considered as an improvement in principle upon the share. As with the participation of shareholders, so with the stake of the company

---

*By Vilmar.

directors and partners, the investment is irredeemable. However, there is no factitious development, no paper which can be traded on the Stock Exchange. As shareholders the company directors and partners possess a claim on the total profit which is in addition to their salaries and wages and to the interest on their capital stakes. According to section 48 of the Ahrensburg constitution, the application of profit is so regulated that all the members of the company as a whole have a claim on profit. Up to 75% of the profit may be put towards self-finance by the general assembly of the members. The rest of the profit is distributed to members in proportion to their incomes, taxes having been paid, and 2% having been given to the Karl Backhaus Foundation. This distribution to an institute of the *Geistesleben* is remarkable, although of course its sphere of activity is limited to one company only, aimed as it is at the development of the members so that they can participate in the self-management of the company.

All this prevents the development of any direct substantial private ownership of the company's means of production. There is only private ownership of the counter value of the working capital paid in, which can, as already mentioned, only be realised by leaving the company or in a liquidation. In such a liquidation the reserves and other property of the company would not be shared out, but would pass to the Foundation, and so are "neutralised". How then should this kind of ownership of the means of production be characterised—who is the owner of the physical capital? Generally it can be said that in the Ahrensburg example, there is only a group ownership, which however is not materially tangible, and moreover cannot be judicially divided up, but is, so to speak, suspended over the whole enterprise, and can or must be financially "re-commercialised" only in the event of liquidation, should that be necessary. Therefore this type of ownership is effective only in respect of the *usufruct* of the means of production. The ownership "experience" that is formed in this way realises itself only to the extent that it becomes a living part of the consciousness of those using the means of production, that is, those working the means of production. This is the point at which the whole matter of subordination and ascendancy originates, in the working relationship.

Vilmar is right when he states that this form of associative partnership ownership of the plant means of production does not abolish subordinating relationships. Effective freedom and self-reliance can only be reached through conscious awareness. Fred Blum, in his book on Scott Bader, to be considered later on, brings out this point, that everything depends on the development of consciousness, on the ability to think and to express the results of thought. So long as this stage is not reached, it is not possible to achieve the *Aufhebung* of the wage system with its subordinating relationships. Anything outwardly contrived towards this end, such as profit sharing, rights to consultation and participation, shares in ownership, at best produces only an outward socialisation of the still-remaining wage relationship. Thus with Backhaus, the wage relationship remains, and is expressed in the accounting system, in that wages and salaries are considered as costs against the company revenue, at least as far as the partners are concerned, though not the "cut" of the directors of the OHG. It is through this accounting calculation that profit appears, out of which the directors are paid, the size of the cut being determinable by the assembly of the members. The then remaining profit is, as already mentioned, divided among the employees. What this arrangement amounts to is nothing more than a socialisation of the wages system; it conceals in itself a deep intensification of it. Complete *Aufhebung* of the wages system however requires a higher development of consciousness. It was in recognition of this that Karl Backhaus established the Foundation, as a training ground for the development of consciousness among the workers.

In the Ahrensburg example, three community spheres are active. These are the personal resident directors of the OHG, the sleeping partners, and those workers who are not partners. On the 12th of September 1974, 19 workers were given notice, because of the recessionary business situation. It was reported that among those thus laid off were to be found even partners. One would think that those who had become partners in the plant could not simply be made redundant. Since this was so, however, partnership provided only a loose kind of works community. These redundant workers, whose situation resulted from an agreement of the works council, without any consideration by the assembly of the members, called for dissolution of the partnership.

In this situation, two different issues were manifest; the economic issue of the profitability of the concern, and the social issue of the effectiveness of the works community. The economic problem hinged on this, that any new-style company is embedded in the capitalistic economic system, and must follow the laws of that system. It has to be recognised that the social reshaping of the inner structure of the company in the economic system cannot alter the fact that the new company is still part of that system and subject to it. It is in the very nature of that system that any unneeded labour force becomes redundant. It is precisely this fact that contradicts the essence of the true works community. The question arises, whether one can simply push out some members out of such a community of workers by means of redundancy. The conflict thereby arising would of course take another form, and would be differently resolved in a socially arranged economic system. In it, in particular, the occurrence of economic recessions and business downturns would not appear in the rankness customary today; and, to the extent that they did occur, they would not be dealt with by making some of the workforce redundant, nor by leaving the future of such workers to be provided for by state unemployment insurance. Such a way of doing things makes the responsibilities of the economic system into a burden on society as a whole. The problem of a social economic system will be examined further from a different aspect.

The situation of the Ahrensburg example and its social level should be judged from a fundamental consideration of the conditions of a properly-socialised economic enterprise.

Given the levels of individuality of most people today, it is possible to develop a socialised company to the extent permitted by the various social "fields of force". These forces could be comprised under the concept of "social consciousness", which must be cultivated in the following three ways:

1 In the teaching of the ideas that will make possible an intellectual grasp of the overall activities of the company. Every worker must be not only outwardly informed about these activities, but must in addition be able to understand this information and firmly grasp it into his consciousness.

2 The most powerful mental force arises in the development of a sense of community, which kindles an objective interest in the well-being of every fellow worker. This would find the way to fulfil the removal or release of a member from out of the organism of the enterprise in a social manner; then it would no longer be possible for for the member to be expelled out of the organism of the company by a formal redundancy, any more than one could make redundant the partner in a marriage.

3 The directly active force shaping society grows out of the will to take responsibility. This willingness to take responsibility, that develops in varying extents, must be present in all members of the enterprise, so that it becomes an organic structure consisting of various spheres of responsibility, thus expressing the self-management of the company at

various levels of responsibility. A socially structured enterprise can take different forms on the three levels of consciousness mentioned. In the development of the three social "fields of force", the Ahrensburg example is at a relatively early stage. Properly construed, Backhaus made the development of the workers' understanding the centre-piece of his reform, in establishing his Foundation for that purpose. However, the results of such a task depend upon *what* is taught, and on *how*, as well. The policy problems involved cannot be more fully dealt with here.*

The matter of the social constitution of the enterprise is closely bound up with the way in which ownership is structured, ownership, that is, of the means of production, of the substance of the company. This is really a question of jurisprudence, the content of which is the material ties between the workers and the company. These ties can lead to substantial ownership of the means of production, which is individualised as private ownership; or it can, on the basis of the general human possession relationship to the means of work, be structured as "functional" ownership by establishing group corporate possession. Backhaus has not yet attempted this. In this respect he has made use of the conventional capital investment procedure, with a limited stake. This abstract financial tie is not really a *social* tie. Socialisation of the ownership of capital can only be the *result* of the social awareness which pervades the enterprise; it cannot be the *cause*. The Ahrensburg example can be characterised as the beginning of a corporate community, but this is not the same thing as a community company —an example of which can be seen in the self-management by the workers of the Süssmuth glassworks.

3   The Süssmuth glass company—a community company

This glass manufacturing company was taken over by its workers in 1970. The impulse for this came when the 250 employees were threatened with redundancy. The initiative for this radical socialisation came from a section of the employees, stimulated by contact with students at Frankfurt University, which gave them the idea of managing the company themselves. The trade unions also encouraged this idea. In

---

*Professor Livegoed of the NPI, a Dutch educational institute, has analysed this.

particular, a local trade union secretary, Franz Fabian, played a key part in this, and has written about it, in his *Arbeiter übernehmen ihren Betrieb*, published by Rowholt Taschenbuchverlag in 1972.

To some extent the outward social structure of the company corresponds to that of the Ahrensburg example. Karl Backhaus assisted in the establishment of worker self-management there, and is still* a member of the council, which has oversight of the whole, giving advice and support. (The workers sent Backhaus a message of greetings on his seventieth birthday.)

But whereas the three organs of the Ahrensburg example—the assembly of members, the council and the board of the foundation —exercise only a general consultative role vis-à-vis the directors of the OHG, in Süssmuth the corresponding organs have advanced to the point of complete self-management of the direction and administration of the enterprise.

In order to assess what this advance from consultation to self-management signifies, one must start from the basic structure towards which every company, every plant tends. In any working group there can be seen the force generated by a basic tension between the managerial *Geist* and the working activities being carried out under its direction, that in the framework of the company are the subject-matter, as it were, of management. At one end of this tension, the role of the managerial *Geist* is to centralise; and at the other end, the working end, there is the decentralised work force, collaborating organisationally and technically, and tending towards a unity of its own within the company. In this situation it is necessary to bring these two ends into relationship—since, without their co-operation, no economic product can result. This relationship is not only organisational but *human*—and in it lies the basic issue of modern times. Bitter conflict can arise here—or a truly human community can develop. In the case of Backhaus, on the one side there are the four independent resident directors of the OHG and on the other the company of partners, who legally speaking are sleeping partners, albeit with wide-ranging consultative rights vis-à-vis the management of the company.

In Süssmuth, this tension between the management of the company and the work activity has become more deeply socialised; this is because the ensemble of the employees and the controlling body of the company are one and the same. The ten directors of the company

---

*At the time Wilken was writing.

confront the union of the employees, ten members being chosen to make up the company executive committee, who run the company and choose the chief executive. Thus the company executive committee and the executive of the union of members are one and the same. This blurs the tension between the two poles—but does not bring about its *Aufhebung*, in spite of the degree of worker self-management involved. The tension remains, with the technico-economic formation of the enterprise confronting the legal structure of the administration which has to regulate the human relationships involved. Between these two opposite poles, the productive economic body and the legal-administrative body, a social circuit is completed, the motive power of which was provided by the decision of the Süssmuth employees to continue running the company when it was on the point of collapse, and to form the union of members (the *Verein der Beschäftigten der Glashütte GmbH*). The union, therefore, votes for the executive of ten members, which is the same as the executive of the enterprise, and which holds the original capital of the company in trust for the members, thus "neutralising" it, so that it cannot be disposed of by any individual, but is available only to be used, in a manner answerable to the membership. Deep down, the Süssmuth employees must feel this as a possession relationship.

Compared with the Ahrensburg example, the Süssmuth system of ownership is more complex, more intricate. Complex because the responsibility for the use of the means of production is borne by the substantial unified communal body formed by the interweaving of the union of workers and the members of the company. Of course, the fact that the directors of the company and the executive of the union are one and the same brings about a high degree of institutional unity, but this needs in practice to be pervaded by the right human spirit. Ownership thus constituted, with only usufruct ownership, answerable to the group, has taken on a totally new character, which we will term *transubstantial* ownership. Only in the event of liquidation would this transubstantial ownership be changed back into a substantial money capitalistic ownership and be shared out among the members.

However, notwithstanding the communal ownership, the polarisation of the relationship between the business directors and the workers doing the actual work persists. The human ties between the two poles are expressed in the fact that those responsible for the management have not taken it on by their own decision, and do not constitute

what might be termed a separate "field of force", in opposition to
a workforce chosen by the administration of the company; on the
contrary, they themselves come out of the latter, and are accountable
to it. A neutral organ has also been constituted to ensure the proper
management of the company, the *Beirat* already mentioned. This has
more outside representation than the equivalent Ahrensburg body. It
has ten members:

    3 from the company
    3 union officials
    1 representative of a local development trust
    1 representative of the Hessischen Landesbank
    2 others, one of whom is Karl Backhaus*

The management and ownership of the enterprise is vested in the
group as a whole, not in any individual. The management has no
authority based on private ownership, but its authority rests solely
on its abilities, and it must answer to the group for its decisions.

In analysing the Ahrensburg example, the key characteristics of
a social enterprise were set out. In order to make such a company
work, three types of awareness were needed, and would have to be
developed—intellectual ability, a sense of responsibility and a group
spirit. All these three types have been developed to a considerable
degree by the leaders of Süssmuth. A survey revealed that it had
been recognised that the development of awareness was essential
if the experiment of worker self-management was to succeed. This
is in fact very much a matter of conscious awareness; no practical
success can ensue, without a special and scientific understanding of
the *Geist* forces at work.† This understanding is necessary to develop
the degree of altruism necessary to a proper social way of doing things,
without which no real common ownership can come about. The
simple proclamation that the means of production now belong to
everyone (or that, as in the socialist economies, they belong "to the
people"), does not produce any real social effect. Unless the ownership relation is really experienced by all, common ownership is just
a phrase. An unavoidable precondition of common ownership is that
it should be felt as a relationship by every individual member, moreover as something sustained and brought about by the individual's
own will. At Süssmuth it can be seen that each of the ten leaders

---

*At the time Wilken was writing.

†The implication here is that an anthroposophical approach is needed.

has a strongly developed awareness of the new type of ownership relationship there. Thus Hans See found out, as reported in his essay included in Fabian's book already referred to, that the members identified themselves with the company and with its problems to a very considerable extent: "Their own interests are already overridden by the group interest of the company. Their desire to learn is considerable. And the real possibility of having an insight into the decision making process in the company, and of playing a part in it, certainly stimulates the members towards self-management and self-determination."

One of the ten executive members explained that by no means all the members had yet reached the necessary level of understanding. This man, a glass-maker named Bilo, in pointing out this limitation, said: "I mean we want to be clear about one thing, that our colleagues' understanding is not so developed that they know for sure what is going on. So, each of them tends to put his or her own interests and advancement in the foreground and the group interests into second place, and an enormous effort is required to make it clear to them that the company belongs to them and that their advancement comes through us."

A radio play was produced, describing worker self-management at Süssmuth, using actual situations and documents. The most interesting part of this was the debate between the workers. This cannot be dealt with fully here, but something can be said about the attitude of mind of the workers, and their way of speaking. One cannot help getting the impression of an inborn urge for justice among the workers and a common determination to achieve this. This is put over in a straightforward, hearty and commonsense way. Their drive for self development and to resist authority has been awakened. However, it is striking that their thinking is hardly comprehensive, being based on sentiment, connected with their group will. This thinking can on occasion grasp a concrete situation step by step. It tends to judge matters in relation to the inborn yardstick of social justice already referred to. Their knowledge is insufficient and largely got from trade union education; but they want to learn, because they sense that the development of their intellectual powers would help them.

However, it has to be pointed out that this co-operative way of managing the company could run aground.* The basic tension between manager and the managed will reassert itself. As with any other form of creative leadership, the management of a company calls for inde-

---

* As has since happened.

pendence and free decision-making; it finds control, in this case by the workers, irksome. However, the workers, in turn, are inclined to blame the management for falling sales. This causes a disagreeable debate between them. This is, of course, closely connected with what the managing director meant when he said: "Unfortunately, we still live in a capitalist economic system. This is a matter of life and death for us."

To conclude, it can be said that if each member were to have reached the same level of understanding as the ten members of the executive committee, then the trade union type of thinking about wages could be overcome; this type of thinking raises the same question at every stage, namely, "What do I get out of it?". Once this thinking is overcome, then everyone can genuinely begin to experience common ownership. It is the awareness of joint responsibility which enables each member to identify himself with the group and with his functional ownership of the means of production. Only thus will he achieve an interest in the group objectives, which makes it possible to put his own interest in his personal share of the product into a secondary place. When this has happened the working member will no longer feel dependent upon the managers who are responsible for the conduct of affairs. However, in any common ownership company it is inevitable that the tension common to all forms of company will appear. At one pole will be the management and at the other pole will be the working members who feel themselves as sharing in the responsibility; which will always be a cause of debate.

The difficulties with which the new-style of company has to reckon with, are indicative of the fact that it has, so to speak, crossed the threshold into a future form of society; and it may be that the individual project may not survive.* That depends, on the one hand, on the maturity of those working in the company, and on the other hand, on the fact that the capitalist environment tends, in principle, to work against them. However, it is of course true that something new may have to be attempted more than once—not because the new thing is wrong, but because its execution must be improved until it has become completely practical. The highest peaks in the Himalayas were not scaled on the first attempt, but only after several failures, each of which led to an improvement in method.

It cannot be overlooked that reforming the individual company is

---

*As Süssmuth itself failed to survive, at least in its original form.

not the same thing as socially re-structuring the economy. They merely form one of the preconditions for the development of an organic social economic system; this is because they stimulate the power of altruistic responsibility with which a future economic structure can be realised.

4 *The Scott Bader Commonwealth*

The intention behind the reform of the Scott Bader Company was to activate the individual workers. Thus, they were supposed to be co-founders of the company constitution and of its management structure. From the side of the workers, this co-founding is seen as helping to ensure their wages and as bringing about the "inversion" of private shares and private control over profit. New-style companies aim to involve the worker consciously in the running of the company, thereby strengthening their position. Various ways of involving the worker are possible. Thus Karl Backhaus retained the private capitalist form, in which the workers were involved in a rather capitalist way. The position of the workers was given the legal form of partnership in the company, so institutionalising the union of the workers with the company. Thus the workers were, as partners, trained for the task of active joint participation. The Süssmuth company, on the other hand, took the form of a private company, which, however, arose out of the initiative of the workers. The company acts as trustees of the capital and provides the economic management. The union of the workers is meant to run the whole business.

With Scott Bader the two poles, the management of the company, and the group government, are each organised in formal company institutions. Thus, the Scott Bader *Company*, operating on business principles, works together with the Scott Bader *Commonwealth*, which governs the whole by means of a fully fleshed-out system, and which disposes of the company revenues. Reflecting something in the English national character, the financial aspect of the business is placed to the fore: thus, the means of production were given a money value, and taken into ownership by the Commonwealth in the form of money capital. This transferred the ownership out of private hands.*

---

*A sentence about the best German translation of "common ownership" has been left out here.—Editor, English edition.

Scott Bader Company was originally founded in 1923, and later started to manufacture plastic materials. At the time of writing it employs 350 people. In 1951 a new group institution was formed, to which Bader progressively transferred ownership of the enterprise. This group institution was the Scott Bader Commonwealth, formed as a holding company. According to English law, such a holding company can be established without itself having any fixed assets. Bader assigned all the shares of Scott Bader Company Limited to this holding company. Thus the Scott Bader Commonwealth owns, as holding company, the entire capital of the business, controlling its use and having disposal of the profits, within the framework of the articles of association. This holding company is of course different from the usual capitalistic holding company which seeks domination over capital assets, and is instead based on democratic control; in other words, it is those working in the business, not some group of capitalists, who, through the Commonwealth, control the capital. Thus, the capital does not belong to individual capitalist shareholders, but *indivisibly* to the Commonwealth as a whole; and the members of the Commonwealth are those working in the Company. The ownership thus transferred to the Commonwealth is purely functional; this is seen by the fact that in the case of a liquidation, this capital would, under the articles of association, pass to some charity, and so not be shared among the members.

The tendency is thus to form a compact social organism, namely the Commonwealth, which, as a legally independent group, enfolds the business company within itself and pervades it. The central position of the Commonwealth as the holder of the company's capital is further strengthened socially by the fact that only those employees can join who fulfil the conditions laid down for membership. The Commonwealth being the sole owner of the whole assets of the business, it is in no way the individual but the group of members as a whole, who possess the ownership rights. The original owners, by irrevocably transferring the share capital, have thus ended their ownership of the means of production, thereby laying the basis for developing a conscious awareness of responsibility among all members working with the means of production. In order to realise this responsibility in practice, a number of organs have been formed, so that the strictly business operations should mesh with the social aims of the set-up. The German language does not have the same variety of expressions to convey the particular economic associations of such words as "council", "board", "committee", "meeting", "chairman", "management", which can only with difficulty be put into precise German equivalents.

The organs of the group "government" and of the company management at Scott Bader consist of a number of intercommunicating and interdependent committees—a more complex arrangement than is the case with either Backhaus or Süssmuth. The working members' "pole" is represented in particular organs by their delegates. Through this interacting process, a powerful group force is generated. This organic group structure is—to the extent it has yet been fully realised—reflected in the group ownership.

So as to safeguard the intentions of the Scott Bader Constitution, a supervisory body of trustees was established, including Ernest Bader himself* and various outside personalities. Its task is to prevent any breach of the constitution, to make binding decisions upon conflicts in the group, and to initiate correcting action should the company enter into a loss-making situation.

However, the social effectiveness of the Commonwealth can only be realised to the extent that the Commonwealth lives up to its ideals.

5 The aims of the Scott Bader Commonwealth

Bader's aims in establishing the Commonwealth came from deep within him. A strong moral imperative pervaded his setting-up a community opposed to the existing economic system, based as it was on self-seeking and on the development of power centres based on capital. A Swiss citizen, Bader came to England at the end of the First World War, and personally experienced the wage system and the sense of being chained to a hierarchically-controlled private capitalist enterprise. He felt the urge to found a company in which social working relationships would be shaped by practical application of the spirit of Christianity, based on principles of justice and brotherly love. This means, economically speaking, that workers must be freed from the wage relationship, and must be brought to feel responsibility not only for the company in which they produce or sell goods, but also for the effects of the use of these goods. On the basis of his Christian outlook, Bader is opposed not only to the competitive battle which pervades the

---

* Bader stayed on as a trustee until the age of ninety.—Editor, English edition.

economic system, but also to war. Hence Bader and his colleagues will not accept orders which directly or indirectly serve military purposes. As the antithesis of the competitive principle which dominates the capitalistic economy, Bader is trying to realise the principle of mutual self help advocated by Kropotkin and by Rudolf Steiner, to whose basic principle of social development he attributes the whole "wisdom" of the Commonwealth.

His unshakable determination to change the economic system from a competitive one into one based on community and on the individual renunciation of personal ownership rights calls to mind the work of Robert Owen. As with Owen, so Bader has enjoyed exceptional business success. Bader has recognised that any social arrangement such as profit-sharing, workers' shares, or politically-compelled voting rights, would bear little fruit, either socially or economically. To create a viable new form of ownership would require great efforts from those involved. Courage and devotion, and indeed self-sacrifice, are needed. Bader sees the renunciation of ownership made by himself and his wife as being based on Christian belief about ownership. It should be noted, however, that he has made the ownership of the capital over, not into any form of substantial group ownership, but into a *transubstantial* form, so that the assets are held in trust by the Commonwealth for the use of the enterprise and for the realisation of its ideals, and these assets cannot be materially realised.

Bader considers that to be realistic about economics means that one should invest in men rather than in money. This means that the possession relationship of men to the means of production must be properly structured. Above all, all members, including the managers and the founders, must have equal status in relation to the use of the means of production, and to the business revenues.* The realisation of this equality must be developed by cultivating the awareness of responsibility for the company as a whole in every member. In place of the kingdom of the owners of capital, Bader sees the Common-wealth as founded with the long-term aim of turning the workers into responsible owners. He says "they must be freed from the wage system, just as I freed myself from it"†. The founder directors felt it wrong—and against the original Christian concept of property—to take a personal profit in the form of dividends. The directors, including

---

*This does not mean equality of incomes.

†Most workers at Scott Bader are still, however, paid wages.

the founders, receive salaries approved by the Community Council. A ratio of 1:7 obtains between the highest salary and the lowest wage. The same standard of measurement is applied to every job in terms of content and responsibility. The annual bonus which is paid out of profits to all employees, is equally divided between the members, in conformity with the basic concept of common ownership of the means of production.

The aims of the Commonwealth cannot but involve all three levels of the social organism, the economic, the social and that of the *Geist*. Obviously, the Commonwealth has to function economically, so as to serve economic and technical progress and to ensure its profitability. On the social plane, it has the social obligation of ensuring that the needs and requirements of the members are met, and in particular of overcoming the consequences of the wages system as far as is possible under the present system of worker relations.* The incomes of everyone in the company are counterposed against the turnover of the company and graduated according to an established procedure for calculating differentials in a just way. Some of the balance then remaining goes towards taxation and towards investment via self-financing. After these deductions, is left profit proper, of which half goes to be divided equally among all employees as bonus, without consideration of their salary level. The other half is applied to charitable and cultural purposes, as decided by the general meeting of the Commonwealth. This endowment of general and cultural interests is in tune with Bader's concept of the social responsibility of the company beyond the confines of the plant. He believes that business has a real contribution to make towards the well-being of society, locally, nationally and internationally.

Whenever anything is done to serve the cause of progress, opposing forces come into play. At the end of 1975 there was a confrontation between the Scott Bader *Company* and the *Commonwealth*. The exceptional success of the business led the directors of the company to expand in a rather capitalistic fashion. With the help of a loan from the bank, some foreign shares were purchased, yielding profit in the form of dividends. This of course meant that the basic principle of the Commonwealth was being abandoned in favour of purely capitalistic management objectives. For months Bader fought a battle to preserve

---

*Wilken states here that there is no wages account at Scott Bader, but this is by no means apparent from the latest accounts of the company.—Editor.

his life's work, against the board of directors. The peculiar strength of Bader's own religious convictions, together with the help of various progressive friends, came into play. Thus he sought to win the conviction of the directors that the constitution of the Commonwealth was correctly drawn up.*

Bader's pioneering work played no small part in bringing to the British Parliament a law concerning common ownership. This law, the Industrial Common Ownership Act of 1976, defines common ownership enterprises. In the debate on this Act, special mention was made of the part played by Scott Bader.†

One can see that the Scott Bader Commonwealth, due to the special conviction with which it has been developed, carries the development further than Backhaus, and that it also goes further than the self-management of Süssmuth. Neither of these companies have sufficiently developed the aspect of the *Geist*.††

6 *Some other examples*

The example of the von Porst experiment shows that the simple re-organisation of capital and ownership and the outward form of participation are not enough to bring about a genuinely social constitution of the enterprise. This experiment started from a social concern, but lacked deeper preparation. Because of the undeveloped creative powers of the members, it could not but fail.

Without this source of strength, the outwardly organised socialisation of a company has no staying power. This is why the economic difficulties of Backhaus and Süssmuth could not be properly overcome purely from the social side. A purely intellectual training in directly practical matters is not by itself enough. Conventional intellectual concepts lack the socially creative power of the forces of the *Geist*.

People are certainly seeking those creative powers. This can be seen from the multiplication of efforts to reform company structure.

---

*However, on 12 September 1978, a much larger subsidiary was taken over.

†A short section here has been left out, since it has not been fully borne out by the subsequent course of events at Scott Bader.

††Which Wilken considers can be based either in religious convictions, or equally well in the anthroposophical "science of the spirit".

Education for responsibility is being undertaken, and ways of neutralising capital are being sought. Under German law, one way is to form a foundation (*Stiftung*), or can be undertaken by sharing the capital out. Some examples of this type of reform are given below.

Particularly conclusive, because it shows human limitations so clearly, is the self-management example of the Viennese Herz Armature Company, which employed 360 workers. This company practises a participation scheme by which all employees can play a part in all decisions. In 1974 they were offered the opportunity of becoming co-owners of the enterprise. For this a form was chosen similar to that of Backhaus, in that members had a share in the company's capital. It was provided that the head of the company would retain 50% of the share capital, 25% would be subscribed by outsiders, and 25% allotted to the employees. With this basically capitalistic procedure, no fundamental change was envisaged. However, the intention of the head of the company, Lehrner, was altruistic and social, and led to the creation of a group organisation in which each member, irrespective of his place in the management structure, had, it was claimed, consultation and voting rights free from any supervisory "retaliation". The groups established company objectives, resolved problems in the place of work, and controlled the management structure. At the same time, Lehrner developed training in group dynamics for staff, supervisors and workers. This was to enable members to learn how to make decisions participatively, and to develop mature and practical thinking. However, this example has not yet been carried to the extent of neutralising the company's capital, or of socialising the company.

The Staedtler pencil concern has done this, gradually transferring the company capital to a foundation. This is one of the pillars supporting the business. The other is the consultative works management system, embodied in a committee in which problems are discussed. Other tasks are given to ancillary committees. Neutralisation of the capital, and the funding of cultural activities are two of the many matters which have been discussed.

Other companies are seeking what is called the democratisation of industry. There is an association in Germany for this. The firm of Südstahl has developed along these lines, and this will be dealt with further on.

To avoid misunderstandings, it must be noted that neutralisation and functionalisation of prospective entrepreneurial capital is only sensible for the large business. The small productive units created by individual initiatives, being limited in their scope, naturally point towards the private ownership of their capital and means of production.

CHAPTER 7

Consequences

1 The private economic impetus and the class struggle to reform the capitalistic market economy

Both the market economy and the extreme communist system, both their ways of structuring the ownership relationship and control of capital and its product, are equally at variance with the true social nature of the economic system. Both private and state ownership of the means of production are of course a reality and a historical fact, but they are neither economically nor socially *true*. Today, however, great efforts are made in the market economy to socialise, as economic productive capital, the private ownership of capital, in its special role as the basis of creative development. A social tussle occurs between the traditional kind of capital owner and those who by their work make productive capital actually productive. It is the employees of various kinds who want to be joint owners of capital and of the profits it produces, and who wish to control the application of capital, particularly its investment. This results not only from wages policy issues, but in fact goes much deeper, arising as it does out of an elemental and growing self-awareness in the depths of the human psyche, and out of a will to achieve social justice and universal brotherhood. This can only happen if the countervailing powers of class domination are overcome, particularly those exercised by the enterpreneur, who still seeks to satisfy his own economic interests without regard to the interests of others, namely of workers and consumers.

The contemporary social impetus towards class struggle arises from the organised working class, which has developed its power through the unions and the political parties of the left. The parties and the unions work together in the political and in the industrial spheres, particularly in the areas controlled by big business. These two forces give a continual impetus towards the social restructuring of the capitalistic market economy, directed particularly towards productive capital and its utilisation by private owners.

To take the example of Germany, a research group at Karlsruhe University calculated the national wealth of the Bundesrepublik in 1970 at 2.9 billion (million million) marks. A large part of this is factitious, inasmuch as it includes land. This inclusion of land values in the total tends to conceal the extent of true productive property, but the latter can generally be considered as much the same in size as the productive assets, totalling in that year 789 thousand million marks. Of this total, 57% was owned privately by German nationals, 17% by foreigners, and 27% was in state ownership.

It is from this situation that the struggle against the private ownership of productive capital ensues. The abstract totals become real enough when it is a matter of actually transferring capital in order to improve incomes, or to build up political and economic power. In the foreground stands the worker wanting to share in the proceeds of the productive capital. From the standpoint of the personal interest of individual workers, as they are today, there is nothing for them *personally* in the ownership of capital. They are basically interested in consumption. They turn against private capitalism only because it is seen as the force which is always keeping wages down, and this is experienced as an attack on their material standards. The social revolt of the organised workers is directed against the system of the capitalistic market economy and against its aims, against the whole notion of freedom for private owners, against freedom of contract in all markets, and against both emulation and competition in all areas of economic life.

Whereas the ideal of private ownership fulfils itself in the amassing of individual fortunes, bringing status by means of the ownership of material things, which money-wise are valued as capital, the propertyless raise a protest against all these possessions. The aim is to take away this property from the bourgeoisie and make the revolutionary worker its owner, particularly as regards the productive capital of the economy. This has been done in various ways, for example by private projects, mostly taking advantage of laws about capital formation. To this end, a stream of schemes have been developed by entrepreneurs, academics and politicians, in order, as it is said, to "broaden the distribution of property among the workers".

a) Bourgeois experiments, private and public

To an increasing extent, a growing number of individual companies
have gone over to tying their staff to the company, not only by the
wage contract, but also through a financial stake in the company. This
has been done in various ways—by staff shares, sharing the proceeds in
conjunction with a capital stake in the enterprise, and even deductions
from wages for investment. Thus the Bayer chemical company has
established a "workers' fund"; a bonus based on a percentage of salary
is made available by the firm, which can be used to acquire a stake in
the fund. It is administered jointly by the workers themselves, effectively as an investment company, taking up holdings in fixed interest
stock and shares, outside of Bayer itself. Of course, the bonus comes
out of free capital formation. Other German companies have various
schemes for worker shares, but invariably these do not touch upon the
basic constitution of the company.

At a political level, in the Christian Democrat Party various schemes
have been discussed, including one by which a legal union would be
formed in which both workers and shareholders would be members,
which would put them on a more equal footing. The capital formation
laws of 1961, 1965, 1971 and 1974 enabled the formation of workers'
capital, to which a subsidy was added.

A study by the Commerzbank of these various schemes shows that
the number of workers involved in them rose from 380,000 in 1964 to
12.7 million in 1972, who received about 3.8 thousand million marks
extra thereby.

b) Trade union sponsored schemes

Quite different are the aims of the trade unions, but they are certainly
significant. With or without worker shares, they seek participation in
the *control* of capital, in order to modify if not overthrow the existing
form of company. Capital transfers and profit sharing are seen as ways
to bring the socialisation of the company management nearer. Some
unions believe that differences in income and in wealth will be ironed
out by workers' shares, and that these constitute a means of achieving
socialisation. But the tough IG Metall* has come out against this idea,

---

*One of the most important German unions.

fearing that capital reform would weaken the class struggle. It is worth noting that the leadership of the trade unions have developed a scheme for capital which offers the individual worker no private interest, but in which the power over the capital share would be concentrated into funds controlled by the unions, thus making possible an economic concentration of power. The radical unions see the share in capital as useful only to the extent that it is linked with increases in the workers' share of the social product, and with redistribution of profit to the workers. The ways in which they seek control over the private capital-istic economic system are as follows:

1 participation at plant level or above
2 taxing private investments
3 nationalisation of key industries and dominant firms

By these means, entrepreneurial control over the means of production would be limited, industrial power centres broken up and their further growth hindered. Redistribution of productive wealth forms the prin-cipal aim of the present socialist governments, and of the majority of the unions. Political and union concepts of redistribution both derive from thought habits which reflect the emotions engendered by the helpless experience of the burden of the large economic power concen-trations, and of their anti-social heartlessness. The German trade union leader, H. O. Vetter, has suggested a re-shaping of the whole economy by means of democratic control of capital investment, supervised by worker representatives in supra-plant participation. These represen-tatives would have parity with the owners of capital. Final flourishes to the scheme would be the establishment of "economic and social councils"—a point to which we will return in another context.

The socialist government put out a scheme in 1974 for the redistrib-ution of productive capital by means of a permanent tax on profit. This would, in an abstract way, revolutionise the economy; every year this tax would realise some 5 thousand million marks from big business. This would then be distributed among 20 odd state finance companies, who would use the money to form companies. The question arises whether these state finance companies would have greater understand-ing than private companies, although they would certainly not be acting out of private interest. The leader of IG Metall strongly criticised this scheme, briefly, on the grounds that the unions did not want it, the recipients would not use it, the economy would be harmed and the state disadvantaged. The worker could not use his productive capital *individually*, so that the scheme would have no interest for him. The unions wanted simply the democratisation of the economic and social power that lies in productive capital. Moreover, the value of the asset certificates involved in the scheme, on coming to maturity, could fall if large numbers were sold at once, which would mean that the workers lost money and the economy would be disturbed.

It is fundamentally wrong to suppose that the social problem posed by an economy founded on capital and labour can be resolved by the pouring out of vast quantities of material wealth in all directions. On the contrary, this way of distributing capital conflicts with Steiner's basic law of society. Moreover, the unions are against any attempt to propagate the idea of workers saving to buy shares, since this goes against the whole idea of the working class movement; creating employee shares would turn the workers into collaborators with the capitalistic economic system. This can indeed happen in one way; the workers, in helping to finance the capitalistic economic system, can thereby help to restore a falling share price. The unions are opposed to all of this, and instead seek to break the employer's monopoly and to participate in the management of the major industries, meanwhile fighting the owners of capital in order to increase the workers' share in the growth of productivity.

The socialist planned *antithesis* to the diffusion of capital ownership among private individuals is the *concentration* of capital ownership through its collectivisation in impersonal political bodies, such as the capital control fund already described, which would be formed under government compulsion. This would enforce the socialisation of productive capital through the permanent tax on private big business. In this way, the whole of economic life could be in the end turned into a collective system, that would at the same time constitute an endless source of income unrelated to service. Such a system would be an evasion of the social restructuring of the economy that the times call for. Such a form of "socialisation" would leave the underlying basis of the capitalistic economic system untouched, and could not bring about a genuinely social way of life.

2 The positive contribution of the present market economy

Social change grows partly from situations and partly from proposals; for example, in the formation of partnerships or worker participation systems. Such proposals are particularly strongly advanced by those who want to reshape the company in a more developed unity, as a social body, as, for example, in the case of Professor Biedenkopf. The development of a company into a social group would, according to the conventional thinking, be brought about by organising the company in such a way as to give the members specific rights concerning the management of the company, its capital investment and its distribution of profit. Thus it is that Professor Flume has developed the concept of a "company in itself", which concept is not social, but purely a matter of tax technicalities. This whole way of looking at it makes the company into a separate object, which would itself own the means of production, in a manner quite detached from the owners of capital and the managers of the enterprise. Such concepts do indeed point in the direction of the future; but from a social point of view they are limited, since the power uniting and holding the whole together is not purely juridical and organisational. As has already been suggested, this is, from the standpoint of a genuine working community, not enough in itself. But the *Geist* of conventional socialist thinking gives birth only to abstract and mechanical social relationships. All the same, there is the opportunity that these legalistically formed social entities can offer, of being turned into something genuinely human and social.

This approach towards a supra-personal form of enterprise, as we have seen, arises out of the contemporary level of understanding. No social breakthrough results. This level of understanding can only construct new social forms in a formal and purely intellectual way, and then proceed to "organise" them. Indeed, it does not *want* to do anything else. This leads only to the development of forms which circumvent the new organic social awareness that the contemporary situation is crying for. In three different aspects, we can see how such an approach shirks the true shaping of the enterprise, being still imbued with the *Geist* of the conventional market economy; these three aspects are as follows:

1 The legalistic formation of autonomous company constitutions such as those already mentioned which would make the company into a "thing-in-itself". Such companies could only be turned into living social organisms if the totality of the company becomes a *community*. This can only happen if the members develop the social power which would make it possible to work together in a working community. This future goal is staring those people in the face, who would limit reform to conventional reorganisation of the market economy type of company.

Even Professor Flume's "company in itself" can however through the infusion of common ownership acquire a social content which can bring to life the fiction of an organisationally-conceived "legal person".

2 The powers of decision-making which are established for the management of a company do not automatically become community-inspired if they are transferred only in a purely formal manner to some organised grouping of the shareholders and employees.* These formal management functions stay stuck in organisational abstractions, if they are fought over through the exercise of participation rights, whether at a plant or supra-plant level, or if they are organised in political or "parliamentary" spirit, so that decisions are taken by majorities. From this, the lowest level of social co-operation, it is however possible to move towards an organically conceived form of leadership. This can come about through a consolidation of the social group, which causes it to go beyond the stage of contending "parties" in participation, and to develop a genuine collective community responsibility which draws all the members together. Responsibility for the enterprise is then shared, the community debate developed, and the work done to the best of the common abilities.

3 Equally negative, from a social point of view, is the tendency to make a formal legal transfer of the ownership of the means of production into a supra-personal ownership, whether this is vested in the state, in public corporations or in the unions. However, although this form of ownership does not automatically lead to the means of production being used rationally or in accordance with socially-needed working relationships, as a kind of neutralisation of capital it does point the way towards the future economic arrangement of company management, which cannot, of course, be brought about by the interests of private capitalistic profit making, but only by pursuing the aims of co-operation and just income distribution. This cannot but lead towards common ownership of the whole productive capital of the company.†ct This in turn enables the development of a deeply felt kind of awareness of ownership, which will not be imbued with purely pecuniary or material content. On the contrary, it will be much more a matter of wanting to accept responsibility for both productivity and for its social realisation.

---

*As for example with the concept of the German "Aufsichtsrat".

†Wilken is at pains to point out that by "common ownership" he does not mean, as could perhaps be supposed, any form of nationalisation.

With large plants and companies employing thousands of workers, neither self-determination nor self-management can arise spontaneously from some collective initiative. So long as such large companies exist, legalistic constitution of some "parliamentary" form of participation will be unavoidable if new social forms are to begin to develop, but further progress will depend on the "federalisation" of individual departments.

But all legalistically conceived forms of company or of ownership will remain ineffective so long as the members do not invest all their own personal powers to make the thing come to life. Merely working out a legalistic form, and organising it may grant various participation rights, but it can never, of itself alone, achieve any real kind of self-determination. The kind of self-management which will arise from such self-determination needs essentially *social* forms, which may afterwards receive legal recognition. Social organisations which are merely outwardly set up will tend to be used for private ends, and do not form any new social life. Fundamentally speaking, no organic working community, no common ownership, can be created simply by working out an intellectual plan or a mechanistic organisation; but the individualistic peoples of the West have it in them, in the right circumstances, to bring such schemes to life, and to take over responsibility for them. Even within the private capitalistic economic system, it is possible for self-awareness and responsibility to play a part in the field of company objectives and functions, as advanced management theorists such as the best-selling American writer, Peter Drucker, has shown.

Drucker analyses the developments within the enterprise which have been brought about—on the basis of western thinking—by enlisting individual powers so as to attain maximum efficiency on the basis of sound collaboration among all employees. This has been attained by leading the workers towards accepting a share in responsibility for the company as a whole. Each worker is given a personal responsibility in his particular unit of the company, to the degree that his decision-making abilities and will to co-operate permit. This creates a system of graded responsibilities for both individuals and groups. Meanwhile, training, education and the imparting of knowledge are systematically pursued. Those who are thus strengthened in their thinking and in their personalities become participators in a system of shared responsibility for the company as a whole. In order to bring this about, a company-wide system of organisation and management is of course needed. This sort of development will shape the management of the future. It combines all kinds of creative abilities, directed towards continuous improvement of the company's performance. In order to bring about this progressive increase in economic efficiency, there is a continual search for modifications, for innovations and for the detection and solving of problems. Internally, management has the task of leading the many-sided co-operation of the work force and for uniting them in a common sense of responsibility for the enterprise. Zeiss and IBM provide examples of this approach, as also do those Japanese companies that have adopted similar ideas on the basis of Zen Buddhism.

The thing that is striking in this management approach is the development of responsibility. An English teacher once said that when he first gives a pupil a responsibility for something, that begins the story of the pupil's altruism. And that is true, because the ability to take responsibility inevitably involves the strengthening of character, essential if one is to rise beyond mere self-gratification. In this respect, the type of company described by Drucker, with its collaborative responsibility, holds a promise for the future. However, it is limited by the fact that from the standpoint of the economy as a whole, the cultivation of responsibility is kept *within* the confines of the particular company. Hence it retains a taint of group-egoism. Yet the company is in fact only one self-directing cell in an economic system in which every company is constrained to take part in the competitive struggle, in which framework the feeling of responsibility is inevitably focused solely on the company, to the exclusion of all else. (There is, of course, the tendency to form monopolies to work against this competitive struggle.)

In the highly sophisticated form of company, described by Drucker as a great achievement, are incorporated one-sided and extreme forms of Western utilitarianism.* There is also the desire to maximise efficiency on the basis of retaining the competitive struggle of the market economy, as a basis for emulation in performance. In this context, the level of responsibility achieved is, in the final analysis, a veneer of *Geist* over the conventional egoistic and materialistic system; as is indeed revealed by Drucker when he defends entrepreneurial profit on the basis that it is necessary for the self-financing of the company. We have already seen what is to be considered in relation to self-financing and the arbitrary formation of profit. Against this, we have recognised that a genuinely socially effective economic system requires the attainment of a new level of consciousness, and of new human abilities that

---

*The philosophy originally developed in England by Jeremy Bentham.

go along with this new consciousness.

Social forms or structures can be looked at in two ways. They can be observed and described from the outside, in which case the outward form is analysed from whatever is seen to be happening, from the outward behaviour of those in it. This gives a picture of the company at its face value—its legal form, its internal organisation—which can be grasped by considering its structure, the position of its managers and, not the least, its form of ownership. This brings into relief the more formal elements and organisational forms in which the group awareness and abilities are in varying degrees manifested. On the other hand, the level of group awareness, and the drives and decisions arising from it, react in turn upon the outward plant social structure and upon the company. To become clear about this, one must counterpose the formative social forces underlying the outward form. Five levels of these forces can be distinguished, which determine the level of development of the working community they form. The forces which determine the inner group relationships are rooted deep in the psyche; they are the shaping forces of the human will. Attitudes towards the group may be purely self-seeking or they may be motivated by altruistic feelings of responsibility, which latter can vary considerably in scope, from narrow feelings of personal responsibility to broad considerations of the needs of humanity. These attitudes are associated with perceptions about the group which are based in emotion or sentiment, which in turn range from the instinctive to the altruistic. Each of the desires and feelings involved is reflected in a mode of thought, as a level of social awareness. These complexes of feelings of responsibility and perceptions form themselves into the structures we call attitudes.*

This will be easier to see if the five levels referred to are set out, commencing with the most negative and proceeding to higher stages, bearing in mind that in specific cases elements at different levels may be found to be combined. These levels are as follows:

1 An outward collaboration which conceals an inner anti-social feeling, associated with tense relationships.

2 Unconcerned human relationships, with superficially reasonable behaviour; responsibility limited to the immediate place of work; generally an atmosphere of social apathy.

3 *Social attitude, grade I:* (the lowest). Friendly and willing mutual collaboration, capable of material responsibility within the plant

---

*Wilken here seems close to the symbolic interactionist school of sociology.

as a whole, characterised by cordiality and consideration.

4 *Social attitude, Grade II*: (more advanced). Comprises interest in other people, a perception of community, the ability to take some community responsibility, and to look at the community objectively.

5 *Social attitude, Grade III*: (the highest). Human brotherhood. The qualities of level 4 are broadened to include humanity as a whole, and responsibility becomes supra-personal. Only at this stage is the term "brotherhood" applicable; and it is brotherhood which is the best basis for economic life.

Level 1 is, socially speaking, a sham. The basic attitude is antipathetic and belligerent, though this is of course under restraint. However, this does form the commencement of the development of social relationships. In such an arena, devoid of any truly social forces, self-centredness reigns, and antagonisms predominate. The redeeming factor is that there is also the desire to overcome these negative features, and the formation of a socially correct economic system can provide the incentive for the development of the community. The same is true for level 2, which can be seen as the best possible under private capitalistic systems.

The remaining three levels of social behaviour are progressively constructive, and constitute the forces which can shape an organic social company structure, as noted in the new-style companies examined already, in which the highest stage that could be reached was that of working together in a manner based on friendship. The higher concept of brotherhood in economic life embodies that level of humanity to which the example of Christ points the way, and provides the means of attaining. We can say that each of the four proceeding levels of social awareness can be understood as degrees of progress towards brotherhood. It is in this spirit that the struggle for social development in our time should be approached.

Most people living today are inclined to come to terms with existing circumstances, and tend to avoid making social efforts. They are accustomed to let the urge to do something about the social situation die down. The development of an organic economic system is only possible given a level of awareness which goes beyond the thinking that has created the market economy mechanism, or the centrally-planned economy, which are both equally based on self-seeking, whether in the individual or the group.

The development of a genuinely social awareness and the attainment of the abilities associated with it, are hindered by the passivity and apathy often found in modern man, which are encouraged by the superficial equation of pleasure seeking with the quality of life, so current today. Inwardly, there is the insufficient development of independent thought in modern man, the lack of practice in self-expression and the failure to experience the moral aspects of life, coupled with the tendency to enjoy events as alienated spectators. These human weaknesses resist the creation of a genuine working community and of an economic system based on brotherhood. This is discussed in Fred Blum's book about the Scott Bader Commonwealth, "Work and Community".* These same weaknesses will also be recognised from our discussion of the other new-style companies, and were analysed in an interesting study by pupils of the Hamburg Rudolf Steiner school concerning the firm of Friedrich Behrens there, which is an Ahrensburg-type company. This study went in depth into the social aspects of the Ahrensburg company constitution, particularly into working relationships and the structure of wages.†

Finally, there is something which must be said concerning capital policy. It is erroneous to consider that physical ownership can somehow be a substitute for genuine social relations, as for example when it is hoped to pacify the opposition to the private ownership of the material productive assets of the economic system simply by a capitalistic widening of this ownership. This cannot lead to social harmony as, as can be shown, the concentration of capital and power cannot be eliminated by the diffusion of capital ownership in small transfers. To follow this procedure to its logical conclusion would bring about a distribution of the entire social capital to everyone in society; but, under contemporary conditions, it must be asked, how could such a procedure alter the capital power of, for example, the large oil companies? When the share capital of companies has taken on a life of its own, such a distribution would not touch upon the actual companies at all. The existence of millions of small shareholders would do nothing to dismount the monopolistic power centres. While the shareholders would be interested in influencing the management of the companies to increase the amount of dividends, once this was achieved they would lose interest in the question of power. Influence on the policy

---

*Published in London in 1968.

†This study was published in German in the Karl Backhaus Stiftung's "Informationsdienst" for April 1973.

holding; such a majority holding could arise through the commercial activities of individual capitalists, or through the capital policy of a group, either politically or economically motivated.

Many working class objections against the diffusion of capital ownership reflect the natural attitude of the worker towards life in general. The worker sees the allocation to him of capital ownership as being a sham. And that is exactly what it is; it neither frees him from the wage system nor develops any social outlook in his psyche. If anything it would make him as materially-minded as the private capitalist, which could reconcile him to the existing economic system. There is indeed the hope in certain quarters that this enlargement of material ownership could help to avoid the social restructuring of the economy which is now necessary, and keep the present system going unchanged.

Our analysis shows that a genuinely social system cannot simply be "organised". It needs moral qualities and social abilities as well as intellect. Only determined shouldering of economic responsibility can bring about the development of the forces capable of realising the new transubstantial ownership of the means of production and of their money equivalent. Transubstantial ownership can be thus defined:

Seen from the point of view—

of *Geist*:   the ownership is no longer felt to be attached to the *substance*, but goes beyond this.

of the law: ownership or possession with the power of *control*.

of the economy: operational ownership.

Each of these three aspects of ownership possesses a social character, which is however created by individual forces. To develop such a social arrangement, synthesising individual and social aspects in all the organs of the social organism—that is the mission of Central Europe.*

3 West and East: thesis and antithesis in ownership

These critical characteristics can be understood in a deeper sense if looked at from the point of view of the world political situation. The

---

*Anglo-Saxon readers may find this hard to take, but should bear in mind the special situation of partitioned Germany. The substantial point is that this synthesis will probably first take place in an individual country in which the circumstances are particularly suitable. It could equally well be, say, Ireland.—Editor.

economic complex which has developed in the world lies behind this. Under the influence of the Marxist doctrine against the private owner-ship of the means of production, mankind is divided into two parts. In one, private ownership is pronounced to be the essential prerequis-ite of economic activity, and considered as a human right; and because of this principle, of decentralised ownership of the means of produc-tion, the western part of the world comes to be under the domination of England and America. However, the other part completely denies the right of private ownership of the means of production. This part is mostly in the east, including Slavs, Mongols and some of the peoples of South-East Asia. Here the ownership of the means of production is centralised, which was the direction in which Marx pointed. For this to take place, the ownership of the means of production had to be taken over, the previous egoistic owners having been dispossessed and eliminated. What authority then should direct the economy, and in whom should ownership now be vested? This had to be in a social form; hence the state took on this role, as the sole social power. As the im-personal representative of society, it was to take over the substantial ownership of the means of production, and control the whole of economic life. If the state and the people it controlled were equated, then it could be said that the productive capital, the means of produc-tion, belonged to the people. So this would then be the social solution of the issue, what to do after the private ownership of the means of production had been abolished. What this meant in effect was that the means of production came under the arbitrary rule of the controllers of the state and of the state power they wielded. But since the people in the state are not valued as individuals, only as an anonym-ous "people", a mere physical species, free decision-making about the utilisation of the means of production was withdrawn. In its place was state control of the economy, which acts not from any real under-standing, but in the political interests of the government. It is at this point that the free will of independent Western man takes up a stand.

Where no social forces are developed, there will be conflict—that is a social law. In fulfilment of this law, a characteristic antithesis has developed between the economy of the West and that of the East. The basic principle of the Western economic system is the struggle for money, between various parties seeking it. The economy of the West has therefore become a battlefield—and this although it really needs social harmony and the maximum possible development of social powers. The Eastern economic system seeks to end this battle by putting all economic processes under the sole control of the state. This involves the suppression of the competitive urges of the egoistic economic system, in the place of which the state's aim is to use the economy in the struggle against the capitalistic economic system and against the individualist entrepreneurial class. This policy of engaging in this struggle has become the dominant tendency of the collectivist states of the East.

However, neither can the market economy of the West manage without the collaboration of the state, which is on the contrary indispensable. Enough examples of this fact have already been given, but in Chapter 8 the fundamental causes of it will be analysed.

The two economic systems, the individualist and the collectivist, the private capitalist and the socialist do not in fact form a real antithesis at all at the level of the *Geist*. On the contrary, they are two children of the one mother, who is *matter*, or the *mind of matter*.* The materialist *Geist* has pervaded the intellectuality of the whole of the management structures of both systems, both systems having a mechanistic content which works its way into people's minds. Both have been created by intellectualised reasoning. Both form organisations in which people function simply as components of a machine. This makes for a mechanistic kind of collaboration which has to be enforced, either by the hierarchical organs of the state power or else by the technical or marketing entrepreneurial *Geist*. It is the latter system in which the relationships are such as to tend to bring about the undermining of the entrepreneur's authority and to favour the development of a factual debate and of a democratic understanding between the people working in the given economic unit. So long as this tendency remains limited to organisational change, it will embody no more than the minimum social development, and that in an abstract and unenthusiastic way, so that only impersonal relationships develop. But it can be said that through the outward organisation, by men with some degree of equality in rights, of social behavioural and working modes, the basis of an objective social fellowship can nevertheless be laid, which can prepare for the development of genuine community-building.

In looking at the world political situation, we have seen that the demarcation line between West and East divides humanity into two halves, which are in opposition to each other. In one half it is the indivi-

---

*In the German, "der Materiesinn".—Editor, English edition.

dual which forms the centre-point, whereas in the other it is society as a whole, in the form, usually, of the state, which has this role. Between the two are interposed the peoples of Central Europe. Their position is analogous to that of the Pacific Ocean on the other side of the world, which, as its name suggests, is there to separate the two halves so that they may coexist in peace. It can be seen straightaway that both principles, the individualist and the collectivist, have their proper place in the scheme of things, and must indeed be developed. This development is needed to bring them to the point where their true essence is brought out*, so that they are not only mutually reconciled but become able, moreover, to build the human society of the future. It is to achievement of this goal, that the peoples of central Europe are both suited and indeed called. Therein lies the mission of central Europe—to build a real European Community, in the place of the present one, which is orientated only to economic matters and to power politics.

4 *Shaping disinterested capital ownership—a question of awareness*

If, as we have seen, capital is in essence a matter of *Geist*, even in its manifestation as physical means of production, it therefore appears both economically and socially incorrect to vest capital in either private or state ownership. Of course, there is always, in both large and small industry, a functional possession relationship in the minds of those who work with capital, particularly with its material form in the means of production. This possession relationship can, in large industry, be brought out into the open and socialised—as seen in the example of the Scott Bader Commonwealth. Now, the vesting of capital in a *substantial* form of controlling ownership is in fact quite superfluous, and does nothing for economic productivity; on the contrary, the *natural* form of capital ownership is in fact *transubstantial* in its social content, and involves only the *use* of it. In this way it is, as it were, put into *suspense*, so that legally speaking it is only the rights or duties associated with its use which need to be defined. Thus, what usufruct and responsibility ownership really mean, is that there are these rights and duties incumbent upon those who use the thing owned. The communal development of such a form of ownership is

---

*Exactly what "Aufhebung" means in the dialectic of both Marx and Hegel.—Ed

only possible when it is carried out by a group of people whose members have reached the level of personal awareness that is necessary if they are to undertake responsibility. Responsibility as to use means a disinterested attitude like that of an engineer who is simply concerned to get the best out of a machine entrusted to him. This is just how it should be with the economic use of the means of production, if their utilisation is not subjugated to private interests, but is guided purely by considerations of objective productive purposes. Thus purely egoistic interest is broadened into a concern for humanity as a whole, and the instinct for self-betterment broadens into the desire that the whole should go well. In this spirit individual wills can and must work socially together, so that a level of group awareness forms, developing the social forces which can carry through the group ownership of capital.

Only through such a group sense of ownership can it become possible to supersede the authoritarian management of the entrepreneurs with their private ownership of the substance of the means of production, and put to work a decision-making process orientated towards the optimum economic running of the company. To realise this totally unbiased and objective decision-making, the essential thing is the necessary sophisticated expertise. This can come from a single talented individual or from a collegial group with the right abilities. In the final analysis, it can be the will of the whole group of all members of the enterprise which exercises the overall control, each individual taking a share in the responsibility which may vary in extent. It is from such individually graded spheres of responsibility that the social body of the working community can proceed. The means of production then come under the common responsible ownership of those using them, in which the powers of the working community find their expression. These social powers of responsibility are powers of the *Geist*, which develop productivity, so providing the basis for the formation of free capital; so that the more these social forces unfold, the more the company flourishes. This can be seen in the examples of both Robert Owen and the Scott Bader Commonwealth. Such a social group, with its capability to shape the company, needs to be constituted in a closely-knit company body in order to work with the management, so that what may be termed a socialisation of responsibility ensues. In this social structure the legal framework of a much improved type of democracy comes into being.

From all this it is quite clear that the new style of socially-correct forms of ownership, and the form of management orientated towards objective economic purposes which the said new style makes possible, is in no way a matter of outward organisation, but entirely dependent upon the development of the necessary awareness. Moreover this is not so much a collective group consciousness, but an individual awareness which in growing transcends the instinctive self-preservation of an individual who is working with others in the works community. The issue which must be resolved first of all is that of putting the common ownership of the means of production into effect. Now it has to be pointed out that in the three companies examined in Chapter 6, that some of the members have not yet been able to go further than their private concerns, that is, in the wages they are paid. Members of this kind, who are formally part of the common ownership body, are only passive in it, and contribute nothing to the awareness of ownership. They may be able to take responsibility in their own place of work, but not to give responsible consideration to the whole of the jointly-run means of production. So as to raise such insufficiently developed members to a higher level of awareness, Karl Backhaus, as we have seen, established his Foundation with the purpose of developing the understanding of the partners. This development of intellectual and moral qualities is vitally significant for the social future, particularly for the shaping of economic life. One can only work responsibly and participate in respect of things which one understands. It is only in matters of what is *just* that the ability to understand and weigh things could be considered as being inborn in all men. As regards events in the company, and the processes of production, it is only those who have developed the necessary understanding and abilities who can play a part in handling technical, economic and capital matters. People with such understanding will possess a natural authority over those who have not yet developed a similar understanding, and this authority is quite natural and humanly needed.

In a fully-realised working community, in which the direction and the execution of work are in social harmony, and where the capital is owned in common, the basic motive for work ceases to be the wage, and focuses consciously on the totality of the enterprise. As for those workers who are still egoistic in outlook, the commonisation of the means of production has only a formally satisfying effect, inasmuch as they will at least be aware of the absence of any exploiting capitalists or entrepreneurs, but "wage-centredness" will persist. For the rest, money income, since it is assured by the strength of the community, recedes towards a secondary position. This social power of insuring income replaces the purely abstract quantities of "wage" and "profit", and is rooted in members' awareness of the capability which the common will possesses.

The wage system is the socially critical heart of the unresolved social issue of the contemporary economy. This issue can be posed in two ways. Subjectively, it can be asked, in what spirit the work should be arranged, so that people can do it happily and with enthusiasm? Objectively, it can be put, how must the company constitution be framed, so that the worker gives of his best? Conventionally, work has been seen as an abstract quantity, so that some quantitatively measured service is to be motivated by an equally abstract sum of money. Now this is not the motivation, for example, of the true administrator, nor for that matter of the soldier. It is, moreover, inapplicable in the case of the intellectual worker, and with all the self-employed. In all these cases, the motive is the inborn drive towards self-actualisation, and this free drive is not really linked to the matter of compensation, but to the satisfaction derived from the work. On the contrary, it fulfils itself through that kind of enthusiasm which forgets to measure performance against reward. The social future will be built by this truly human attitude. On the other hand, "wage-centredness" inhibits work performance. Only if the objective circumstances make enthusiasm possible can the wage system, and the inhibiting factor of reward-orientation, pass away. For this to happen, a just system of income distribution is necessary. The other condition is that it must be impossible to form power centres based on private ownership of the means of production or of money capital, and impossible to put all economic activity under the yoke of profit making.

When this is achieved it will be possible to fulfil three major aims in response to the challenges of our times, namely:

1 The separation of the urge to work from pecuniary considerations.

2 Achieving a just distribution of the company's added value.

3 The *Aufhebung* of the private appropriation of free capital.

In the constitutions of the companies described there is the possibility of realising these three social aims. Each has established its own social body, which could develop its social efficiency provided that it does away with substantial ownership of capital and with the authoritative system associated with it. Since private ownership is an egoistical category, it is essential to develop a disinterested form of capital ownership. This is achievable by establishing transubstantial ownership, which provides only for functional rights and duties. Proper ownership relations cannot be established by "organising" them; not, that is, if they are to express the "socialness" needed. On the contrary, such relations have to be based in human maturity, capable of disinterested social responsibility.

Of course, the selfish instincts cannot be ignored, let alone abolished. Rather they must be limited by restraining their activity to the sphere of consumption, and preventing their intrusion into the field of the ownership of the means of production or of money capital. However, a kind of private ownership of the means of production is brought about, prior to their actual deployment, through an economic act of purchase, since they are, of course, produced as goods. However, they lose their character as goods, the instant that they are linked with human labour. With that, their private ownership has to collapse, since they take on a new phase of their existence, in which private ownership makes no sense. So what are they, then, at that point of time? The minute that human work is applied to use them, they become a matter of justice, especially as to the application of justice to work, and in the final analysis as a subject of company jurisprudence, and so lose their character as privately owned objects. It could be said that their form of ownership becomes a social one, though not in the false sense that this is claimed, when the substantial capital is nationalised in a Marxist way—which is the highest form of authoritarianism. It is not through nationalisation, but through the transformation into functional ownership that the *Aufhebung* of capital power is achieved. The formation of a non-material responsible ownership makes it possible to achieve the merging of the plant and the company into a group social unit. This can be likened to the rose, which shows us its foliage, the leaves of which exist side by side, and outwardly are linked only by the stem. But the bloom is a unity, quite beyond the mere sum of the separate petals. And its scent bears witness that there is something more in life than just the material things.

5   Forming the enterprise into a legal organism

It is essentially a social structure which is capable of making transubstantial ownership of the means of production workable as a way of running a company; but this social structure can be given a proper legal form. This has the effect of giving support to the whole company,

in every aspect, and to the transubstantial or functional form of ownership in particular. This legal form lays the basis for objective responsibility for the best use of the means of production, and thereby also
for the economic prosperity of the company and for the well-being of
the members.

The most striking development of the common ownership company
as a legal organism that I have come across is to be seen in the example
of the Scott Bader Commonwealth. The Commonwealth can be
envisaged as the mirror-image of the economic enterprise. There is thus
a polarity between the responsible chief executive and the workers, who
have their separate legal body. The ownership of the money value* of
the means of production is vested in the socially formed legal body of
the members. This legal body thus has an independent existence in the
framework of the company. This needs to be brought into harmony
with the business operation of the company. In order to ensure this
a board of trustees has been established, to act as the supreme controlling body. In particular they have to see that the constitution is not
breached, from an ownership point of view, and that harmony between
the two aspects is preserved.

The moral substance of this legally constituted form of transubstantial ownership pervades the inner workings of the company as
represented in its business objectives. This includes all the company
activities, management and technical and labour. Of course the
company management has to relate the goods produced by the technology of the plant to the values given them on the markets in which they
sell. This involves the acceptance of responsibility beyond the confines
of the company, towards the users. At the same time, the distribution
and pricing of the goods produced raises the issues of income formation
and of the application of profit. In this, responsibility has to be taken
for effects on the social economy as a whole. The interconnections of
this responsibility extend worldwide. It is for this reason that a socially
responsible management is needed, one that derives its motivation from
some deep source, perhaps ethical, perhaps religious, perhaps based on
knowledge and experience of the human psyche.†

No one company can bring about an economic system single-handed.
In the production of goods under the division of labour, it is necessary

---

*Strictly speaking, of the nominal capital of Scott Bader Company, which is, of
course, much less than the actual money value of the productive unit.—Editor.
†Again, it is reasonably clear that Wilken has anthrosophy in mind.

for the company to reach out into the rest of the social organism. The works needs the enterprise—and its marketing function. The marketing work of the company is not concerned with the production of goods and services but with the commercial sphere, turning the said goods and services into articles of commerce, into commodities. Commerce performs a circulatory function, for which money is necessary; thus the transfer from production to consumption is made possible. The movement of values involved is complicated and hard to see into. The goods created in production receive a value in circulation, which is then used up in consumption, so that the production value and the circulatory value cease to exist. This process of "disvaluation"* in consumption has not been fundamentally studied by economists, who tend to brush it aside as a sort of datum relative to further production. There is a single dynamic circuit, from production, through circulation, to consumption. The enterprise (as distinct from the plant) stands in the middle of this.

There are, then, three levels or spheres of activity, which are to be fundamentally differentiated; men encounter them in every enterprise, as the task of management, in the work-process, and in the associated social relations. All three spheres interpenetrate. The social relationships have formative effects upon the technical and managerial spheres. Social problems arise here; these are intrinsic in the human condition; and their resolution is always a matter involving justice. So far as the sphere of production is concerned, there are the laws and duties of men working together, and also the legal form of ownership of the means of production. In the circulatory sphere, where values are put upon the created goods, there is the issue of the just distribution of incomes among those engaged in the undertaking, as well as the matter of deciding to whom the profit should go. Juridical issues of this kind cannot be settled solely by reference to the interests of the individual company, not even solely in relation to the economy as a whole, since the just distribution of free capital can only be arrived at by considering the role played by all three organs of the social organism.

Economic events spread beyond the individual company, so far as to form a world wide socio-economic organism, through the activities of the commercial sphere, in which the distribution of the product is organised by means of money. In this world-wide economic organ-

---

*This whole matter is particularly well-treated by the English Steinerist economist Christopher Budd, in his "Prelude in Economics", West Hoathly, 1979.

ism, the individual companies form but cells, which again contain organic socially formed structures. The material basis of these cells is the technical production of goods and services; this technical organism becomes as it were, the tool of the trading organism of the enterprise, which fulfils the marketing function, through which the goods produced are valued, become commodities and are exchanged against money in the economic circulation process. A third company organism, which tends to develop a life of its own, is the legal form of the company. This deals with the social relationships necessary for the functioning of the company; this internal social dimension is necessary in order that the company should have external social relationships in the world of commerce, and is a microcosm of the whole social sphere of producing and trading. This legal organism has the capability to resolve social issues affecting the company, which is why there is this tendency for it to develop an independent life; we have seen an example of this in the Scott Bader Commonwealth, in which there is an attempt to form a company-wide judicial organism. In this context, the judicial function relates—as it did originally—to the concept of justice as meaning right social behaviour. We described this separate judicial organism in the Commonwealth as the mirror of the whole company; one can feel how well the English word "Commonwealth" expresses the social nature of this company.

Both the production and the trading functions each want to make a social form, the human content of which would, on the one hand, relate to the management, and on the other hand, to the work being carried out. However, the nature of management is such as to comprise not only the physical issues of the production and trading processes, but also the development of social matters. In the works both the intellectual management and the practical control are carried out by the production manager, whereas the business and commercial functions lie with the entrepreneur. Of course, there is equally physical work to be done by the trading function. Both in the works and in the business function, even the most major decisions depend upon human work, in conjunction with the means of production, for their realisation. The kind of managerial abilities required for the technical and commercial development of the company lie in a form of informed responsibility, underlain by technical expertise, and orientated towards production and that systematisation of the goods produced which is reflected in the organisation's accounting system. The whole management process in fact resides in the taking of responsibility for the commercial and economic use of capital.

The abilities and attitude required to carry out work consist of more than just practical aptitudes, whether innate or learnt. Work has a special value; it brings out something of the best in people. Basically, this happens if the work is done on the assumption that it is *given*, since this involves the *Geist* in the person doing the work. The real principle of work is self-surrender. This is spoilt by the exploitation of the work for materialist profit.

The social, that is the legal, organism of the company needs neither management nor labour to run it. The social activity realised in it is nothing but social, being dedicated to the common good and to reciprocity; and this is quite inevitable, since in this organism the original human essence of work cannot but be realised. And it is only in this way that Steiner's law of social development can be realised—namely that the work which is the most fruitful is the work done reciprocally for others. It is by the reciprocal arrangement of work that the brotherhood of man can actually be realised—and this, while an ideal, is nevertheless an essential prerequisite if humanity is to reach its goal.

The fundamental nature of the social and legal sphere is such that it cannot accommodate the kind of leadership so unsociably practised in companies and factories. In its place must come a pattern motivated by a considered love, which is indeed the basis of all living social relationships.*

6 *The impact of individualisation on economic processes.*
   How effective community spirit fosters the growth of a company.

The world historical event affecting human development was the impact of Christ. This brought self-awareness, the experience of freedom and individualisation to the human psyche. The basis of this development was laid by various cultures—the intellectual contribution being from the Greeks, and the juridical from the Romans, while the Teutons developed the powers of the will, and the Jews laid the basis for the universalisation of religion. The powerful trend of individualisation had effects which were divisive and against authority. We encounter the first

---

*Some Marxists, notably the English Christopher Caudwell, have taken the same position; see Caudwell's "Studies in a Dying Culture", London, 1948.—Editor.

manifestations of modern individuality in the absolute princes and in the free entrepreneurs, who all exercised great personal power.

This is in sharp contrast to the original formation of society in which people lived out their whole lives in consanguineous groups. Thus each person experienced in his own life the same life experience that other members of the community, as his brothers and sisters, would experience. Such a community would be ruled by the force of religion, or by a theocracy. These religious and consanguineous ties were weakened however by the progressive development of the individual, which placed the *self* at the apex of the personality, as Steiner put it. As part of this same process, people acquired the capacity for individual thought. By the power of his intellectual thought a man comprehended the world he observed around him in terms of a thought creation produced by himself personally. It was precisely these powers which shaped modern social life, the structure of which has been realised by such thought, the effect of which has been progressively to weaken the original social structure. The contradiction between the abstract concept of "society" and the reality of community has been analysed by Professor Tonnies in his book "Gemeinschaft und Gesellschaft". Society converts the community into a consciously desired structure of human groups and associations. Society, in this sense, developed side by side with the process of individualisation, and involved ever larger numbers. This is shown by the way that the force of individualisation has developed in the working class to the point that they want to take over control. Some examples of this are Süssmuth in Germany, the Lip Watch factory in France, and the occupation of the Daily Mirror by the employees.

So long as there were only a few people capable of taking on the total responsibility for a company, there had to be free entrepreneurs with their intellectual powers and their risk-taking, if the modern economy was to be built. But, in the meantime, the capacity to take on responsibility, and the desire to do so, have both been awakened and have grown, as is shown outwardly particularly in the continuous pressure for *participation*. The aim of participation lies normally in the field of legal forms of the working relationship. If participation is to play a part in the decision-making process of business management, then a certain business expertise and leadership qualities are going to be needed. Now, in order to characterise and justify participation and joint working in the affairs of the company, reference is made to the concept of democracy, which has thus been borrowed from the political sphere, for use in economic life. For example, the Ahrensburg constitution speaks of "democratic principles in the completion of industrial power"—thus bringing into play the political concepts of power which apply in the arena of the class struggle. What the demand for democracy means in economic life is that the individual personalities of the employees play a forceful part in the direction of the concern.

The individual personalities that wake to the full force of their conscious powers rebel against all authority. In this respect, one must distinguish between those management postures which have become outmoded and those which are justified. Now, the rebellion against authority extends to include the rejection of the management pyramid involved in the working relationship; however, the hierarchical system of practical activities brought about by the division of labour is rooted in the fact that different men have developed their capabilities to different extents. Those who are more developed will always have authority as a result; while someone might reject this authority, it nevertheless persists. It is not sensible to struggle against authority if that authority is based on *Geist* rather than on "politics". However, this struggle is justified if authority in social matters is misused for personal ends. All management hinges upon intellectually-conceived decision making, which is a matter of individual creativity. However, it can also be exercised jointly through some collegial understanding, to reach which is the social purpose of debate between equals. In matters of the *Geist*, authority rests on its own inner strength. But the technique required socially to organise the sphere of the state, the *Rechtsleben*, is essentially different from that needed to run economic life. In the state and in the *Rechtsleben* the principle of authority has to apply, and with it a hierarchical administrative pyramid; whereas in economic life the principle of individual co-operative self-determination and self-management comes to the fore. The only hierarchy in economic life depends on intellectual qualities, and on the technical execution of various specific tasks in the context of a division of labour which is both horizontal and vertical.

By drinking in the full content of economic life and its structures, one can discover that democratising management does not touch upon the real nature of the company form of economic life, which does not work through votes or majority decisions. On the contrary, the intellectual content of decision-making about the factual management of the economy and its companies is on the far side of parliamentary head-counting. Only if social issues—as distinct from economic ones—have to be resolved, will the economic system need to adopt procedures proper to the *Rechtsleben*. In that case, voting may need to be adopted if there is no unanimity.

The combined effect of individualised will-power and a theoretical approach can bring about the conscious formulation and organisation of completely articulated social structures. But the forms and company structures arrived at in this way embody only the ultimate lifeless fantasy of the old ways, and have none of the communal spirit of losing oneself in dedication to the common prosperity. All there is, is the intellectually conceived and money-minded economic system of the mammoth concerns. Moreover, those people involved in these concerns who make no higher claim, are satisfied enough if they are treated politely and receive ample wages. It requires a deep sense or awareness of what is objectively to the common good,* if any interest is to be developed, even to a limited extent, in the prosperity of any big business organised in this way; and such an interest has to be developed for the whole trading economy in the future. In order to understand this it must be recognised that the future economy and with it the future company must be put together by considerable thought, of a type which however, must be distinguished from the mechanistic kind hitherto employed—it is organic thinking which is needed.

The *mechanistic* way of constructing companies derives from egoistically motivated intellectual drives, which are of a rather cold-bloodedly objective kind, and directed only towards self-preservation. This type of company is characterised by three traits which are essentially a-social and indicate its internal social decay:

1 the leadership function is warped by the self-centred power drive involved in the domination of capital.
2 the work force similarly becomes obsessed with self-centred wage struggles.
3 social relationships lose their content and their potency.

The resulting social vacuum can be papered over by the intellectual type of organisation, but this mechanistic system works well only when sales are good. In such companies, if there is respect for people and economic security, it is possible that for the time being the workers may, on the whole, be satisfied—a gratified egoism creates a sort of contentment. All this changes, however, as soon as there are economic

---

* See Rudolf Steiner's "World Economy", London 1949.

difficulties. This has been seen to happen even in new-style companies.

Now, even in the framework of these mechanistically conceived companies, although they are somewhat the result of individualist drives being flung together and underpinned by rather rigid legal concepts, it is nonetheless possible to grant ownership rights in a form of a legal claim upon the distribution of profit and along with other material benefits. This cannot bring about any real common ownership, nor any organic group relationship in connection with the use of the means of production. This type of legalistic usufruct relationship can be brought about by dividing up the ownership of the assets in a formal way; for example each working member may be given a percentage of the productive capital, so that in the case of a membership of one thousand, each member will have a one-thousandth share. This procedure becomes even more remote if this is done by the actual issue of legal company shares. Dispositions of this kind have no community-building potential, but can form elements which can be used if a real community system is later brought into being.

The organic way of constituting a company, which belongs to the future, requires an approach which goes beyond mere self-orientated intellectuality, and cause for, as it were, a living way of thinking, based on an objective sense of community and on the will to recognise social necessities. This organic character reveals itself by its inner integrity, its concern for justice and above all, by its determination to realise the material existence of the whole community. A company that is formed in this spirit of awareness of community arrives at the definitive constitution of its social organism by having a separate legal body. Just as in the primitive social relationships, which were based on a subjective feeling of community, so equally in a consciously formed legal body the decision-making process will work through individual members' innate feeling for justice. Fundamentally, the social activity of this legal body will be carried out by social administrative techniques, and only day to day matters will be handled by commercial management. The point of the legal provisions of the company will remain the arrangement of the working relationships, the structure of the company, and the stipulations needed concerning the ownership of capital. Further tasks will be the structuring of the management function, the fair distribution of incomes to members, participation in the application of profit, and particularly of free capital, and, last but not least, arranging the ownership of both money and physical capital. Beyond the confines of the company there are the social issues of the wider economic system and of the control of the earth's resources, and of the land.

It is the actual experience of the correct social relationships, and of the way in which they build towards a whole, that will develop in the human psyche the ability both to feel and act in a community spirit. This social awareness provides perspectives which stretch as far as the human mind can conceive, and have the power to bring mankind into brotherhood. A human group soul would then come into being formed by the social awareness of each individual, and will hold people together in the same way that ethnic or national groups were held together by the ties of consanguinity.

A community thus created by the efforts of individuals can become the medium of an effective common ownership of the means of production, and of a form of ownership, moreover, which is limited to their responsible use. Thus, substantial ownership of capital is superseded and replaced by a living social form. This can then take legal shape in the body of the company so that the common ownership is made effective in the three aspects mentioned, management, labour and administration. This supra-personal and independent form of company ownership was foreseen by the entrepreneur and social philosopher Walter Rathenau, who said: "A large business in reality no longer belongs to the shareholders—it belongs to itself. Its aim is not to increase private possessions but common ones." Rathenau's insight indeed suggests the common ownership of capital and the human dimension of economic life.

CHAPTER 8

Transforming Economics

Anyone who is convinced from the analysis so far that new living forms must be created to bring about a genuinely social economy, will see that realising the necessary social forms will have a radical effect on the traditional contemporary economic system.

This effect will go well beyond the concepts to be found in the financial sections of the leading daily papers, which discuss, every day, such issues as business trends, tariff policies, the labour market, and the full employment policies which so encumber the state, the situation of the various industries, their sales and profit prospects, the size of the various large concerns, all from the viewpoint of the market economy.

The point of all this concern with economic activities is to be found in the Stock Exchange quotations. The stock market's valuation of the economy merely points out the lack of an economic over-view such as could only be worked out jointly by suitable economic associations. The stock market view is only a substitute for such a realistic appraisal of economic trends, and the interplay of the buyers and sellers of stock market valuations can be considered as no more than a caricature of the collective awareness which an economic association could develop.*

Anyone caught up in such economic events and unable to see over them, will be, as it were, hypnotised by the powers of suggestion exercised by existing market relationships—which seem destined to go on for ever. Those wanting to keep things as they are, those with a conservative attitude of mind, will be confronted with the need to change this attitude, as tendencies towards social renewal of the economy, as we have described them, come into play in the fairly near future.

---

*Such associations seem not unlike those advocated by Hegel.—Editor, English edn.

1   A general view of the three constituent parts of the social organism

In order to understand just what the economy really is, one must see it in its context as one of the three parts of the social organism, each of which is independent, each of which supports and penetrates the other parts. The threefold division of the social organism is a creative concept, which is indeed the key idea, the law rather, according to which each nation—and eventually humanity as a whole—should be differentiated into three parts, as the condition of social harmony. These three mutually supporting and interpenetrating parts are:

1   The independent and self-managing *Geistesleben*, in which mankind has to make all the gains attributable to the *Geist* its own, in order that the *Geistesleben* should reach its destination, which is for it to be a totally free entity, answerable to itself alone.

2   The *Rechtsleben* as realised by the appropriate political constitution, which has the purpose of arranging and securing social life according to the idea of justice.

3   The self-shaping economic system* which has the purpose of making all the various material goods and of distributing them in society, and which is so arranged that it is based on the power of a universal and self-transcending social mode, the essence of which is summed up in Steiner's general social law.

These three summary definitions stand for three fully differentiated spheres of life, each of which has its own specific tasks, and its own means of carrying them out. In the *Geistesleben*, the point will be to find ways of managing its own affairs without being any longer under the influence of either the economy or the state, so that science, art and religion can be developed and fostered in complete freedom. As for the *Rechtsleben*, it will find its true essence in the attainment of a purely justice-orientated state, in which the aim is not to strive for political power, nor to prepare for war, but to provide for the recognition of human equality, and of every individual's right to his or her own life. The *economic system* has the most social content, since it embodies the principle social law, according to which it is necessary for economic units to be formed capable of organising mutually reciprocal work, mutual assistance and mutual provision. Thus it is in the economic sphere that social life reaches its peak of development; in the *Geistesleben* it is the individual which predominates, and in the *Rechts-*

---

*In German, "Wirtschaftsleben".

leben the social structure needed is more impersonal and legally conceived.

Let us therefore go more deeply into the economic system. Its proper organisation can only be achieved, on the one hand by practical economic expertise, and on the other by socially just human relations. The expertise derives, of course, from the *Geistesleben*, and the justice from the *Rechtsleben*; however, this double relationship can only be properly achieved when the economy is correctly—and organically—related within the social organism to the other two parts thereof. That is to say, the economy cannot prosper without a deep and intimate relationship with the cultural sector, with the *Geistesleben*; and on the other hand, its constitution needs the legal backing of state laws whose content is based on proper understanding of the economy.

The *Geistesleben* has its effects in the economy, not only as the source of economic expertise in the strict or narrow sense, but also in a wider sense, as the sole source and motive force behind economic development. We have already noted two areas in which the *Geist* thus induces progress. In consumption it provides creative stimulus through the invention of a continual flow of new products for the satisfaction of man's material needs. In production and circulation it is active in the development of labour-saving technology. Moreover, in circulation particularly it has the role of developing the monetary system by means of techniques for regulating the money supply. Economic necessity is continually presenting new tasks to be solved by the human *Geist*'s ability to contrive means of saving labour.

One particular such task arises from the necessity of achieving justice and meeting social requirements in the structuring of economic relationships. Humanity is always under the compulsion of the law of the division of labour, to work, that is to work for each other, so that the economy must always have reciprocity—which entails the application of the principle of justice. Reciprocity involves responsibility for ensuring both the just distribution of income and the just allocation of work. Finally, as mentioned already, the social use of the means of production raises the universally important issue of the right way to arrange ownership relations. The subjective feeling of possession is made into a reality by the establishment of usufruct rights and by legal provisions for the distribution of the product produced by the social use of the means of production. Recently legal claims have been made increasingly on behalf of the workers, for participation in the management of the means of production.

Two quite different things have therefore to be brought into harmony
—the attainment of economic discernment, and of a just social order,
both as regards human labour and as regards the distribution of the
product—if the problem of restructuring the economy is to be solved.

*2 Economic associations as organs of economic planning**

These two things, economic understanding and economic fraternity,
stand in a unique relationship to each other. It is the special characteristic of the development of a general conscious appraisal of the
economy, that this cannot be properly, that is to say concretely,
achieved by any one person. On the contrary, it can only be attained
by the collaboration of all those who are active in the practical economic sphere, and who are informed about it. For this collaboration
to come about, suitable forums must constitute themselves, and for
this organised bodies will be needed.† These are indispensable if
adequate economic data and analysis are to be assembled, and they
form a natural focus of social debate as well. If economics is fertilised
by the science of *Geist*, it will form these associations as the centre-
piece of the economy. It is they who will direct the self-structuring
of the economic sphere of society. They are the organs of deliberation in the service of the realisation of all the economic processes
needed for the satisfaction of demand. The reason for this is that the
judgement of individuals is never sufficient to develop the kind of all-
round awareness necessary for effective planning. This applies whether
the individuals are entrepreneurs, managers, academics or businessmen. Nor can the awareness needed be developed by the type of
planning carried on by state planning bodies. Rather, the information and appraisals needed for economic activity can only be developed by the meeting together of a sufficient number of individual
practical experiences and pieces of information. These can then
produce a common assessment, out of which the right economic
action will result. If economic activites are to be correctly organised
and if a correct appraisal is to be realised, then a fully-articulated
social dimension is needed, which will in fact form itself as a

---

*German "Vernunft".

†These seem a little like the English "little Neddies".—Editor.

complete universe of these associations.

Thus the associations form the heart of the social planning of the economy. However, other social forms will also play a part in economic life, and these forms will be equally based on the necessity for collaboration in achieving economic ends. Examples of these forms are provided by the three companies studied in Chapter 6. In these companies, comprehensive processes of combining individual talents are taking place. Such processes are, of course, universal, though in other places they are not carried out in the same way. They are typical of economic activity. But they do not constitute associations in the sense meant. Associations have a scope which comprehends the whole economy. The necessity for this lies in the dialectical* relationship of the contradiction* between the interests of producers and those of consumers, which requires to be harmonised, as regards the exchanges between them. In the infinitely complex intermeshing of individual needs, there arises the practical requirement for reciprocal harmonisation, and for a common understanding, as to what is economic, and as to what should happen. Associations are there solely to reconcile different interests and groupings. This is done by bringing together one-sided experiences, assimilating them, and thereby developing an overall plan, as the basis for practical decision-making. Members of the associations will come from production, consumption and commerce; and as they will be working together to meet demand, they will—and must—understand each other.

This then is the social principle which epitomises the planning procedure for the economy. As such it is the antithesis of the self-orientated market economy. The dialectical* nature of the associative method lies in the fact that it makes possible the common development of a workable economic plan and that it brings together people who can jointly reconcile economic aims and tasks. The understanding obtained in this debate could not be achieved by any individual in isolation, were he scientist or practical man. The associative economic view takes as its basis the dialectical* principle that the opposing poles of the contradiction* are synthesised, so that each pole contributes its particular experience to the common understanding. This dialectic is a product of the *Geist*. Each pole, of course, incorporates a limited understanding, and has one-sided interests; but in the associative debate, there develops the dialectical force of a social synthesis of

---

*See glossary for the explanation of these crucial terms.—Editor.

the different individual points of view into a solid and effective overall plan.

It is reciprocal understanding which forms the guiding social principle for the development of this economic plan and of practical means for implementing it. The process of reaching this understanding must be continuous, since the economy is in constant movement, with new impetuses continually taking place in both production and consumption, and old ones continually dying away. Hence, disequilibrium is always being generated, to the point that just when a balance is being reached, it will then turn into imbalance. Similarly, each achievement of social harmonisation represents the point of departure for new social processes. This dynamic aspect of the economy can only be handled effectively by means of the associations, who alone are in the position of being able to develop an overall plan capable of dealing with the changing patterns of economic events. The whole social issue is, as a matter of socially shaping the economy, dependent upon consciousness, and that at a level unattainable by the individual, and reachable only by joint effort.

The irresistible nature of the necessity for the economy to form these associations was put this way by Rudolf Steiner, that one would not actually have to set them up, one would just watch them form themselves. This will happen by freely developed moves towards a common understanding. Something of this sort has already tended to happen in recent times, with suggestions emanating, for example from the United States in 1974, for the formation of a common transatlantic energy pool. But for this to be an association in our sense, it would need to have been formed on the initiative of people in the economy, and quite divorced from politics.

The work of such associations constitutes the *Geist*-form of the social law of reciprocal rights and duties, and it is for this reason that they can become the formative force in economic planning. For example, they will be able to ensure balance between production and consumption, between the sum of commodity values and the amount of money, and between the trend of capital investment and the need for work. By following the principle law of social development, and the law of the division of labour, the economic system will be able continuously to adjust all aspects into a harmonious balance. The economy is therefore being drawn towards the formation of associations.

*3 The universal nature of economic life, and the question of how to
meet the needs of the other two parts of the social organism*

Each sphere of the social organism is universal, and affects every single
human being. Everyone is born into a social group, and always lives in
one. In particular, everyone is a citizen of a particular state. Cultural
life educates and informs every person, and indeed gives him the
content of his existence. Thirdly, throughout his life, he continually
develops economic needs. All this is regardless of his generation group,
his job or vocation, his religious beliefs or his ideology. Thus every
person exists in three different spheres:

1 economic or material
2 national or political
3 cultural or to do with the *Geist*.

The economic system provides the universal material support for man's
physical needs. Now with reference to the other parts of the social
organism, the economic system has to provide not only its own requirements for economic goods, but must also meet the material needs of
the *Geistesleben* and of the *Rechtsleben* and the state. That is, it must
supply large groups of people who are not themselves economically
active, but who contribute—if at all—only indirectly to the production
of economic goods and values. The state, of course, helps the economic
system by providing its members and institutions with the necessary
legal services; similarly, the *Geistesleben* contributes to economic
activity through its development of technology and productivity.

Strictly from an economic point of view, one can consider the economy as a self-contained entity, isolated from the other two members of
the social organism. On this assumption, that the people working in the
economy produce for themselves. Were this the only task of the economy, it would not need to produce more than its own requirements.
This position is, of course, unreal. The needs of those working in the
other two members have to be met, as to both individuals and institutions, in both the *Geistesleben* and the state sector. For example,
buildings, equipment and apparatus—all of which has to come from the
economy. These are necessities, and they raise the issue, how can the
demand of the other two members be met, in other words, how the
distribution is to be arranged? The circulation process of the economy
works on the assumption that the managers and workers therein supply
themselves; but if economic values are to be transferred, free of charge,
to the two spheres which themselves produce no economic values, how

can this be done? The other two spheres, producing no services, have no economic counter-values to offer in exchange, so that the economy as well as satisfying its own demand, must also satisfy this considerable external demand. There has to be a non-reciprocal transfer of values.

Given this social necessity, the production of the economic sector has to be divided into own demand and "transfer" demand, that is, demand from the other two sectors. This touches upon one of the major social problems of our time, which up till now could either not be resolved at all, or else only in a distorted fashion.

This issue extends to include the fact that within the economy, as well as outside it, there is a further kind of non-reciprocal demand. This demand is made up by the needs of the so-called *pure consumers*. The extent of this factor is somewhat hard to fix. The basic form of pure consumer is the family dependent member, who has to be supported by the breadwinner. This may sometimes involve not only close but distant relatives. The calculation of income must take this factor into account, so that this support can be given by the worker.

However, it does not end there. In addition to the dependants of workers there are also many others who cannot supply their needs through their own work, such as the elderly, the sick and the disabled. In West Germany in 1972 there were some 1.6 million such citizens requiring varying degrees of financial support, and in some cases protection. And, even in countries who have continual economic surpluses, there are institutions of the *Geistesleben* and others having more strictly social purposes, who have to struggle for support. These include children's homes, nursing homes, and all sorts of charitable institutions; to which must be added, private research and educational bodies in both arts and sciences. All these are pure consumers, and produce no commodities; but these must nevertheless receive some share in the social product, whether through voluntary donations or through taxation.

Providentially, the productivity of the economy goes well beyond the capacity to meet the needs of those at work in it. The productivity of natural forces and the productivity of the *Geist* both combine to increase industrial production to the point where there would be super-abundance, were there no pure consumers, no social or state sectors, no *Geistesleben*, to provide for. Indeed there is a tendency for the economy to produce too much, which otherwise could only be disposed of by the massive and non-reciprocal free distribution of goods. Of course there would be no renunciation in such a case; but the existence of this potential does make it possible to think, financially speaking, of donations being made, which could cover the needs of the *Geistesleben*, of the state, and of all the pure consumers. If a responsible social view is to be taken, then, it can be said that all these have independent claims on the economy—quite separately from whether or not they make any contribution to economic productivity.

The division of income among the community can be seen schematically as follows:

1 to productive activities, within and outside the economy
2 a) administrative activities of the state
   b) social vocations and institutions
   c) cultural life—art, science, religion, sport and leisure activities
3 Pure consumers
   a) support of family dependants and social security
   b) money payments to non-dependants—e.g. pensioners
   c) theft

Meeting the economic needs of pure consumers is in most cases a matter of providing for distress. However, the claims of the *Geistesleben* and the state are fundamental in character. The way in which these transfers of economic values can best be arranged can be seen by considering the example of the *Geistesleben*.

4 *Providing for the* Geistesleben

The details of the relationship between the economy and the *Geistesleben* have already been analysed. From this analysis, the issue arose as to how the economy could give enough to finance the *Geistesleben* without the necessity of taxation. The self-orientated logic of the market economy, aimed as it is at profit maximisation, develops no incentive to finance the *Geistesleben*, except in particular cases, mostly out of self-interest, when specific services are directly purchased. In these cases, these services are treated as commodities and paid for. While the claim of the *Geistesleben* to share in the results of its contribution is indisputable, it cannot be quantified, and hence no systematic way of accounting for this is possible. *Geist* values are incommensurable with material values, lying as they do on a different plane.

This is why the mode of structuring the *Geistesleben* raises such fundamental issues. It has to be independent of the other members, and needs a legal basis. It needs not only consumer goods but proper accommodation, the need for which is continually growing, to cater for schools and for research and other cultural institutes. If the *Geistesleben* is to call itself fully into conscious existence, and to provide for the provision of its material needs, it must constitute itself, along with all its institutions, into a fully self-determining member of the social organism. Only then will it have the confidence to justify the claims it has to make, on the basis of its dedicated authorship of its services. No countervalue can be put on this supply, which must be made as a donation. At present this is done in a circuitous way by the state, but not on an adequate basis.

Three possible practical sources exist for this funding:
1   The product of labour
2   Free capital formation
3   Superannuated capital

Source 1: this can be put very simply. If one wants something to prosper, one will make a contribution. Economically, this is the same thing as working for it.

Source 2: this form of contribution is more impersonal, and can be socially advocated on the basis that the formation of free capital is the result of the contribution of the *Geistesleben*.

Source 3: this is a rather difficult issue, dealt with more fully after the analysis in the next section.*

5   Limiting the life-span of capital: the associative system of capital deployment

The money form of capital appertains to the spheres of production and commerce, as producers' money, or as what could well be called commercial money, circulating on a different plane from the purchase money used in the sphere of consumption.

In the traditional capitalistic market economy money retains its value in perpetuity, and there is no time limit on its use as a medium of exchange or payment. However, this unlimited life span in fact runs counter to the continually changing and developing move-

---

*A fuller account of this will be found in Appendix 6.

ments of the real economy.

This problem has not been recognised by orthodox economists. It cannot be fully dealt with here, except to the extent that it can be considered in relation to capital money. Capital money plays the part of providing for future capital investment in a specific use. Once the investment is made it is, of course, transformed into physical capital, that is, into the means of production. However these latter do not last forever. On the contrary, they wear out. And when they do, their economic efficiency comes to an end. This happens with all means of production acquired by money capital. This does not apply to the capital money employed in the means of production, not that is, according to the primitive legal concepts at present applied. which would see it as going on in perpetuity. Having, indeed, an abstract character as money capital, which is continuously valid, it carries the title to a profit, particularly to the appropriation of free capital, and to control of the company management.

However, the necessity to limit the life of this capital function of capital money arises out of the dynamic movement of the economy, and is based on circulation; and it cannot be ignored. On the contrary, this must be "dis-valued" along with its physical equivalent, and must expire when that wears out.*

The point is seen when we consider what happens when an investment capital—a money capital that has been put to work—goes out of service because the means of production acquired with it are used up. Nominally the capital is still there—but from the viewpoint of the social economy it is no longer at work. Its function as capital is over. The life span of the money capital is in fact connected with the life span of the physical means of production, and it is the essential task of the monetary system to bring this connection out into view. In order to understand the extinction of the capital function of a productive investment, it is necessary to consider in what practical form this extinction can normally be brought about. At this point we will only make a few indications about this, as to the direction in which the solution is to be found.†

One must start by considering the fundamental difference between

---

*See Appendix 5.

†Steiner deals with this in his "World Economy", and it is treated more intensively in the second volume of this work, published in German, as *Das Kapital und das Geld*, Schaffhausen 1981—Ed.

the two levels of the economic structure. These two levels reflect the material part and the *Geist* part of the economy, respectively. They constitute two different levels of economic processes. On one level the consumer goods process takes place, in which products for ultimate consumption are bought and sold with consumer purchase money. The other level is that of the production and capital goods, the capital sphere. Now, the expiry of the life span of a productive capital could be seen in this way, that its money function is transferred from the capital to the consumer sphere. Thus, the original subscriber of the capital would have this capital paid back to him on the condition that it was either used for consumption or donated to the *Geistesleben*. Of course, the latter might be quite common once there is more *understanding* throughout the economy.

It is only by such decapitalisation of money capital that the monetary system can, as far as possible, be adjusted to the age structure of the capital assets of the economy. Thus the varying ages of the different assets still in productive use would, to a certain extent, find their expression in a corresponding structuring by age of the corresponding money capitals. The practical techniques by which this age structuring can be put into effect, and the procedures by which the transfer of capital money to the consumer goods sphere can be effected, requires a more detailed explanation of how an organic economic system would work, and particularly how the monetary system would adapt to the actual needs of the economy. Such an explanation would have to begin with the fact that the methodless issue of money—such as takes place under the conditions of the capitalistic market economy—causes an uncontrolled increase in the money supply. Now the extent of the increase in the money supply hinges upon the material security that the borrower offers, which forms the collateral security for the repayment of the loan. Such a creation of money in a way which is unconnected with the needs of the economy, must, inevitably, bring about an uncontrolled inflationary expansion in the private economy. Such a mechanistic expansion of the money supply can, moreover, never be rectified by the subsequent adjustment of the money supply by means of the banking system—to say nothing of the matter of getting the total money supply back to the correct amount needed by the economy. (This point was explained earlier in connection with the discussion on profit.) A deep understanding of the economy, and a comprehensive approach, are needed, to get this right.

The way in which capital should be terminated depends upon

which of the three sources it came from—savings, free capital, or the creation of money. All three raise the same question of how they should be transferred into the sphere of consumption; for each there is the possibility that after repayment it could be reinvested back in the capital sphere. Given the present-day level of development of the economic system, and in view of the way in which the legislative framework encourages egoism, this is scarcely to be wondered at. What is needed is a system in the economy which has a real appraisal of capital, such as would be developed by the associations described; the said associations would have an assessment of the pattern of capital flows, and could deliberate as to exactly how, in the light of this insight, time-expired capital was to be transferred to the consumption sphere.*

As regards capital from savings, as already discussed, this is only split off from consumer incomes and generally is intended as a deferment of consumption: so that there is seldom any need to make a special transfer back into the consumption sphere. The periods for which consumers save are variable and randomly divided between short and long term. At present, of course, all deposits paid into banks are recorded under the one heading, so that consumer savings are mixed up with sums deriving from private profits, of all the various kinds discussed earlier. This would not be so, however, in a self-determining organically arranged economic system, in which the confusion between different kinds of deposits would disappear. When savings proper are withdrawn, because of the whole nature of the savings process, this is almost always after a comparatively short time period. The investment of long term savings in banks and similar institutions largely regulates itself. Thus the repayment of loan capital takes place through the banking system and stays within it. In the overall savings process there is a continual interchange of deposits and withdrawals. Thus, refunded capital investments are continually set off by deposits, and vice versa. All this is, of course, separate from the main lending operations of the banks themselves. In the consumer sphere there is no age-structuring of money, since it would not affect its purchasing power.

---

*There are various ways of doing this which are not discussed here. For example capital money which is being repaid as cash could be in some way marked with its age. This could be used to control its further employment, so that it could not be reinvested as capital. This, of course, presupposes an age classification of the quantity of money as explained by Steiner in his "World Economy". This understandably is out of the question in a mechanistic economic system.

It is to be borne in mind that this question of the time expiry of capital relates only to the purchase of the means of production and capital goods, by industrial enterprises—and not to the financing of property or share deals, nor to any other factitious or consumer capital transactions.*

The repayment or decapitalisation of *share capital* makes use of the same method as the decapitalistion of a long-term investment financed out of *free capital formation*. Before its investment as productive capital, the free capital would have been in a suspense account, that would be legally conceived as "transfer property"; this would mean that some arrangement would have been considered, at that stage, so that the free capital was transferred in relation to an economic overview, and with social responsibility. The theory of the market economy is that profit-making employment of free capital in private interests will coincide with the objective needs of the economy for capital. However, this happens only to a limited extent, and then only by a circuitous route; mostly, it does not happen at all. This is because self-orientated and social urges are incompatible. The former can only bring about superficial and mechanistic social forms.

A socially aware transfer of free capital has to consider various social groupings who could make a claim for it. These can be classified as follows:

1 Primary applications
   a) investment in the economy
   b) financing the *Geistesleben*
2 Secondary applications
   a) as bonus payment for those working in the economic system
   b) financing the state.

There are thus four interests, whose competing claims have to be met. This necessitates deliberation in the associations, in which the participants will need to modify their subjective claims to arrive at objective decisions about that division which is both economically correct and socially responsible. Industry will have valid claims to make for investment—and the workers will equally be wanting more income. These two divergent claims—which at present engage in industrial conflict—can be satisfied through the proceedings of the association, in which the *Geistesleben* and the state would take part as well. The other claims would have, of course, to be borne in mind. The transfer of free capital

---

*See Appendix V.

would be neutralised, vis-à-vis the economy, in respect of those parts which were given, without reciprocity, to the self-determining *Geistesleben* for the use of such institutions as educational establishments, research institutes, clinics, welfare bodies, etc.

Within the relationships of the Western market economy, donations to individual institutions within the *Geistesleben* do of course occur, sometimes in the form of the establishment of foundations. However, these donations are somewhat spasmodic, since they are not intrinsic to the system of the economy as such. Naturally, the present-day economy is glad of the demand attributable to the *Geistesleben*, which helps it to stay in business! Hence some arrangements have to be made and of course this gets to be pushed on to the state, which transfers the necessary finance via taxation. Through this makeshift and circuitous way, the state acquires an unfortunate power over the *Geistesleben*—unfortunate because it opens the way to political influence.

Returning to the problem of how to transfer time-expired capital back to the sphere of consumption, it makes no difference whether this capital derives from free capital, from the creation of money, from shares or from capital deriving from savings. The interested parties likely to make claims, in order to receive their necessary means of existence, are mainly pure consumers, such as the *Geistesleben*, social institutions, and perhaps the state. With so many consuming groups involved, there are various ways in which decapitalised capital could be applied. For example, it could be dealt with on the level of the individal company. This seems possible if one calls to mind the new-style companies already mentioned. In these, at least in the early days, it seemed that the company members were able to confront matters of management and revenue in a dispassionate spirit. Thus the awareness of responsibility could grow to the point adumbrated for the associative system, in its readiness to supply the *Geistesleben*—or its individual institutions —regularly and on a planned basis.

As it is, the financing of the *Geistesleben* and its cultural bodies has become the concern of the state. This follows inevitably from the self-orientated nature of the economic system which, today, lacks both the ability and the will to do it, except on a narrowly business basis. If, from time to time, the economy has supported research or education, then that has been mainly for technical reasons, in order to lay the basis of further growth for the particular business concerned. Where such privately motivated help has been insufficient, then the state has had to step in. This it did by turning the people working in the *Geistesleben* into civil servants, and endowing the various cultural bodies itself. However, this endowment has been generally inadequate, because other government purposes, particularly military ones, tend to get priority. The political dependence of the *Geistesleben*, brought about by this roundabout way of financing it, runs counter to its whole basic principle, which is that it needs freedom of thought. The subjection of mind to an all-pervasive state power is a social evil, which can only be eliminated by separating both the economy and the *Geistesleben* from the life and control of the state proper.

6 *The economy as a constituent part of the state: the state proper*

Under a heading which is the exact opposite of the above, the German Federal Statistical Office publishes from time to time,* as part of the detailed national economic accounts, a statistical analysis of the administrative services provided by the state for the economy and social life, and of the claims made on the economy in return. This analysis includes, on the one hand, financial payments, mostly taxes, and on the other hand, government revenue from state economic activities, including fees for the performance of administrative services. Thus the finance which the economy provides to the state throws back again into the economy. Details are shown in the following table:

THE GERMAN STATE AS PART OF INDUSTRY, IN 1966

Source: "Wirtschaft und Statistik" Vol. II, 1967

	thousand million marks
1 Total government expenditure:	193
Of which:	
2 Total purchased from the economy (incl. goods, land [sic!], plant and services), roughly one third of total state expenditure:	62
3 Incomes paid to state employees, and so made into consumer money:	39
4 Current financial payments to pure consumers, against no counter-value, i.e. the so-called "redistribution of income", mainly pensions and social security payments, equal to nearly a half of state expenditure:	81

(Total national product for 1966: 490.7 thousand million marks)

---

*In the government review, "Wirtschaft und Statistik".

Obviously, the state, in so far as it is economically involved, is in fact part of the economy, within the framework of the national budget. However, it is less obvious that the economy equally forms part of the state. Nevertheless, it is part of the development of modern times that the state and the economy tend to merge, and this increasingly so the further east one goes. But it is also characteristic of the western economic system that more and more of it should come under state control. Indeed, all modern states see themselves as compelled, not only to take over a larger and larger part of the private economy but also to maintain the overall economic equilibrium. Thus, we find the following forms of governmental economic activity, in areas previously purely private:

1 in government-run industry,
2 through subsidies and other assistance to the private economy. The government has to step in wherever the traditional market economy lacks the ability to perform the task. Thus, 27 per cent of the German national capital is in the control of the state. Particular areas which the private sector does not find profitable and so fall to the government are: roadbuilding, much of transport, and municipal housebuilding. Thus in 1966 the German state invested 7.8 thousand million marks on roads, waterways and bridges, and 18.2 thousand million on buildings, and a further 10.7 thousand million on various subventions and capital grants to private industry.

Far more important still is
3 the role of the government in respect of the overall economy, responsibility for which is left to it. This includes
   a) stabilising the value of money
   b) counter-cyclical policy
   c) maintenance of full employment
   d) development of international trade.

This raises the point that the functionally centralised state* has, as a matter of policy, become hypertrophied, and spans and stands over the entire social organism.

Important raw materials, for example, oil, are managed by states, so that the political means of power such as tariffs and other controls on international trade are used as a means of this management; and it is only this situation which makes it necessary for governments to pursue an international trade policy that is dictated by national interests. It is

---

*German "Einheitstaat"—see glossary.

then governments who deal with each other economically and who make various settlements in respect of the international exchange of goods and movement of capital investments. Political actions of this kind are also part of the arsenal of counter-cyclical policy. It is the fear of a cyclical decline—the so-called recession—which motivates the state to struggle to remove all the symptoms of this decline, such as shortage of capital, unemployment, falling production, etc. The elimination of these manifestations of a cyclical downturn goes far beyond the competence and capability of the state, as is shown particularly sharply when the state tries to stabilise the value of the currency.

Responsibility for the stability of the currency has become the state's, simply because the contemporary economic system is so established that it is unable to achieve this stability itself. On the contrary the sitituation is such that the depreciation of money goes on continually in all economies—even those who were not involved in the World War, and even in the relatively stable economies which existed before it. For example, in Germany, which at that time had a currency fixed to the gold standard, there was a depreciation of 60 per cent between 1895 and 1913, a period of eighteen years.* The causes of this lie deep in the monetary system: They are not, at present, grasped from a causal point of view. Hence, it is that the continuous depreciation of money cannot be stopped. Instead, the best that can be done is to adjust the quantity of money marginally and this can only be done after the inflation has already commenced. Thus the state is expected to eliminate this economic disorder yet not only does the state not know its cause, it, in fact, cannot know it; no more can the central bank, the guardian of the currency. Even if the functionally necessary quantity of money were known it does not lie within the power of the authorities to bring this quantity into existence centrally, for fundamental reasons—which, so far, have not begun to be grasped in their true essence by economists. The knowledge cannot be got from them, how to bring the quantity of money in the economy into the correct functional relationship and amount. It will have to be recognised that the control of the quantity of money is only possible if the life expectancy of money is limited both for consumer and producer purposes. The latter require a time limitation on the capital function of the invested capital money.

Even if the minister responsible for the stabilisation of the value of

---

*See Wilken's "Volkswirtschaftliche Theorie der landwirtschaftlichen Preissteigerungen in Deutschland 1895–1913", Berlin 1925.

money had the knowledge of the law governing the functionally necessary amount of it, he would still not be able to act from this knowledge. The practical management of the monetary system, if it is to follow this law, depends on specific knowledge of the way in which it can be carried out in the economic system; this knowledge can only be obtained after full studies by the economic associations. The foundations of a proper monetary system will be laid to a large extent when a social procedure is adopted, for the investment of productive capital. Here the problem is to establish the correct relationship between savings, free capital and the creation of money for capital purposes; and this has to happen in the light of the broader consideration, that the total of these must be adjusted for their functional life expectancy. The practical management of this depends on the development of the correct concepts and analysis, which can only be done by the associations. No single minister, no single manager in the economy, can form the necessary judgement for this. Hence the primitive and unconsidered system of contemporary monetary management has to go for good. It is easy to see that the quantity of money is increased in a way which is both unreal and not thought out, whenever an individual is granted credit money on the basis of some security, usually a factitious one, such as property or shares. Another source of inorganic increase in the quantity of money comes from the celebrated "deficit spending" of the state, aimed at relieving unemployment.

People today who stand perplexed and helpless before the unceasing devaluation of their purchasing power, demand from their governments that they should stop this endless depreciation and stabilise the value of money. The real statesman has to go against these demands and say to the people, "You are asking something of the state that does not lie within its competence, something for which it is not qualified because it does not and cannot understand it. So you must go to the *Geistesleben*, if you want a monetary system with a stable value."

It is in the *Geistesleben* that the understanding of the money function, both as to consumer and capital use, has to be attained. What has to be carried out in the light of this understanding can only happen once the economic system has reached the associative level of development. The state can never know how the issue of money should be managed so as to have that amount actually needed for circulatory purposes. The state cannot create the social bodies which are to be created in the economy, whose task will be to limit the life of money, both for capital and for consumer purposes. These organs must form

themselves out of the inner necessity of the economic system. The state
cannot do more than secure the legal form of such bodies—the
associations, that is—and keep a watching brief to the extent of seeing
that they are run in a just manner.

At present, the state has to involve itself wherever the market-driven
economy does not have the ability to solve its problems, in connection
with such matters as production, capital formation, capitalisation,
income distribution, and particularly the financing of the *Geistesleben*
and of other pure consumers. This kind of state integration of the capitalistic market economy has been described, in Germany, as the "social
market economy". This designation is contradictory, in that what is
thus, euphemistically, called "social" comes purely from the state, and
not from any fundamental movement in the economy itself. The state's
social practice must of its very nature be limited to the theoretical
regulation of the outward organisational forms of such structures as are
needed, either for economic or for social reasons. Thus political forces
interfere—a self-determining economic system would on the other hand
be able to develop, out of its own resources, the right social formations
to cope with economic matters; whereas the state, being overloaded
with economics, becomes estranged from its proper functions—although
these proper functions are themselves perfectly social, namely to ensure
justice in all human affairs.

As the trustee of human rights, the state has the fundamental duty
of protecting the liberties infringed in the economic battles between
entrepreneur and worker, and between traders and consumers, as it has
done, on the employee side, by means of social policies and labour
legislation. Also, on the business side, commercial law was developed, as
were laws concerning the extent to which competition could be carried.

As for capital and monetary matters, in a self-determining and
associative economic system, the state would have to attend to the legal
framework for the special institutions formed for this work. This would
apply to every kind of institution that the associative economy needed
to develop as one of its organs. These would all need to have the sanction and supervision of the law, in the appropriate spirit.

Such a state would be, so to speak, unalloyed, wholly devoted to its
proper purpose. This can only happen if the state and the economy are
disentangled. Taking its place as a member of the social organism,
freed from the encumbrance of functions not really proper to government, the state would still need to be financed; but it would not need
to make any claims upon free capital. Instead, this would be done

largely through taxes on expenditures.*

Only a few years after Steiner had put forward the idea of the three-fold separation of function of the social organism, its significance was recognised by Professor Wolzendorff, of Halle University, whose article on the subject was republished in 1969.†

7 *The redemption of competition by the need-orientated economy*

Emulation is not quite the same as competition, since it is to do with a fundamental principle of the development of mind. What it purports is that any given level of development is always the departure point for the next step forward, that every achievement of the *Geist* is prelude to a further and greater achievement. We are all, both individuals and nations, engaged willy nilly in a contest concerned with the develop-ment of the *Geist* and with progressively higher standards of attain-ment. Thus there is emulation in every imaginable sphere—athletics, art, science, etc. The truth is that all intellectual development takes place in the context of this process of emulation; it is a basic principle.

Now when this idea is related to the economic system, it is necessary —if emulation is to do good—that the economy is orientated towards the satisfaction of *needs*. But, in any economic system motivated by self-orientated economic competition, neutral emulation of perform-ance will inevitable take second place to the competitive struggle for survival. The achievements of the *Geist* thus become mere weapons, with which to drive competitors out of the market. It is thus the principle of competition which has become the mainspring of the conventional market economy. All competition is aggressive; whereas emulation proper lacks this feature, and is pursued purely for its own sake. The importation of the competitive principle into the economy distorts the nature of emulation, and leads to a situation in which the whole point of economic activity—namely the satisfaction of needs—is lost sight of. The optimum satisfaction of needs cannot therefore be achieved, the individualised economic units of the private economy being more concerned with maximisation of production and sales as an end in itself. There is thus no limit to the self-orientated striving for

---

*See Wilken's "Reform des Steuerwesens", Freiburg i. Br. 1968.
†In "Sozialwissenschaftliches Studienmaterial" I, "Der reine Staat", Berlin 1969.

material reward, and hence no limit to the competitive struggle either. On the other hand, there is the situation that the demand for goods is restricted, and it is of course to this restricted level of demand that the competitive maximisation of profits and of production has to relate. This makes difficulties for industry, and the state has to help.

Thus in 1974 the German government intervened to help the sale of cars by a package of measures which would cost the taxpayers milliards of marks. The relationship between the state and the economy is thus in a dilemma. On the one hand there is the threat of rising unemployment, on the other the cost of trying to maintain car sales. These measures helped car manufacturers locked in a competitive struggle to maintain or even increase their already high turnover. Such a counter-cyclical policy keeps competing firms in existence without consideration of the need for their products. To anyone with common sense, looking at the streets packed with cars, a further increase in their number, and particularly in the number of commercial vehicles, must appear contrary to economic rationality. This contradiction is seen particularly sharply when one contrasts the superabundant road traffic with the underemployed railways. In the competition between the railways and road traffic, the position of the latter is strengthened by the fact that a massive new branch of industry stands behind it, in which each individual concern is trying to outbid the others with a succession of new models, from fear of being driven out of the market.

The transport of people and goods by the motor vehicle has led to the situation that the capacity of the railways is neglected. This transfers the profitability of the railways to the motor vehicle industry which, from an overall economic point of view, makes its profits out of the railways' costs, so that the large deficits of the latter have to be paid for by the general population, as a sacrifice for the equilibrium-shattering overgrowth of road traffic.

When a downturn in sales is expected, the car manufacturers are threatened with losses. Now maintaining profits is necessary, if the good opinion of the stock exchange is to be retained. Sometimes in such a situation the directors of the car manufacturers try to cheer up their disenchanted shareholders with the hope that profits will rise, with the appearance of new models. Any detached spectator of this sales forecast might feel that the said increased sales could only be at the countervailing expense of the other car manufacturers. Profits thus won at the expense of others are justified, in the view of the market economy, but this is not so for those who base their thinking on economic rationality, or who live in a broader consciousness of the national and world economic system. For such people, the decisive question will be, how can the economy be so run that it keeps step with real needs? Sound economic thinking will lead to the same conclusion that economists have always reached—without the latter drawing the obvious corollary. Of course, the point of economic activity is to satisfy the need for material goods—*from which it follows, however, that this cannot be brought about properly through market profit.* What the orientation of production to need requires is this, that production will be geared downwards if the quantities needed decline, and that this will be socially and economically justified, that is, if production for need is meant seriously.

But in the market economy, there is the compulsion—because of the individual interest in profit-making—always to expand *beyond* the point needed by real demand; and this tendency cannot but bring about a shortage of capital. For this reason, the formation and/or expansion of companies under the compulsion of competition must inevitably entail a struggle to obtain investment capital. In a proper need-orientated economy, new undertakings would only be worthwhile if there was the demand there. Such a limitation of the economy is only possible if the economic associations develop the right awareness of the total of all demands and of all productive possibilities able to gratify the said demands. Consequently, a need-orientated economy could not, under normal circumstances, experience a shortage of capital.

Companies—like all things created by men—grow old and lose their efficiency. This is true not only in a market economy but also in an organic, need-orientated, one. With any human creative activity, there is the fundamental principle at work, of a polarity between building up and using up, between growth and decline, which polarity expresses itself in money terms as being between capitalisation and decapitalisation.

Once a socially structured and self-determining need-orientated economy gets a grip on the processes of building up and using up, on both the consumer and the capital side, then there could be no more bankruptcies (which are socially speaking pathological). A need-orientated economy will no longer be under the compulsion to over-produce or to over-capitalise. What will stop bankruptcies happening is the exercise of social responsibility, which applies not only to the overall economy, but beyond that, to the social organism as a whole. This kind of overall social responsibility can only be put into practice by people whose level of awareness and motivation have gone beyond the self-orientated type of responsibility and moved towards the experience of the common right to work of all men and of joint responsibility for this. People of this kind would be able to form associations capable both of deciding policy and managing the development of new enterprises and the closure of outmoded ones. The problem with economic closures is, of course, what to do with the redundant workforce; a need-orientated economy has to grapple with the problem of full employment, just as do today's government and economy. Moreover, this concerns not only the economy proper, but also the entire social organism. With a need-orientated economy, there will certainly be rather less essential work to do, not the least reason being the development of labour-saving technology. One must try to imagine how an economic system would operate, where production is carried on only to meet needs. In such a system, the economic principle will be adhered to so that the least possible work will be done to meet consumer demands. Out of this arises a major social issue as to how people can be active within the social organism so that, on the one hand, the necessary work can be done, and on the other hand, how people can be employed in a dignified way—which every person needs for his own mental and spiritual development. Today this issue is handled only superficially, by means of the dole, which does little to meet people's need for real work.

The whole nature of the economic associations lies in their ability to find a balance between different and opposite interests, and between various economic situations. Thus, it is only through these associations that divergent lines of development in commerce can find the right equilibrium. In these associations all concerned would come together— not only the representatives for different economic proposals but also the representatives of the general population. The thing would be to find a balance between growing and declining developments, which would require economic knowledge and recognition of social needs. Various ways might be agreed, in the light of a detailed assessment of the situation. For example, in a particularly severe case, it might be decided that growing sectors would help declining ones to adjust with an equalisation levy. Such a responsible approach and such solidarity could only come about through the deliberations of the associations. The adoption of such a levy would be the genuinely social and sensible thing to do, from the standpoint of the whole economy, utopian as this may seem in an economy in which each individual can carry on at the other's expense of another, and think that the right thing to do.

The future economic system will not consider the main aim to be the maximum possible social product, whether this is sought with a view to deliberately stimulating over-consumption, or to maintain full employment. Rather, the starting point of the future economy will be to manufacture those goods and services which are actually needed. That is what a need-orientated economy means. It completely supersedes the profit-orientated market production system with its fragmentated individualism and its obsession with sales. Money-making —being the principle concern of this system—pushes the economy into the competitive struggle, with its price strategies and its compulsion always to produce more, so as not to go under. The exploitation of emulation to make private profits becomes the driving force of the whole system, witness the processes of the so-called science of advertising. Thus, the competitive principle puts the leaders of the separate companies under the yoke of the individualistic self-actualisation drive, often to the point of personal exhaustion. None of this need be, if the economy is re-orientated towards what is actually wanted—which would in fact bring harmony into the economy, and enable man's competitive instincts to be used constructively as a spur to real human progress in matters of *Geist*, in something like the way this happens in sport.

8 Reconciling social and individual aspects

We have seen that the need-orientated economy cannot be organised by any collective or impersonal authority, but must in fact develop out of individual efforts. Social structures produced by individual impulses —particularly those of an associative nature—are by their very nature not *organisable* since they are rooted in human wills, and in the instigations of practical economics. It is in fact because of the great development of human society which the market economy has brought about that the individual has become capable of running the economy properly. This attainment will be secured for good by the need-orientated economy, which will use it to develop its procedures.

Those who want to alter the market economy, but who seek salvation in the conformist and omnipresent collectivist economy on

the Marxist or communist pattern, are in fact reverting in their thinking
to the social forms of pre-Christian times, and taking as their pattern
the unindividualised societies which predominated everywhere in that
stage of development, based as they were on consanguinity and on a
deeply religious *Geist*. Men were then born into, and, so to speak,
taken over by the forces of this society, for the duration of their lives.
This type of society lost ground as humanity lost its sense of religious
purpose, and developed instead the awareness of self, and the capacity
to make personal judgements. For this it was necessary to develop
individualised intellectual powers, so as to develop a clear conceptualisation of the tangible and perceptible world. This process has been
going on for over two thousand years beginning with classical times
some eight hundred years before Christ. By the beginning of modern
times, the religious and consanguineous ties of the old society had been
almost completely dissolved. Thus it is now necessary when people
want to negotiate the formation of social groups which will not be
dependent on kinship or racial ties, that they can only do this by means
of the free exercise of the will-power of their individualised selves.

The main problem of the economic system is, therefore, to express
the nature of modern humanity, so that the polarity between individual
and social aspects should be resolved. The starting point for the recon-
ciliation or synthesis of these two polar forces is, in fact, the individual
nature of humanity as it has taken shape since the fifteenth century in
conjunction with the development of independent powers of thought.
It is out of this individual nature that modern economic life takes its
shape. The historic character of this development was, philosophically
speaking, formed by "liberalism", that proclaimed freedom as the
highest manifestation of the human individual, and as the guiding principle of the modern social economy. The creators of this liberal economic system were, historically, the early entrepreneurs, tough, self-
aware and daring. Thus this system sprang from the earliest stage of
human individualisation, so that it was at that stage that it was formed;
now the earliest stage of individualisation is characterised by the fact
that it pursues only the aim of personal self-actualisation. Hence, all
economic relationships are arranged with this interest as the guiding
principle. The drive for self-realisation subordinates all economic relations to the self-orientated desire for personal acquisition. Under the
influence of this self-orientated economic system, the private ownership of the means of production and the competitive market economy,
both developed. The natural ownership of consumer goods was ex-

tended to cover the private ownership of the productive basis of the economy, both as money and as physical capital.

This ownership of capital has the tendency to develop a contagious form of self-intensification, brought about by the innate right attaching to capital, to appropriate the values it creates, significantly including free capital. This right is in sharp contrast with the way in which capital would be managed objectively and in relation to the requirements of overall economic considerations. Once capital is separated from its private control, its management becomes objective in the sense that it aims at the optimum economic operation. Superseding the self-orientation principle and making capital objective, means that a new social procedure for managing capital will be needed. This must develop itself out of a truly human form of community. Thus, this kind of capital management is fundamentally different from the authoritative and mechanistic form. An organically formed community system is much more developed, socially speaking, than one which is mechanistic and intellectually organised. The advocates of the latter have failed to recognise that it is the basic tendency of man to become independent and that with the help of abilities deep within his personal being, he will create new social forms. Only through such social forms will it be possible to change economic life from a struggle about money into a living community, the realisation of which is the mission of the individual liberated human spirit. It is imperative for him to use these powers in this way.

The fulfilment of this task may be obvious to the detached thinker, but is faced, as we have seen, with great difficulties from a human point of view. In discussing the three new-style companies, we saw how in most people, the sense of dedication and responsibility is, as yet, under-developed, and we saw also both how necessary and how difficult it is to change this. Karl Backhaus saw this when he established his educational foundation as the spiritual centre of his company. Because many of the members of this company had not yet developed the necessary maturity to take over greater responsibility for the company as a whole, it was, at first, unavoidable that the method of democratic will-formation should be employed. This is a makeshift, by which, at least outwardly, equal rights are set up for all members and exercised for the main decisions. It will, in practice, be necessary for similar new-style companies to start by creating such democratic arrangements which will take the under-development of responsibility into account. This will mean that the form of organisation will be rational rather than organic, so as to make some progress by means of the democratic system, pending the attainment of more dedication by enough members.

The one essential subjective force in the psyche, by means of which the formation of a completely human community will be brought about, is the individual spirit of freedom. Some things in man may hold him back from this, the true freedom. One has to want certain things —to face the truth, both about oneself and others, to accept responsibility in the light of what one has learnt, and above all to do the thing which one finds to be necessary. This has little in common with that form of freedom which wants nothing more than the unhindered satisfaction of instincts. All freedoms, all demands for freedom move between two poles; one is self-orientated and the other, the antithesis, is altruistic concern for the well-being of one's fellow man. Only from this latter pure freedom can the power be developed, to take responsibility for the correct management of society. The moral perceptions which develop from this true freedom, are needed for the shaping of social life; these perceptions are not generated by the intellect, which can only organise outward relationships. They arise, rather, from deep inside the psyche, which possesses conceptual powers relevant to social living and to justice, although these powers are not recognised by conventional psychology.

These powers which are essential if a genuinely human community is to develop, could be seen in an early stage in the examples of the style companies considered. But it must also be recognised that these "powers of the heart" are not yet enough by themselves at the present time. There has also to be a knowledge of what physically and objectively has to be formed in the social organism; in this connection, it is particularly the economy—as one of the areas of society particularly needing objectivity in its shaping—which needs to be permeated thoroughly with the right understanding. This is a matter of the realisation of the very core of an organic system.

The social organism, just like a biological organism, forms a complete whole, in which each member, each organ and each cell, humanly speaking, is interested in the social whole and in its well-being, since that is also its own well-being. The operation of this organic social law governing the collaboration of all members, organs and cells for the whole and for each other, can only be brought about for the economy through the conscious understanding of Steiner's social law. This provides the method by which the social arrangements for the common work can be shaped by economic understanding. The conventional business spirit of private profit-making must change itself into a socially orientated self interest, that is based on the achievement of the optimum economic operation, and on complete conviction about the necessity for deep economic understanding of the whole process. The spirit in which this must be realised is just like that of an engineer who is, of course, totally convinced that his machine will not work unless it obeys the scientific laws of the appropriate technology. The personal interest of both entrepreneur and worker, for so long centred on narrow self-satisfaction, can in this way be raised to a higher level. In such an objective economic spirit can the social structures develop which will form themselves as associations giving overall direction to the economy. Through them the economic impulse which shapes economic activity will be raised to a higher social level so that in the place of the profit motive, there comes a concern with the fruitfulness of the economy as assessed on a rational basis. Of course, personal and material satisfactions will still be there, but no longer in the foreground, and they will be satisfied in more social forms. Thereby, the original social forms of the economy will be reshaped by individual awareness and determination. At this stage, then, the ownership of capital takes on the supra-personal form already described, and the egoistic management of the economy will have to put its inner drives into the service of economic and communal operation. This leads, naturally, to the formation of associations in which different interests and experiences can be brought together and reconciled.

It is through a universal and associative system of economic activity, which is the radical antithesis of the market economy, that the economy can develop an objective way of working. Whereas the social forms of ancient times were religious and impersonal, and based on consanguinity, society can now develop on the basis of the wills of individuals who are conscious of their mutual responsibilities and so form communities based on the spirit of brotherhood.

9 *Three economic conversions of matter—commodities, money and capital. Increasing or reducing production*

The power of individualisation has developed a threefold structure in the liberal independent economy. As yet this process has not fully unfolded, because of the nature of the individualised materialist *Geist*. This secular event in the development of mankind has brought about an economic system which can only be explained by the deflection of the focus of human consciousness away from the *Geist* and towards the material. Now it was only in this way that the first act of personal individualisation was able to take place. This impulse towards independence and awareness was produced by the strength of the material ties; and became so general, and at the same time penetrated so deeply into human thinking, that all human progress has been, in these conditions, aimed at the development of a material culture and of a technological mastery of the whole material world. It is as if a magic power had brought man to the earth, in truth a technological power of the *Geist* that seeks to seduce men into constructing a technical empire and to bring the whole earth under its control. Within this transformation is contained a particular kind of penetration of matter by the human *Geist*, especially in the economy—in which this process fulfils itself in three stages. The first stage consists in the production of commodities; these are based on human labour in its broadest sense. The second stage is reached through money; in which commodities are transformed into economic values in order to arrange their social distribution. The third stage takes money further, and transforms it into capital. This stage presupposes the other two stages, that is, both the production of goods and their money-organised distribution. Similarly, the production of goods—formed out of natural elements by labour—forms the precondition of the money stage. These functional transitions—from goods to money, and from money to capital—reflect the human activities that bring them about; that is, they involve progress from working abilities to social abilities and from thence to abilities which spring from the individual human *Geist*. Those familiar with anthroposophy will recognise in these three stages the reflection of the three human systems—digestive, heart and cerebral.

To put it more precisely, in commodities matter is continually their basic substance, but in money it disappears. But money—not the actual substance of the monetary tokens, but money itself—manifests a specific character of the commodities in a form which is quite separate from their actual substance, and which distils, as it were, the essence of that character only, which subsists in their social function. Money is experienced as the impersonal social symbol of matter in itself, to the extent that matter has been worked into goods, and forms an ingredient conceived as an abstract material value quantity. This essence, lying at the basis of all matter, is [that same essence to which] the principle of differentiating matter by dimensions number and weight refers; but [in this context] it is limited so that only number, as the expression of the relationship of differences in value, is made use of.* It is through a numerically differentiated money system that the social exchange of goods is carried out. The function of money consists only of this social function of enabling exchange, in accordance with the varying value quantities involved; this began with simple primordial acts of isolated exchange, and found its full realisation in the exchange process of the whole economic organism, in which all members of society are linked with one another. In the latter case, the essence of exchange is not in itself altered, but is the same, whether the objects exchanged are consumer goods or means of production or capital goods.

The economic value incorporated in money by means of the individual acts of exchange realises in itself the material essence of the objects exchanged, in the form of the values places upon them —including the case where the objects exchanged are legal titles. However, the capital form of money begins to exist only when the essence embodied in the money is separated from its relationship with commodities, thus becoming as it were its own thing, quite abstract, so that it then sets about its own life, totally divorced from its origin and from its previous application. It cannot be said that money originates from goods, since it is not brought out of the commodity system, but has to be introduced into the economy as having a legal basis. Capital, on the other hand, comes into being as a result of intentional economic initiatives, and arises independently out of the putting into effect of a creative economic idea. Any money lying unused can be used, whether it is free capital, savings or the result of credit creation. It is its application as investment which puts it into the more advanced category of capital.

In modern times, it is the institution of the private ownership of capital which has given capital a private existence of its own. Through this private appropriation of its substance and function it was able to become an instrument of the development of economic dominance and social power. It is of course only a small section of humanity that have

---

*The words in square brackets have been inserted in this important sentence in editing, since it seems as if something is missing in the German text.—Editor.

brought this instrument under their control, thereby exercising power over a large part of the earth's resources and peoples.

A social and economic science which respected economic rationality and social justice would have to recognise that persons in possession of capital ought not to use its function for private ends. Invested capital should not be privately owned—though of course it must be managed. It can be understood that the private use of capital is in conflict with such management.

If the social and *Geist* powers of capital are set to work to put into practice an economic idea, and this idea is then however taken over by the spirit of materialism, this means that the holders of power are thereby led to make the economic values of the world over into their own possession, so that they can turn them into money. If materialism is pushed to the absolute limit, then an absolute character is also invested in these material economic values. This motivates their acquisition, so that they can become united with the person owning them. An economy driven by this materialist spirit will come to believe it to be the whole point of life, and will be pushed towards unlimited expansion. This is then elevated to become the basic principle, and the premise upon which all economic activity is based.

Growth is an organic conception, but making growth into a permanent and absolute factor is contrary to nature. The materialist concept of growth is borrowed from the organic principle, but is perverted into a quantitative and mechanistic notion, and so takes on the form of a continuous outward expansion of the material aspects of the economy. However, since even a mechanistically shaped economy still has to deal with the necessities of human life, the principle of mechanistic growth will find itself corrected by the law of organic growth. This striving—based on an anti-organic conception of things —to secure a continuous expansion of the privately managed economic units in the overall economy finds itself from time to time exposed to recessionary tendencies which compel production and sales to cease expanding, but instead to contract or even to stop altogether. Moreover, while it is quite natural that firms and industries should not go on for ever, unless substantially reshaped from time to time, in a mechanistic economy based on the price mechanism, their closure takes on the anti-social form of bankruptcy.

A practical if rather ponderous reason is often advanced to show that continuous growth is necessary; according to this argument, growth is necessary to create employment and so reduce unemployment, which results from the continuous growth in the population on the one hand, and from the continuous development of labour-saving technology, thus producing a tendency for the continual dismissal of more and more workers. Hence it appears necessary for the economy to grow, by the increased production both of consumer goods and of the means of production.

This situation has only been briefly outlined here. But anyone who grasps it and finds it irrational to expand economic production beyond what is individually or socially needed, will understand that the control of the development or run-down of economic facilities from an overall economic point of view can only be achieved by an economic system that makes its aim the recognition of needs. Of course, adjustment of production would be necessary for changes in population. But supposing the population to be no longer expanding, say because the birth-rate was falling, the notion of continuous growth would become quite unreal. In that eventuality, sales would decline, there would be redundancies, losses instead of profits, amounting to a near collapse for big business; economic activity would have to be adjusted if only actually existing needs were to be met. The recognition of such needs could only be met by free associative groupings, involving all those concerned. Such an economy would not be aiming at the highest possible demand or at endless expansion of sales. It would have to be capable of adjusting production as required by needs, whether this went up or down. Once demand was satisfied, the situation would call for rethinking of objectives, in an economy orientated towards simple satisfaction of needs. For, example, to take the case of cars, an idea would have to be developed of how many cars were needed. There would never be any bringing in of the state in order to help boost sales.

In 1974, a German paper reported a conversation between two car chiefs who both came to the conclusion that steps should be taken "to overcome the obstacles to car sales at home". In this request they were still bewitched by the logic of private capitalism. If one were to take them through the city streets filled with cars, surely they would begin to understand that a worm's eye view of the economy was not adequate?

Imagine—this would be a revolutionary departure—that representatives of the whole transport industry, the railways, motor transport, car manufacturers, airlines, shipping companies, the Post Office, etc came together with representatives of the users to form an association in order to understand the various diverging points of view. In this endeavour it would be possible and necessary to rise to that level of social development in which a feeling of responsibility for the whole transportation system would be developed. This is otherwise forced on the state. It then has to create a balance between the profitable and unprofitable concerns, the latter, at present, being the railways and the postal services. The state supports their losses in this way, that part of the taxation on the community is diverted to finance them; but the population is not in any meaningful sense aware of the application of these taxes, and so bears collective losses which, if borne individually, would not be borne willingly. It would be a step forward in the matter of social responsibility if the general public could feel itself responsible, in a spirit of solidarity, for the functioning of economic events; even if, at first, this was not for the whole economy, but just for a particular sector, such as that of transport. Such an association would, for that sector, be able to form clear concepts as to how those undertakings operating at a deficit could be carried on, seeing that they were meeting essential needs. This could be done in various ways, for example, by establishing a correct price structure for the various transport services. In other cases, there would be subsidies paid by the profitable concerns which could be wholly or partly passed on in prices.

There are a number of issues in connection with the social adjustment of the economic balance between growing and declining companies. These issues cannot be dogmatically prejudged, but must find their solution in the practical life of the associations. The form of these solutions would, however, depend on the social maturity of the people, in this case transport experts, in the association. We have seen what this means in the case of the new-style companies, in which there are inactive members who have to be carried along by those who are socially active.

Of course, the practical discussions of the solutions to such problems could be treated as seminars in which the level of understanding could be raised, so that people in the industry could develop their awareness of the various possible methods of solution available.

A need-orientated economy forms a higher level compared with the two dominant and rival private and state systems. In the private capitalistic economy demand is met according to the business logic of each company being in isolation. This means that a decline in sales causes losses, redundancies and a decline in profitability. The antiindividualistic collectivist and state-controlled economies try, in the name of socialism or communism, to overcome these difficulties by nationalising the entire economy. This imposes on the state the tasks of determining the amount of production, and of planning investment; this means directing labour—and fixing, and planning, demand. However, this is not a true need-orientated economy; the practice of the eastern countries cannot be seen as being anything else but the rigid control and planning of needs by means of anti-individualistic, state-collectivist economic management. A self-determining economy, on the other hand, cannot but set aside the market principle and replace it by a system which not only retains individualism but develops it still further and makes it socially effective. In it, people would still work for sub-jective motives but they would have to collaborate with one another and maintain a common understanding about economic trends. The technique of forming associations would enable a self-determining need-orientated economy to deal with declining economic tendencies effectively.

To anyone whose eyes are focused solely on present-day relation-ships, much of what has been said may appear to be wishful thinking, and a need-orientated economy may seem both utopian and unreal-isable. However, anyone who familiarises himself deeply with what has been said, particularly about the nature of capital and its various aspects and relates this to the revolutionary events now breaking out throughout the world, can now see that there is a world-wide conflict with materialism, which has become the focal point of human destiny. It is only when man has conquered matter and brought it under his control that, in awakening to personal independence, he can become directly and consciously his true self. It is for this reason that the eco-nomic system is the area in which every nation becomes progressively more and more involved in the material world. The Western world began this. By bringing materialism into its dominant position, in the form of the capitalistic market system, it penetrated matter to the fullest extent in the industrial economy. In so doing, it developed a hasty but continual acceleration of productivity, based on the material power exercised by technological and organisational thinking. This happened because it was recognised that this same thinking was the source of extra productivity, and above all of the first formation of capital—out of which profits would result. This intellectual materialism motivated the Western industrial economy to expand throughout the world. At the same time it developed a social system based on the market, in which the so-called price mechanism governed economic processes.

It is, of course, the natural sciences that provide the intellectual basis of this kind of domination over all economic and social relationships through a mechanistic social system.

It is in the highly sophisticated powers of thought developed by the scientists and used to grasp the content of the outward perceptible world that man experiences something from inside himself as being his established personality. This material consciousness of self is based on intellectual thinking and comes into being quite independently of whether he appropriates economic values to himself, thereby developing the will-power side of his personality.

This materialism, which today is developing its overwhelming power over humanity, nevertheless contains a particular paradox. While on the one hand materialism stirs man to involve himself in the material world, so as to become conscious of himself, on the other hand the historical challenge arises, that in the longer run he begins to find materialism spiritually empty. Thus, the situation arises wherein his consciousness, though strengthened by materialism, subsequently tries to free itself from it. It is precisely when materialism is pushed to the limit that the personal awareness and the self-orientated drive for freedom which it has awakened begins to find it oppressive; it turns freedom into its opposite and hinders further progress. This oppressiveness of matter, its soulless power, awakens a strong desire for something more spiritual and for the will-power to achieve liberation from materialism. Thus, the capitalistic economic system has, in fact, done human development a service. The examples which we have studied illustrate the attempts which have been made to achieve liberation from the old materialistically conceived form of company, and to establish a social system based on mutual collaboration in work. These attempts are motivated by the continual wish to go beyond the self-orientated economy. At all events, they started in this spirit.

There are many signs today that the tendency to move the centre of human gravity away from the material and towards the spiritual is becoming stronger. The spell of the materialist philosophy can only attract people who have lost contact with the spiritual source of all things; in the words of Novalis, they have not soared to a "magic idealism". Hence, they are tempted by the atheistic counterpart of that idealism, which involves the attempt to turn the world into a technological universe, and it is only with this approach that the economy can be given an absolute value, as if it were the whole content of human life. But the social future can only lie in the control of economic values by a society formed into a social organism in which the economy, as a member thereof, is run by organically conceived social forms. These need to be formed by people who are spiritually aware and have the good will to work together with others, for which the ability to empathise will need to be developed. It is only by that power to empathise that the ill effects of materialism upon society can be overcome and replaced by truly human communities. As Rudolf Steiner said, "If men were endowed with nothing more than that which is today allowed to be according to the materialist outlook, then social life would degenerate rapidly towards complete chaos. But in fact, all men and women carry with them an element of ideal thoughts and concepts." This was said seventy years ago, in which time the chaotic element in social life has continually increased. Only by bringing into play our endowment of idealism, can the trend towards chaos be halted. The means by which this can be done have been revealed in our investigation into capital.

C H A P T E R 9

The Motive Force of the Economy

1 Capital as the organising force in the economy

Our investigations into the phenomena and the functioning of capital show that its nature cannot be pinned down by any one single definition, but that it has to be understood through concepts which are flexible.

An important distinction is to be made between the source of the formation of capital, and the intention to form it. This is a matter of the two time-aspects of all *Geist* developments; the original formation of capital deriving from the past is in a polarity with the future function of capital, which will introduce new economic processes. The productive aim of this capital investment is to produce and socially distribute economic goods to the extent that these are needed. The capital in money form put to work for this purpose is given its impulse by the intellectual ideas of technologists and entrepreneurs, which ideas can only be put into practice if they have the necessary money capital available to them. Money capital is "crystallised social *Geist*", that constitutes the organising force in an economy based on the division of labour. This force is produced by the combined effect of all entrepreneurial initiatives. Behind these initiatives money capital is at work; again there are the two time-aspects involved. On the one hand there are the three different ways in which capital is accumulated, and on the other hand there is the way in which the invested capital then affects the social economic organism and its processes.

Capital can be accumulated from three sources. It can come from the formation of free capital, that is, financially separated out as the result of the productivity organised by the *Geist* and put into effect by human labour. In addition to such a fundamental form of capital, savings can be invested, which, of course, result from deferring expenditure out of income. Thirdly, the enterprise may be financed by capital derived from the creation of money, usually in the form of bank credit.

The capital character of all these three kinds of money is at rest, up to the point when it is invested. When that point comes, it is activated into capital proper. Just as there are three kinds of capital formation, so too are there three kinds of capital effectiveness to be distinguished. These can be understood if one calls to mind the productive basis of the enterprise; this is explained more fully in Appendix I. In the construction of a company one finds at its lowest level the materials and forces of nature; at the next level, human labour extends itself over the surface of the natural basis; above that, is the human *Geist* directing the thing as a whole. All economic activity originates in the creative ideas and wills of men, with the aim of meeting human economic needs. The way in which this aim is put into practice is to make a new living cell of the social organism; which is, of course, the enterprise, that has the productive works and plant as its material core.

The enterprise and the material plant incorporate two quite different impulses of the *Geist*. This is revealed in the different *Geist* powers used in management. In the plant, it is the engineer who manages, in the enterprise, it is the entrepreneur. The engineer, as works manager, grapples with nature and fashions its productive forces; whereas the entrepreneur makes use of the product of the plant and introduces it into the social commercial organism, in which the said product is given an economic value and transformed into a commodity. Economic value is a social creation, and results from the combined effects of the operations of all enterprises.

The productive activity of the commercial sector thus involves value productivity, whereas the plant has to do with physical productivity. The direct activity of the plant engineer is focused on the mechanical organising of the combination of natural processes with human labour. Machines are constructed, the work is organised according to what is required, and both consumer and production goods are produced. The objects that the company produces come in in three ways. First, there are the raw and accessory materials, which must be purchased. Also to be purchased are partly manufactured items, components and suchlike, all of which are produced in other plants, a form of the division of labour known as specialisation. Contrasted with these are a particular kind of manufactured product, qualitatively different from other kinds, namely the means of production, and ranked as capital, so that they are appropriately classified as *physical* capital.

Physical capital includes all kinds of means of production. These are goods that are not meant for consumption; hence, from the point of view of the circulation process, they are purchased not with consumer money but with producer money. In this way is constituted a separate production and trading sphere, qualitatively different from the consumer sphere. Because of the need for means of production, a whole army of enterprises has been formed, to manufacture such productive equipment. This has the consequence that a more advanced development of the division of labour is brought about in the economy as a whole, and this needs its own monetary circulation system, set apart from that utilised for consumption purposes; it is to be seen as the capital money circulation sphere, quite distinct from the consumer money circulation sphere. Of course, there will have to be exchanges between these two spheres; in these exchanges lie certain difficult problems of economics, which will not be further considered here.

From these reflections it can be recognised that the economic role of capital is universal. In its threefold conjugation is revealed the key position of capital—in which is embodied the *Geist* that pervades the whole economy. The essence of capital is *Geist*. It works as the managerial *Geist* of entrepreneurs and directors—the two forms of which can, perhaps, be wholly or largely focused on a single person, or else may be exercised collegially. When the *Geist* that leads industry sets natural materials and human labour to work for a purpose, it unites with both nature and labour and infuses them. Now the transfer of the impulse of the *Geist* into the economic system takes place through the medium of money. It is money that is put towards investment and in it the active entrepreneurial *Geist* is crystallised. It is the *Geist* that raises money to the status of capital. It is only outwardly that money capital incorporates matter; its function lies in the social utilisation of the material world for economic ends.

Beneath the sphere of money capital lies the realm of the technological utilisation of natural productivity, in which is found a gigantic world of machinery which takes over or reduces human work. This veritable arsenal of produced means of production and of systems for arranging production acquires its capital character through the *Geist* at work beyond this technical world. The kind of *Geist* involved is that of inventive and scientifically-trained human intellect. The physical capital it creates is materialised *Geist*. If one surveys the whole, capital appears as the all-pervading principle of the economy in the following three propositions which concern three levels of activity of the human *Geist*:

The essence of capital is *Geist*.

Money capital is *Geist* as crystallised by the working group.

Physical capital, which enables production, is materialised *Geist*.

This overview can be further elucidated if one places these propositions in position in the capital side of the three divisions of the enterprise. This can be established through consideration, from the point of view of the economics of the firm, of the various courses of the flow of capital investment.

The capital investment which is necessary when the company is founded divides itself, according to conventional terminology, into fixed and working capital. Fixed capital is used to acquire the means of production, and appears at the start of the company's life. The fixed capital, inasmuch as it is used to acquire the means of production, is a special form of purchase capital, qualitatively speaking. In it —in conjunction with the organising human intellect—the formation of the *Geist*-produced free or original capital is made manifest.

Working capital appears when actual working operations commence and divides itself into two parts; on the one hand it is used to purchase materials and components, etc, and on the other it is expended in money payments that the market economy calls wages. These two divisions of working capital can be called purchase capital and work capital respectively. The author has explained these two concepts more fully in an earlier publication.* Also in that book, a detailed account was given of the question of the distribution of income, which is realised through work capital (conventionally known as wage capital). The sum allocated for incomes forms the money equivalent of goods still in production and not yet put into circulation.

The whole financial input of capital, commonly called "capital investment", embraces all these various kinds of capital. The money capital used for the financing of this investment disappears with its being set to work as fixed capital in the means of production, as working capital in the various goods needed to be purchased, such as raw materials, auxiliary materials, component parts, and so forth, and finally as work capital in being allocated to money incomes. The last-named category is of course transformed into consumer money. Now the market economy misconstrues working incomes to be *costs*, for

---

*"Metamorphosen der Wirtschaft", Jena, 1931, untranslated as yet.—Editor.

the commodity, labour-power; which means that the market economy, through the struggle over wages, conceals the real nature of this process —in spite of its significance for monetary policy. Working incomes (including the entrepreneur's drawings for consumption purposes) form the equivalent money sum as counterpart to the total aggregate of all commodities that are manufactured in the economic process by human labour-power and management skills. The total of incomes and the total of the produced consumer goods interact with each other so as to move towards a balance with each other. The solution of the whole problem of employment depends on this. It is the setting to work of productive capital which forms the essential precondition for the enlistment of people into the economy and for their subsequent employment therein. Following the organic logic of the overall economy, to the performance of all the employees there must always be a corresponding quantity of purchase money of equivalent value, which the goods brought into the circulation process will tend to absorb. This means that whenever people become employed there must first be a capital sum so that they can live until the products are completed and sold. Herein lies the particular circulatory significance of work capital.

Each economic unit forms itself within the economic organism as a whole and therefore, in the overall social organism. Consequently, a key role falls to capital when, in its money form and by means of the money system, it spreads out throughout the system. The capital set to work in a particular economic unit incorporates indirectly the living social forces that shape it. Through the investment of capital an economic enterprise is brought into being. The economic processes it sets in motion spring from the creative conception of the free individual human *Geist*. Those who are to put this creative idea into effect are responsible for the capital invested and for its continuing effect in providing social livelihoods. The form in which it realises itself is the technical plant organisation of commodity production on the one hand and on the other hand the commercial organisation of the financial side of things. The focal point of the whole system is, however, the risk-capital investment. It is this investment which acts as the comprehensive organising force behind all economic processes; and which has to precede all manufacturing and sales processes, it being their motivating force.

The creative mind behind a capital investment embodying a new economic unit is, before anyone else, the bearer of responsibility for the continued existence of the enterprise. (The mind may be that of one individual, or of a collegial group.) It is through this bearer of responsibility that on the one hand the inner workings of the enterprise and its works are organised, and that on the other hand the whole is related to the overall economy—so that the capital investment is subject to the general principles of society. The capital relationship between the individual enterprise and the overall economy extends itself in three directions and into three corresponding areas of the economy:

—on the production side these are,

a) the provision of the means of production,

b) the purchase of production goods (raw and auxilliary materials, etc.) and also various manufactured components, that is, natural materials which have already undergone manufacturing processes.

—on the money side,

the transfer of money in the form of income distribution to everyone working in the company.

All economic happenings are first made possible by the investment of money capital, working through the above functions, which pervade and make up the overall economy. However, various options thereby arise. Increasingly, these days, capital investment is carried out by multi-national combines, all in sharp competition with each other for control of the market. This is done from the market-economy standpoint of profit maximisation. In an article written in 1972 by the financial head of the German company Philips-Holding, Doctor Kandlbinder wrote a veritable hymn to profit. He characterises profit as "pure profit", if it derives from an on-going position of future profitability, in a growing economy. He speaks of a "modern renaissance of profit", as the motor force of the economic dynamic, and so necessary for social welfare. The conception of profit as the engine of economic dynamism contains a partial truth; the author of the article has, of course, experienced in his company how technological developments lead to continual formation of free capital, the nature of which he nevertheless does not and indeed could not correctly understand. He speaks of profit as if it were an in-dependent active principle—indeed he almost personifies it. Profit is, however, simply something which can be used for either good or bad purposes; this depends entirely on the people responsible for managing the capital investment. True profit is not true profit simply because it recurs over a period of time; it cannot be defined on that basis. From the standpoint of the overall economy, the question is, how did this profit come into being?—from the formation of free capital—or did it arise artificially from monopolistic pricing, which can accumulate money privately at the expense of the community? Even if one does consider profit as the engine of the economic dynamic, that does not mean that the essence of profit is defined solely by its producing still more profit when used to finance capital investment. There is also the question how the capital which is invested affects the economy, particularly when it is motivated by profit in the context of the capitalistic market economy.

At present capital investment is made on the basis of the private drive for profit. This results in a competitively-induced over-investment of capital, with ensuing over-production—as seen, for example, in the motor industry. At the same time, this over-investment brings about the premature decapitalisation of still useful means of production, in extreme cases leading to company liquidations, as at present in the building industry. A further consequence of the private competitive capital system is that some branches suffer from a chronic shortage of capital while others, particularly the large multi-nationals, build up their own capital excessively, through their pricing strategy, or can obtain any amount of credit capital. Imbalances of this kind disturb the economy still further when aggravated by continual depreciation of money and the recurrent threat of unemployment. Since the market economy, with its principle of rational egoism, cannot deal with these faults, the community is obliged to tackle them, via the state. This confronts the state with problems it cannot solve since they run counter to its proper function. The state control of capital investment has recently been considered; the demands of the unions for participation have moved in this direction. The state is further pressed both to stabilise prices and at the same time to ensure full employment; but this makes for a particular kind of contradiction. To stabilise the value of money requires a reduction in its quantity, particularly restraining the excessive formation of capital from the creation of credit, which tends to increase the quantity of money and generate inflation. But employment policy requires an increase in jobs which, generally speaking, is only possible through increased capital investment. These demands on the state are misdirected and would be better made on the economy, which, in the main, is alone capable of meeting them—and must in the last analysis do so. However, this cannot be done through an economic system driven by the asocial profit motive; such a system does not develop any objectivity in its capital management, and is forever stumbling against social obstacles. There is no salvation from this situation, until capital is put to work with a full awareness of needs as opposed to consciousness of profits, with its concomitant ignorance of real economic necessity. This is why the economy needs to be orientated towards need and based on social co-operation; only thus can capital fulfil its mission as the organising force of economic life, and form the means whereby economic ends are realised.

2 Capital as the gateway to employment and as the basis for stipulating the quantity of money

The threefold nature of capital reflects the three investment functions — fixed, purchase and work capital. The significance of capital for the overall economy—as its organising force—is seen particularly in work capital, in two ways. Work capital is directly essential, if labour is to be brought to the means of production and to the materials to be processed. It is by setting work capital in motion that the gate is opened through which those wishing to find employment must pass. This employment is put into effect by a labour contract which ties the labour activity to a system of income distribution in which a money payment establishes a social balance between the two. All consumer money is a creation of that portion of the financing capital which is used as work capital—as opposed to that used for the purchase of the means of production and of raw materials. The economic organisational function of work capital—which, in the private economy, forms the basis of income distribution—is to provide the quantity of money necessary for circulation purposes; through this means the distribution of the goods which have been produced to the people needing them is brought about. This is the objective social function of income distribution. The value system is what balances the amount of goods and the amount of money; on the commodity side this works through pricing, and on the money side as abstract value quantities, reflecting the legal right to claim goods. The total value of the total production of goods—the so-called social product—should be in harmony with the exchange function of the circulating quantity of consumer money.

This financing of the total economic sale of goods must, fundamentally, be so arranged that the value of money is not lowered. It can only achieve this aim if all economic processes are brought into reciprocal balance in accordance with the basic organic principle. Such balances are formed, for example, between the quantity of commodities and the quantity of consumer money and also between the formation and utilisation of various kinds of capital. Above all, the prices which are formed must be in harmony with one another throughout the whole economy; the equilibrium is upset if, for example, arbitrary price increases are one-sidedly forced through—as has happened recently with the oil producers.

It is the quantity of money made necessary for circulation purposes which is the precondition for stabilising the value of money. This applies not only to the market economy, but fundamentally to an economy that is self-determining and orientated towards need. If such an economy expands it does not do so because it can only survive by continuous growth, but in response to the needs calculated by the associations. It must, therefore, develop methods of financing investment and of providing purchasing power so that equilibrium is brought about, or at least tends to be brought about, for the whole economy. The difficulty in ensuring this balance is considerable, because the quantity of money is flexible and internally elastic. It is not simply a matter of the number of notes or coin in circulation, because the economic supply is varied by the speed of its turnover. When this speed—the velocity of circulation—changes it is not the number of tokens which alters, yet the effective operation of the system is such as to mean that there will be a change in the total number of exchanges. Some acceleration can be induced or some restraint exercised by varying the amount issued, but as the possessor of money is free to spend it quickly or slowly, the total effective supply cannot be quantitatively fixed. Correcting the number of money tokens in existence does little therefore to control the supply.

Thus the central problem which arises in further pursuing our enquiries into capital and into the monetary system, is how to control the supply of money. Today, this problem is at the centre of economic policy throughout the world. The inability to solve the problems of inflation and of stabilising the value of money are seen in the way that corrective efforts are made. These consist in seeking to reduce an already expanded money supply subsequently, through the fixing of banking deposits and through the increasing of minimum reserve requirements through higher interest rates and credit squeezes. All these are simply corrections after the event, and they cannot really stop the inflationary increase in money; at best they hold it back for a while. Any systematic regulation of the quantity of money must take place in advance rather than afterwards. Beyond a certain point this is only possible through a fully conscious system of capital investment; an essential requirement of this is knowledge of the needs for consumer goods, and arising from that, a conception of the production which it is necessary to undertake. From this the needs for means of production and for raw materials will then be seen. The aim of investment is to produce goods; and the creation of a corresponding quantity of consumer money is needed, as the social instrument for the distribution of the total of goods, the so-called social product. Thus the quantity of money created needs to correspond to the total of goods for sale.

A particular problem affects the monetary system when pricing strategies bring about an increase in the money supply. This happens mainly in the sphere of purchase capital which can be exploited to accumulate a trading capital. This is what happens when, for example, oil producers unilaterally increase their prices. Economically unjustified increases of this kind are estimated to be costing the consumer countries some fifty thousand million dollars annually. One could well consider this as one of the greatest examples of exploitation in economic history. This is why the quantity of money is increasing against the direction of the trade cycle.

The quantity of money that is correct and necessary from the point of view of circulation is not a fixed or well-defined sum. It cannot be mathematically or statistically calculated, since it depends, above all, on the changing velocity of circulation of all forms of money. However, various measures can bring about an indirect control of the money supply. These lie in the conscious planning of capital investment which would have regard to the various types of capital formation in relation to their effects. Quite a different sort of indirect control over the quantity of money can be achieved by structuring it, so that various quantities of money have various expiry dates. That is, the quantity of money is classified according to its expectancy of life. This necessitates that the money tokens put into circulation would have a limited and legally accepted period of validity. This would conform with the unavoidable organic principle that all parts of a living organism must have a finite life-span. It is the neglect of this limitation which brings about the need for such traumatic corrections of the economy. Usually these happen through a continual depreciation of money which, from time to time, brings about a complete currency breakdown. From this point of view, the world-wide depreciation of money can be understood.

This organic law was foreshadowed by Silvio Gesell. Rufolf Steiner dealt with it in his "World Economy". He developed Gesell's materialistic concept into an organic one, by which the expiries would be functionally co-ordinated. Thus, for example, donations to the *Geistes-leben* would, in Steiner's scheme, be made with money near to its expiry date.*

3 The associative system for the transfer of free capital.

We have already looked at the question of the ownership of free capital, which originates in the on-going economic process; and we have shown that the only socially correct solution is to put it into a trust or transfer form of ownership. This is a very topical matter, as it involves the neutralisation of capital power and the prevention of the private misuse of capital. This raises the question of the limitation of the life-span both of consumer money and of capital. In Appendix V, this issue is related to the example of the ownership of the Suez Canal. The question there was, what happens to a capital when its capital function comes to an end in the cycle of the economy. The same question arises when free capital is formed. To whom should it belong? In what way can it best be allocated? How is it to be transferred both legally and with justice? This brings us to those relationships between the three members of the social organism which make it necessary that the product of economic activity must to a considerable extent be passed over into the non-economic spheres of life, and be, as it were, transfused in them; these two spheres being, of course, the *Rechtsleben* and the *Geistesleben*.

The state provides for its employees, and for its administrative buildings by means of enforced contributions in the form of taxes, which take a significant part of the product of the economy without there being any countervalue in return.

The *Geistesleben* as well is at present financed and economically supplied by compulsory payments via the state. This impinges on the freedom of the *Geistesleben*, and needs to be replaced by something more in the spirit of freedom. We can show that a system of donations will be necessary. An organically constituted money system would no longer deal with this matter in a makeshift way, but as an intrinsic part of the system. This must be so arranged as to effect a countervalue-less transfer of part of the money amount constituted by both income and

---

*For reasons explained in his "World Economy", Lecture XII.—Editor.

capital sums. Such a system of systematic donations can only be realised when the social organism is fully deployed in its three parts, each run according to its own particular principles and tasks.

There is a contemporary example of the transfer of free capital, in which the associative character of such a system can be studied. This is provided by a foundation in Bochum, the "Neuguss Verwaltungsgesellschaft", in which twelve companies combined to give their surpluses, essentially free capital, to a trust which devotes part of the funds to people in the *Geistesleben* and invests part in companies. This could be seen as a precursor of the principle of capital administration suggested. The trust encourages the formation of new-style companies similar to the Ahrensburg model, and lays considerable stress on the development of the capabilities needed for the solution of technical, juridical and economic problems. This body makes use of the anthroposophical approach.

Another example is provided by the Donauwörth company of Südstahl. The owner, Frau Tangerding, after her husband's death, made over 90 per cent of the capital to a foundation having the aim of advancing professional and cultural education, with particular stress on the development of understanding vis-à-vis freedom, self-development and responsibility. In order to fulfil these aims, it is enjoined on the foundation to make particular provision for the re-training of young offenders, including educating them in art and culture. This example therefore shows how the system of providing for cultural development may be started in a small way. In this case this is done wholly by a private initiative. A systematic financial provision for the *Geistesleben* would hardly otherwise be possible. Free social initiative can found the sort of institution in which capital can be properly administered. The new-style companies we have considered all have the right spirit to embark upon the creation of such institutions.

4 *Freedom the creative force and community spirit the structuring force in the economy.*

Freedom is the great force shaping human life on this planet. The part it has played in shaping economic life is fundamentally incalculable, although it is possible to appreciate the quantitative changes made at a given point in time. These quantitive changes have grown in importance as time has gone on. Since the beginning of our present time reckoning, that is, since the beginning of the age of freedom, it is the liberated *Geist* that has become the source of economic developments; whereas in earlier times these were directed by priestcraft, or by hereditary rulers. Thus, the modern economy has been built up by the free powers of human self-awareness. The full self-orientated enjoyment of these free powers was sanctioned by the philosophy of liberalism, to the point of making it the basic economic principle. However, this has brought about a rather deceptive scheme of things; the incalculabilities of which have increased to the extent that the self-orientated market principle is less and less able to control things. As a result, there are continually growing maladjustments in the spheres of capital invest- ment, of pricing, of employment, of international trade and of the monetary system. The helplessness of the market system in the face of these uncontrollable economic developments has obliged governments to interfere in economic affairs or, as in the east, to take over the econ- omy completely; there a complete state economy has been forcibly brought into being, so that all economic processes take place within it. This is supposed to make them calculable so that needs and their sat- isfaction can be fully estimated in advance. Thus by eliminating free- dom, more calculability is brought about.

But for the west the question remains how to achieve an economic system in which human freedom can be maintained—since it is rec- ognised that this is the most vital of human values. However, this vital value can only be realised if it is raised above its lower, self-orientated form. Only then can it develop the necessary social forms for the econ- omic system. It is because this has not been done that increasingly great distortions have developed in all aspects of economic life. So as to con- trol them economists are always trying to make economic trends cal- culable. They hope to do this by means of mathematics or graphs; latterly, econometrics has become a separate science. However, its sub- ject matter only yields information about the past. It is indeed possible to extrapolate from this information, i.e. to assume that past trends will continue into the future, but this inevitably leaves human creativity out of the calculation.

This temptation to quantify economic trends, and to "flatten out" the monetary processes which underly them, has become compulsive in this era of thinking based on the natural sciences. This kind of thinking seeks to provide for all human relationships by the laws of dimension, number and weight. When it is applied to economics it has a completely deadening effect. Only the material substructure of economic activity can be made calculable in this way—which, of course, every works management does. But in the economy there are natural and human incalculabilities.* The supply and discovery of industrial raw materials is quite unpredictable; so is the continually changing supply of labour power—since the will to work changes, as indeed do its financial claims. Equally unpredictable is any commerce conducted in freedom; this affects the use of money, and because of the subjective elements involved, monetary movements are particularly impossible to predict. Where there is freedom there is no calculability. (In his youth, the author found this out the hard way when, in an unpublished study, he attempted to find a way of making monetary processes calculable. After many attempts this was abandoned.)

The freedom which has taken possession of the economy has been proclaimed by liberals as being a basic human right, hence as the basic principle of the economy. The problem, however, is to harness freedom to the service of economic and social requirements. The principle on which the economy needs to be based is not quite freedom as conventionally conceived. Certainly, individual economic actions are free actions; but powers of social control must arise out of them. Such powers cannot, however, spring from the lower, self-orientated form of freedom. The economy requires a general and detached sense of the common interest, and it is this which should be at work in a fully comprehensive system of associative social structures. This sense of the common interest is vital for real freedom. An economic system founded on it and on economic and social necessities would be able to dispense with state help and thus relieve governments of tasks which they cannot and are not meant to solve. The whole point of such an economy would necessarily be to satisfy human needs. By contrast, in an economy in which satisfying need is only brought about by pursuing personal aims, talk of meeting real needs, such as emanates from both economists and businessmen, is just an illusory gloss on the self-orientated system.

In a self-determining economy created by an objective sense of common interest and orientated towards the satisfaction of needs, capital can acquire the position due to it as the organising force thereof. It is precisely capital which is on the one side a product of and on the other side an instrument for the free human *Geist* in the economy.

---

*See Schumacher's concept of "meta-economics", in "Small is Beautiful".

Capital sprang out of the *Geist* in a twofold and dynamic form; this happened once and for all when technical intelligence brought about the creation of labour saving means of production and the organisation of the work force. With them appeared, quite passively, the original formation of capital; in its other aspect, the active called-into-life form of capital came into being when free human decisions about investment started true economic processes going. (An active capital is constituted when neutral sums of accumulated money are used to realise a creative economic idea.) These two capital forms being creations of the human mind can only attain their correct form when they are realised out of the spiritual force of a common will. In this way the economy takes shape through the universal development of social bodies working in association. In the last analysis—as Robert Owen knew well—genuinely-meant social relationships, if they are based on something more than just a purely rational understanding, constitute the greatest factor making for economic productivity, and thereby the principle source of free capital formation.

Appendices

APPENDIX 1
THE NATURE OF CAPITAL

The essence of capital, as founded on the Geist;
how its manifestations are best explained in flexible concepts

This appendix is devoted to a fundamental exploration of the entire phenomenon of capital. It will explain how, in the different forms or manifestations of capital, an underlying unity is none the less to be observed, and how these different forms relate to one another and form a totality, given their location and significance in the overall economic structure.

Leaving the physical means of production—which make up capital in its factual or real form—on one side, let us first examine capital in its money form.

Current pragmatic thinking considers any sum of money as capital. But these are really nothing more than sums of money, which may have been secreted out of various sources to form what may be thought of as money at rest. But capital can be actuated out of these inactive sums, which form a sort of link between the past and the future cycles of economic activity.

The economy is continually in movement, and no part of the system can therefore be understood without being considered in relation to that movement; this must apply to capital, as it does to all economic categories. Capital cannot be understood in a stationary sense, as an isolated, arrested fact; it may appear to be like this in its money form, but this will only be the case if capital is wrongly defined as mere money. This is true even when that money derives from profits.

Looking therefore at the living stream of economic events, rising in the past, and flowing through the present into the future, it can in any instant appear to have no movement; but really its future course is already being set, as it is acted upon by human decisions. As we utilise this vantage point to see what capital is, we can form a flexible concept of it and its manifestations, which will come as near as can be to the actual socio-economic process. In the flow of economic events over time are seen three stages of its dynamic, in which three stages the processes of capital unfold and take various forms.

a   The "past tense" of capital

What we are considering here is the original "primeval" source of capital accumulation. We have already become acquainted with the particular, once-and-for-all form which this took when thought led to portions of the money in circulation being set aside. The capital which freely appeared in this way is the quintessential form. It takes its capital character from the product, expressed in money, of the impact upon the economy of creative human thought. We have already seen that this form of capital embodies the origin in thought of all economic life. The money capital appearing out of consciousness in this way takes on the character of a materially-stamped *original capital*. As such, it separates itself out from the economic process and stands in this form as capital which is—as yet—independent of its subsequent application. All subsequent capital activities are shaped by the free will of human decisions. However, this creation and accumulation of capital brings about not only economically and properly needed formations of capital, but also the extortion of profits formed by market power, and with this the form we have called factitious capital.

Briefly summarised, the money forms of capital formation which are genuinely justified and conform to economic necessity are as follows:

1. the free and primary formation of capital in the sphere of production, that is, the formation of profit in the true sense.

2. the voluntary formation of capital in the consumer sphere, from savings and not from profits.

3. the arbitrary formation of capital through the creation of money in the financial sphere. This can be considered as freely created in counterpart to the primary formation of capital. It is usually in the form of credit creation by the banks. The danger here is that any increase in the quantity of money which is not justified by some real development would upset the balance of the economy, increase

prices, incomes, and capital sums, and lead to inflation. This would be an unjustifiable form of capital formation, which would hinder proper circulation.

We can see three further general forms of unjustified capital formation:

1. the formation of capital through pricing policy, so that prices of goods are increased, leading to what is called "forced savings" on the part of consumers.

2. the formation of capital through the withholding of necessary income formation, for example through paying inadequate wages. Marx considered this to be the primary form of capital accumulation.

3. the formation of capital through unreal and improper profit formation resulting from the sale of factitious goods such as land and various types of property, including factitious capital as already discussed. All this is linked with the speculative accumulation of money capital, which has the effect of impoverishing others by dislocating capital from its proper function.

A further aspect of the accumulation of capital for the purpose of share or currency speculation—which becomes a curious "means of production" for the profitable investment of dislocated money sums—is dealt with in Appendix 3. All these improper and counter-economic capital formations are in most cases effected as a consequence of the concentration of economic power. We have become acquainted with a whole series of such egoistically-motivated and monetarily-disequilibrating capital formations in Chapter 1, à propos of the analysis of profit situations.

Conventionally speaking, all forms of capital at the point of formation are lumped together, whether justified or not; and at this point, they are in a condition of rest. In order to understand this, and indeed to put it right, we must consider the significance of this position of functionless capital sums at rest more closely.

b   The "present tense" of capital

In all cases of accumulations of functionless capitals at rest, one finds them to be in a sort of no-man's-land between the birth process of capital formation and their future capital application. This no-man's-land of passively-existing capital cannot be defined in terms of any particular time dimension—the time spent in this condition can vary quite considerably. What we are considering is a situation which is neutral, that is, in which accumulated capital is neutral in respect to its future use. Such a functionless and inert sum of money could perhaps be used for priming the pump of industrial production; or it could equally well be applied to consumption, perhaps for the satisfaction of ordinary human material needs, perhaps in the financing of the *Geistesleben*, or of governmental activities. In these latter cases, the passive money capital does not find its fulfilment as a productive capital in the economic sense. The realisation of a capital idea by means of the utilisation of inert money sums can come about when at some time or other it serves as the means of developing economic productivity and is transformed into entrepreneurial capital. In the development of modern economic life the gathering together of money capital has been the starting point for the foundation of economic power centres; this, of course, was the focal point of the view which Karl Marx took of the capitalistic economy, and he considered the accumulation of capital to be the central issue in the critique of political economy. However, this forms not only the emotional but also the factual basis for the gathering up of functionally inert money sums as capital, so that the amount of capital which is accumulated is in some relation to the amount of economic and social power wielded.

Objectively speaking, the conception of a possible economically productive investment of neutral capital leads to the idea of a *prospective* capital, that is to say, a capital with a purpose in mind, as opposed to capital at the stage dealt with above, when it is has been born in the course of the economic process. Through it, new production is brought about, with ancillary service and trading functions, so as to develop the economy. If popular usage, because of these facts, calls large sums of money "capital", this is indeed a symbolic connotation for a potential or prospective—that is to say, investment-orientated—application of neutral capital in the form of accumulated monies.

c. The "future tense" of capital

Sums of money that lie functionless, at rest, are available for any use.

In particular, they can be applied for economic purposes. As these sums of capital money are expended, they lose their capital character.

As mentioned, part of accumulated neutral capital is absorbed in private personal consumption, which in this case is supported not by income from work but from various asset values. Private consumption enables existence and enriches life, by meeting the demand for culture and for luxuries. However, neutral capital can also be consumed productively, for example in the *Geistesleben*, in social life or in government. Above all it can be used for the productive development of economic life. The concept of investment capital is commonly applied very widely to include both productive and consumption investment, covering not only economic productive capital but also such things as schools, churches, government offices and sports facilities.

Whether the purpose is economic or non-economic, the act of application decapitalises capital. Any productive application is "value-creating", whether the values created be economic or non-economic —the latter comprising social and cultural values. However only economic value creation creates material values in the form of material objects or of practical outward services, which directly or indirectly contribute to the physical movement of men or goods, or which perform necessary auxiliary tasks in the ensemble of economic activities.

A clear differentiation should be made between i) economic value creation, which is based on the polarity between *Geist* and matter, and which takes its shape from a social organic economic system, and ii) the various forms of non-economic productivity. In spite of the way in which the economy intertwines with cultural, social and political affairs, this distinction can nonetheless be made.

d   The character of economic activities in the strict sense

Mind is set in opposition to matter or nature; and the character of economic activities is formed by this opposition. Thought is applied to nature, to raw materials, in order to move them, or by work processes, change their form into something else. This is done in order to survive, and in order to develop and progress. So all sorts of activities are carried on by the mind, designing and making things, and moving them from one location to another, and of course directing all this. Such activities can only be realised through human effort, which is a basic impulse of mankind, for the reasons outlined earlier. Effort involves both thought mankind, for the reasons outlined earlier. Effort involves both thought and physical work in the strict sense, the latter being necessary to execute the plans which thought has conceived. Even the simplest physical work contains elements of thought. Even in the most elementary task, the worker has to think about the effect of what he is doing.

Thus, we can distinguish three productive forces:

1. The impersonal substances of nature.

2. The ensemble of physical working activities. These activities stand socially between nature and thought.

3. The role of thought which directs and organises all three.

These three productive forces are dependent on each other for their productivity. No particular one of them can take precedence over the other two. No production could occur without the resources of nature; without work no plans could be carried through; and without thought there would be nothing creative to set the work in motion. If any one of these three forces fails, the system then grinds to a halt.

We need to subdivide the activities of the mind still further if we are to understand the nature of capital fully. Thought pursues the following three aims:

1. Controlling and directing the overall economic activity—the entrepreneurial function.

2. Organising the labour force.

3. Technological design and construction of the means of production.

Bearing this subdivision in mind, let us look at the various manifestations of capital.

The entrepreneurial function, the organising function and the technological function together comprise the role of thought in the development of the economic system. The mind is the powerhouse of all this development—indeed, mind is capital.

It is mind which determines the precise way in which nature will be worked upon; this is the trinity of economic productivity, from which the mind has developed all economic forms. The basic nature of capital is thus embodied in mind; it is mind which determines how capital shall be efficient. This source is wholly non-material. Both its power and its "size" are non-material. Beethoven's musical genius was in no sense material—yet it was in no mere figurative sense his capital. The fact that the exploitation of this capital, in the publishing and distribution of his music, was reserved for later generations, does not affect this point. Of course, economics is not concerned with the composition of music, but only with their actual distribution in society; as one would expect given the role of economic activity in securing material existence on this planet. The scope of economic activity is indeed to bring production and consumption into relation, and it is natural that consumption should include all forms of the transformation of matter into objects capable of sustaining man's physical existence. But one could even say that the purpose of economic system is to enable matter to become thought, and more, spirit as well.

In this connection it should be noted that thought processes are not like those of economic life at all. Some people have tried to claim that the mind of the teacher, in speaking to the pupil, is, so to speak, modifying the airstream, which the pupil then consumes. All that is really happening is that the pupil is simply understanding what the teacher says. No economic productive process is taking place here; simply what is going on is communication between minds. Minds are not consumed.

The willpower of the entrepreneur is expressed in his thought, and so becomes his capital, the dynamic of which he directs. Moreover, the physical means of production which serve the enterprise, themselves owe their origin to thought, both on the part of the technologists and on the part of the plant managers who organise actual production. All these thought forms are necessary if production is to take place.

Thought therefore constitutes capital of the first degree. Capital of the second degree has taken a money form. We must also subsequently go into capital of the third degree, but more of that presently.

e. Capital of the second degree: the money form of productive capital

In discussing the accumulation of sums of money to form neutral money capital, we distinguished three types—free capital formation, capital from savings, and capital from created money. All of these are neutral in the sense that they are not as yet earmarked for any specific purpose. They constitute potential capital for productive purposes, and only receive their true capital character at the instant of their application to some productive economic project.

The entrepreneur needs money capital. He cannot achieve his aims without it. As an entrepreneur he does not own either the raw materials or the means of production; these have to be acquired. Similarly, he must hire labour. Major social actions are necessary, as a result of the division of labour in society. Only through social arrangements can the three productive forces be brought together under the control of the entrepreneur. These arrangements are negotiated through the impersonal medium of money. Money opens the door to the forces of production, through the purchase of materials and of the means of production, and through money advances which are negotiated as wages and salaries for all the people working in the enterprise.

Seen from the money side of things, the conventional economic theory of the firm has hit upon an analysis of capital. According to this view, it is divided into fixed capital, for fixed assets, and circulating capital, out of which incomes are paid and production materials purchased. Marx's distinction between constant and variable capital is better; he includes in the latter only the capital for wages, the capital fund out of which wages and salaries are paid. The best division to employ is that between *purchase capital** and *work capital**. Under the former will be included not only fixed plant and machinery, but also the purchase of all necessary materials.†

The power of disposal over money capital is normally—and from the economic point of view, sensibly—arranged by the entrepreneur through the borrowing of neutral capital. Self-financing from profits, whether proper or otherwise, and government subsidy are not normal methods of capital procurement.

The acquisition of money capital enables the inner capital quality of the entrepreneur—in a word, his *thought*—to be transferred into the medium of money. This capital quality which thus appears implants itself in the raw materials and in the means of production purchased with the money capital. Through the investment of purchase capital these physical materials and equipment acquire the quality of physical capital. However, income formation, on the other hand, which is financed by work capital, should not be commercialised in the same way. Out of it is paid the incomes of workers and other employees, and it constitutes the true preparation of income.†

Before its social use, money capital was neutral, unbespoke; now it is invested in economic processes it is realised, or rather becomes concrete in character. Applying it productively makes it into the basis for fulfilling the future aims of the enterprise, as conceived

---

* See glossary.—Editor, English edition.

† See the author's work, *Die Metamorphosen der Wirtschaft*, Jena, 1931. (Unfortunately this work has not yet been translated into English.—Editor.)

by thought, so as to enable the production of goods and economic services.

Thus, through the economically productive investment of money capital, two dimensions of value are brought together, the past in the form of neutral capital and the future in the form of the productive investment, in which a previous and a future value are together condensed. This manifold conglomeration of value becomes, moreover, the physical productive capital which lies at the basis of all economic activity, known as the means of production.

f Capital of the third degree: manufactured means of production

By this is meant all the plant and various types of means of production which were not in existence at all before economic production started. It is the creative entrepreneurial function which makes these items capital and gives them their value, in terms of economic productivity. At the same time, these means of production have their own capital character resulting from the intellectual application of the technologists who design and arrange them. However, this capital character cannot be directly accorded to the facilities constructed for non-economic purposes, such as for example school buildings. These facilities are of course very useful, but not in the economic dimension, and so cannot be classed as productive capital. Naturally, the concept of usefulness applies to created values employed elsewhere than in the economic sphere, but cultural and governmental assets cannot and should not be conceived as possessing economic productivity. So to do would be to obliterate the critical distinctions between the three parts of the social organism. All the same, the investment of money capital in facilities needed for the *Geistesleben*, for cultural purposes, or in social or governmental life, is undoubtedly fruitful in the broadest sense.

My pen-holder can be useful in each of the three spheres of the social organism. Equally well, buildings and so forth can be of service not only for economic but also for state or cultural ends. Of course the production of both pen-holders and buildings results from economic processes, from the combined work of managers and workers. They both start as commodities, irrespective of where they are used or consumed, in the economic sphere or elsewhere. Here we confront the question of consumption, which needs to be differentiated in two ways. It can generally be said that each and every humanly-needed act of consumption is useful. All commodities are called into being to be consumed. This applies not only to the satisfaction of immediate human needs—for food, clothing, shelter, transport, recreation, but also to what is needed by the *Geistesleben*, or for social or governmental purposes. All the goods produced for the non-economic sphere of life are consumed in the same way as economic consumption goods. Both kinds of consumption are recognised by the fact that each constitutes an end in itself. However, another type of consumption, namely the consumption of the means of production, is different, in that it reproduces itself. Though capital goods are made in the same way as other commodities—consisting of matter as worked upon by the human spirit—they are then used in economic production in such a way that though they are consumed, this is not the end of the matter. They reproduce themselves in their capital value. Having been advanced in the form of purchase capital and work capital, they subsequently retrieve themselves in the economic cycle; and it is in this way that they reproduce their own money capital value.

The means of production thus have a unique position among the forces of economic production. Since the fifteenth century they have come to play the leading role in modern economic life. The planet is literally covered with industrial equipment and machinery of every possible kind. There is specialised generating plant enabling energy taken from the earth to be used to supplement physical human effort. Machine tools have taken over functions previously undertaken by human labour. All these means of production have been developed to reduce the material amount of human labour, and to make it more productive. The ability to do all this came from the power of the intellect, through science and technology, opening up the hidden potentialities of matter, and creating not only the world of machinery but also developing the organisation of social labour to the maximum degree of productivity. In all this technology and organisation we can discern productive capital of a higher order, that which produces free capital, that can properly be seen as surplus value.*

The three essential economic productive forces combine with the investment of the appropriate money capital to set these productive

---

* Wilken does not refer to Marx directly here, but the use of the Marxist term seems apt. See the glossary.—Editor, English edition.

capital goods up. This complicates the dynamic of production—otherwise busy making consumer goods—since these same forces are now put to work making the means of production, requiring a specific allocation of money capital to this end. (The physical character of the manufactured means of production is expressed in the term "physical capital".)

The peculiarity of the capital applied to the means of production lies in this; had it been used for the production of consumer goods, these would go directly from the sphere of production to the sphere of consumption, and be used up, but commodities which become means of production stop and turn away from this journey. Productive goods are turned back into the sphere of production, where, while they are indeed consumed, they reproduce themselves, in that they retrieve the money capital put into the economic cycle, and generate free capital.

The way in which capital goods are turned back was studied by the Austrian economist Böhm-Bawerk, who commented: "It is conceivable that less capital (or productive power) enters into the arena of consumption than was originally intended. Many commodities can obviously be used in a variety of ways. This enables goods—which are ready or nearly ready for consumption—to be turned back to a higher level. For example, corn, instead of being used for food, can be used for seed, or in a distillery, wood can be used for heating a smelter instead of an oven, iron for making machines instead of park railings, and so on."*

Economic resources can only be used to manufacture production equipment at the expense of manufacturing consumer goods. However, foregoing these consumer goods enables an increase in productive capacity, which manifests itself indirectly in the economising of labour and the formation of free capital, which, as we have remarked, can be considered to be true profit.

The means of production, as creations of the human *Geist*, have a productive force of their own. Their introduction enables the highest form of the division of labour to be established. This happens in such a way that the means of production make a detour in the course of industrial activity, turning away from the straightforward and simple type of production directed towards consumption. The means of production have constituted an independent realm in economic life, formed by the turning back of productive forces. It is precisely in this

---

* From *Kapital und Kapitalzins* II, p. 146, Jena 1921.

detour that we can see the reciprocal relationship between members of society and the social interdependence of economic life. The social principle of reciprocal interchange of services was seen by Kropotkin as a higher basis for economic life than egoism. The satisfaction of needs, rather than conflict, needs to be the main motivation of social production in the future.

The competitive market principle led to the establishment of the independent sector of the means of production and the production goods associated with it. This raises the question, how the circulation of money is thereby affected. It is from this side that the over-production of capital goods can be tackled. In Volume II of this work* it will be shown why the capital goods sector needs its own special monetary system.

Now it is wrongly supposed today that the economy can only be carried on if there is continuous economic growth.† In order to achieve this growth, capital is needed, and the competitive market system causes a struggle to obtain this capital. Political influence is brought to bear to realise profits which are not really justified; and attempts are made to add to the rate of free capital formation, causing "over-heating" of capital goods production. Large-scale enterprises have developed, whose main concern is to eliminate competition so as to secure for themselves the maximum amount of capital—a development criticised by Galbraith. This tendency has the effect of crowding out the true entrepreneur from management. As an American sociologist, C. Wright Mills, pointed out, "A genius at the head of an undertaking is an impossibility. If he dies, the business flops." Thanks to this trend, the business loses its individual character, being guided by impersonal and highly sophisticated management techniques. The aim has become growth without limit. The independent entrepreneur has to go, and his place has to be taken by the professional manager, with his manage-ment science and his systematic training. This has far-reaching consequences.

The powers in the means of production, which have been "captured" from the powers of nature, are in themselves, so to speak, "neutral". If, as a consequence of private ownership of the means of production, they are privately appropriated, then positions of great power are created, for which many people will be motivated to compete. As this power

---

* *Das Kapital und das Geld*, Schaffhausen 1981.

† For reasons of space, the ensuing section has had to shortened.—Editor.

becomes technocratic in nature, and therefore impersonal, the use of the powers of nature becomes completely dominated by a particular school of thought—the materialist one. This tendency needs to be arrested, since it would eventually lead to a negation of all other values.

It is in fact this very tendency in the economic system which has brought about the revolt of the communist countries, although they do not by any means realise what it is they are struggling against. Their revolt is in fact subconsciously directed, but is channelled into blind hatred. This is because Marx could only see the surface symptom—the distorted condition of capital—without understanding the real nature of capital.

g The intellectual essence of capital

At first sight it may seem odd—particularly to anyone trained in the natural sciences—that the essence of capital lies in the power of the human mind.

Yet intellectual power can be seen in the initiatives which have to be taken by the managers, in the creative technological aptitudes essential if any capital equipment is to be designed, in the organisational and leadership abilities without which no work force could ever be organised. The means of production owe their very reality to the fact that the human mind has flowed into them; otherwise they would be no use to the entrepreneur at all.

Herbert Gross placed what he called "intellectual capital"—to which he devoted considerable attention—alongside the three traditional factors of production, land, labour and capital, as a sort of "fourth factor". This is, of course, a confusion of the truth. Capital itself is the embodiment of the intellectual factor to which Gross was referring. There could be no free capital, no economically productive neutral money capital, without this factor.

h Capital terminology in the firm

Finally we ought to make a brief examination of the manifestations of productive capital within the firm. Conventionally, a distinction is

made between the ownership of the material means of production
—which constitutes physical capital—and ownership of money capital.
Money capital includes not only the cost of financing physical capital
but other value-quantities as well. In limiting the concept of physical
capital to the means of production, it is thus made to coincide with
what is called fixed assets within the firm; of course, in addition to
these fixed assets there is also working capital, divided into work*
capital and purchase capital. Marx counterposed work capital—which
he called variable capital—against physical capital, in the broadest sense
—which he called constant capital, including in it not only the means
of production but purchase capital in addition.

Purchase capital would, of course, include the raw and auxiliary
materials necessary for current production for sale. (The concept of
purchase capital can be widened to include the purchase of the fixed
assets—as in my "Metamorphosen der Wirtschaft". This is of course
a matter of definition.) Naturally, the fixed assets do not in any
way correspond with the nominal capital shown in the balance sheet.
They take their money value from the original purchase of the means
of production, which value remains to represent the company's stock
of fixed assets. Its original value is shown separately in the accounts
from the depreciation applied to the fixed assets.

Thus we have traced the dynamic connection that runs from the
past—i.e. from the initial financing of the means of production, by
means of savings, free capital and the creation of money—to the dispersal of the productive capital in use. Between the two the present
aspect interposes itself, in the form of the current value of the capital
in use at a particular point in time, which could be called the capital
stock. It is the same thing as the actual productive capital of the enterprise. At any time its real balance sheet value can be ascertained. But
it can also be represented in a factitious way. This happens particularly with the capital companies, in the form of the nominal capital
which, it is taken for granted, persists. In big business these separate
accounting valuations of the capital stock, which represent the
company's capital, have become, through their private ownership,
the instruments of economic power.

---

*See Glossary.—editor, English edition.

APPENDIX 2
MARX'S FALLING RATE OF PROFIT

Karl Marx developed this theory on certain assumptions, among which surplus value, and the accumulation of profit out of capital, played a decisive part. Marx, being a supporter of the labour theory of value, divided the capital essential to economic production into constant and variable capital. The latter includes only the capital advanced for wages. Constant capital comprises the fixed assets and plant capital. It was the variable capital which Marx held to represent the crucial cost factor. It was to him the source of surplus value.* Moreover, Marx was aware of the labour-saving effects of machinery, and of the tendency for workers to become redundant when technical equipment was put in their place. Hence it followed that the plant tends continually to grow in size—therefore so does the constant capital. But variable capital is thereby economised. The combined effect of these two opposite tendencies means that the *proportion* of variable capital to constant capital declines. Both may grow, but the variable capital grows more slowly. Hence, the formation of surplus value cannot but grow at a slower rate than the growth of the total capital. That is the law of the tendency of the falling rate of profit.

We see the Marxist account of the formation of surplus value as being like the forced saving which can be extracted from consumers by excessive prices, or from workers by inadequate wages. Certainly there was something like this in the contemporary situation which Marx witnessed, which he extrapolated into being generally applicable to all capital formation under the capitalistic system. Marx's passion for social justice, and his campaign against human exploitation, led him to

---

* Marx thought it was not even possible for wages to rise above their "value in exchange"—i.e. the "cost" of keeping the worker in existence.—Editor.

lose sight of the actual source of capital formation. Things might have been otherwise, if he had not seen Hegel's idealistic dialectic as "standing on its head" and tried to turn it into a materialist dialectic instead. By thus burying mind in matter, he was bound to miss the fact that it is mind which is the whole essence of capital.

It is worth noting that both the author's theory and that of Marx start from human labour. In both cases the technologist and the managerial organiser are brought into association with capital formation. But the source of capital formation is entirely different. The one bases capital on the saving of human labour and the other on the exploitation of human labour, in conjunction with the replacement of labour by machinery. But Marx sees this substitution of labour by *Geist* as leading not to capital formation but to exploitation, so that the workers made redundant by technology become members of the "industrial reserve army". Marx generalised from a particular historic situation and deduced the whole nature of capital from an over-supply of underpaid labour. However, capital formation must really be considered as an intrinsic aspect of economic processes.

APPENDIX 3
CURRENCY SPECULATION

The abuse of money in exchange speculation

When an increase in money supply is unrelated to the real needs of the economy, the circulation of money is disturbed and its management disorganised. If one currency zone increases money supply in a way that is inflationary, i.e. economically unjustified, it brings about a debt situation vis-à-vis other currency zones. For example, the dollar inflation associated with the Vietnamese War put the dollar area into debt in relation to other currencies. This brought about currency speculation on a major, world-wide scale. The dollar inflation of 1973 looked like this: an estimated sum of about eighty thousand million dollars was floating around, looking for a chance to turn a profit. A way of finding such a profit lay in the purchase of currencies which, while highly valued, had their exchange rates fixed under the Smithsonian Agreement of 1971. Under this agreement, central banks were obliged to intervene with supporting purchases to maintain the fixed parities, should one of the participating currencies tend to sink in value relatively to the others. In 1973 the Deutsche Bundesbank, the German central bank, was obliged to make such purchases. Between February 1st and 10th, some twenty thousand million dollars flowed into West Germany and were taken up by the Bundesbank at an unrealistically high rate of exchange. When the dollar was subsequently devalued by about 10 per cent, the Bundesbank thereby lost over 10 thousand million marks on its total dollar holdings. The way in which this influx of hot money had gathered a killing could be seen later when the demand for marks by currency speculators taking their profit led to stocks of notes being exhausted, and new stocks having to be specially printed.

At the end of 1971, an agreement had been signed by the finance ministers of ten countries in the Smithsonian Institute in Washington by which a new set of exchange rates was established. This involved devaluing the dollar. The American President, in a burst of exuberance, described this agreement as a milestone in world financial history. A result of it was that the Deutsche Bundesbank's assets with foreign banks were down-valued by some seven thousand million marks, and further losses were also borne, so that the Bundesbank could make no dividend to the German Government, thus bringing about a loss to the German taxpayer.

These events are mentioned in order to point out the essentially anomalous nature of the currency markets, in which a given currency is treated as if it were a commodity. Money is intended to be used as a means of purchasing, a means of lending and on occasion a means of making gifts. Instead it is bought cheap and sold dear, which is a denial of its true function. This is only possible because of the existence of separate nation-states whose individual economies are cut off, one from another. This poses the practical necessity of bringing the various national currencies into an economically correct value relationship with each other. Differences in the value of various currencies do not arise out of the true function of money, and it will not be possible to relate currencies correctly except in relation to this true function. Now the right parities can only be arrived at when individual currencies are not disturbed by increases in money which are inorganic. Disequilibrium is bound to result from these increases: bad money disrupts the whole economic structure. The currency speculations of 1973 had their root in the dollar inflation and its world-wide effects.

Let us look at some facts concerning this unnatural dollar inflation, and that part of it which became transferred into West Germany. The Deutsche Bundesbank Monthly Review showed a German export surplus for 1972 of 20.2 thousand million Deutsche Marks, of which 2.5 thousand million DM was accounted for by trade with the United States. Dollar balances also accrued from the export surpluses of other countries where these were settled in this currency. The US balance in the same year showed a deficit of 65 thousand million dollars. In addition, deflated dollars came into Germany and were used to acquire German industrial companies. (Only part of the American deficit mentioned above was accounted for by the trading deficit.) The flooding of the money markets of the world with dollars had further causes as well—for example, the tremendous cost of maintaining the war in Vietnam. To a considerable extent, the costs of this war were met by the creation of money. The excess money thus created came out of the war sectors of production through the normal processes of circulation, and was unable to find profitable employment in America, the productive capacity of American industry being already stretched to the limit. The extent of this pool of hot money was confirmed by the results of an enquiry made by the US Tariff Commission, according to which multinational companies and banks had liquid funds of some 268 thousand million dollars, available at short term. The liquid assets of the multinationals were in fact something like twice the size of the entire currency reserves held by the world's central banks and the international monetary institutions, according to the Commission's calculations. Thus even a small number of the multinationals would be able, if they wished, to speculate against currencies to the extent that the central banks would be crippled in their function of regulating the economy. In addition to the multinationals, a further factor in the weakening of the dollar was the volume of payments to the oil-supplying companies. This, it must be supposed, added to the creation of money, which would be likely, given the circumstances of trade, in which massive purchases were taking place without there being a compensating counter-production. Thus a flood of dollars came into the oil producing companies, mainly in the Middle East. To some extent these were put into construction. Saudi Arabia, the leading producer, had however no proper economic outlet for this money, and so sought to purchase more stable currencies with the dollar, thus engaging in speculation against the dollar.

The destructive force of this excessive bidding up of currencies is caused, at root, by the creation of money quantities over and above what is economically justified. This can only be adjusted, once it has happened, through the increase of prices. Artificially fixed currency parities conflict with this adjustment, and as a result countries with strong currencies suffer an influx of hot money from countries with weaker currencies. This influx is maintained by the speculators who trade on the differences between the values of the various national currencies.

In view of these facts, we are brought to the conclusion that the perversion of money into a tradeable commodity must tend to have a destructive effect on the economic system. This is unavoidable under the market-economy, in which the balance between the different currencies is arrived at through the working of the profit motive, so that money is commercialised and displaced from where it is needed in the economy. Economic analysis shows that, unless inflation is tackled at its root, the only way in which the market can adjust to the inflation is to increase prices. In this way, the value of the total stock of goods available is brought into line with total purchasing power, so that the two are in balance. First of all, this balance may thus be brought into a false position by currency speculation—as we have seen, an empty and economically pointless activity. Secondly, it can happen that the disturbance is so great or continuous as to prevent balance being more than partially achieved.

The reason why currency speculation obstructs the normal equilibrating process, why this process can only accomplish itself through price increases, is that the inflationary money is not capable of being applied to the purchase of goods, but is drawn into the business of turning a profit on the differences in the exchanges. Naturally it is non-inflated currencies which are purchased, and the value of these currencies widens on the exchanges, thus widening the differential between currencies. This in turn widens the speculative profit realisable on such deals. Thus the activities of the speculators can turn such a sum of foot-loose hot money as 268 thousand million dollars into a disruptive force in international economics. The disruption is of course augmented when the strong currencies are obliged under intervention rules to buy inflated currencies in order to maintain previously arrived at rates of exchange, under international agreements. In the case cited, the Deutsche Bundesbank in the end lost as much as seventeen thousand million marks. First of all, getting on for five thousand million marks were lost in March 1973, when nine thousand million dollars were sold at a trading loss, compared to the intervention price. But in addition, the currency reserves, which had increased to 94 thousand million marks (compared with a note circulation of 46 thousand million!), of course also fell in book value, entailing a further loss to the German economy—ultimately the German taxpayer—of another 12 thousand million. The speculators were estimated to have made three to three and a half thousand million marks in profit. These figures are the measure of a capital movement which was quite purposeless, from any real economic standpoint.

The effects of this process continue. The influx of hot money into a strong currency brings about an increase in the latter, but this is not related to any requirement of the real economy. This results from the international agreements referred to, by which one central bank is obliged to buy up currencies of other countries. Thus, a strong currency is obliged to import inflation which it has played no part in causing; and this imported inflation brings about price rises in the importing country. What, for example, is the Deutsche Bundesbank supposed to do with the thousands of millions of dollars it is obliged to acquire in this way? The American government has of course found its own answer to this question: the Federal Republic was asked to find eight thousand million marks as a contribution to the support costs of American forces stationed in Germany, as a subscription to American bonds, and as purchase of war material from America, to keep the armaments industry there employed, after the end of the Vietnam war. Thus Germany was asked to pay in advance for 175 Phantom planes, which could not be delivered until a year later!

That is perhaps sufficient about the extraordinary consequences of the 1973 currency upsets. Obviously the lesson is that speculative forces can be so strong that the normal countervailing techniques of central banks—such as interest rate adjustments, reserve ratio requirements, etc—are inadequate to deal with the situation. The three thousand million marks taken up by the Bundesbank on 1 March 1973 in order to support the dollar, were just so much an addition to the German money supply, which would be beyond control by measures aimed at stabilising the value of the currency.

Now the significance of the disruption caused by such speculation will be more clearly understood when the matter is looked at from the point of view of the capital cycle.

Capital investment in another currency takes on this sterile, counter-productive character when it has as its object the exploitation of the opportunities of importing inflation into a given currency. Now in the traditional sense, a currency transaction would take place when a commercially required transaction involving time leads to a value relationship being established between two different national currencies. Up to 1914, there was a currency exchange system, by which the temporary imbalances of payments in and out would be adjusted by reference to the gold standard, which kept exchange rates stable within very narrow limits.

Quite a different situation is created when speculators seek purely financial profits out of an inflationary situation and out of the differential depreciation rates of various currencies. Now to speculate in this way it is necessary to have capital with which to buy the currency to be speculated in. Multinationals who had accumulated large liquid balances through the retention of profits during the Vietnam war, set about using them as capital for this speculative purpose. This is of course in conformity with the basic dogmas of the market economy. These dogmas were in this particular series of events carried to absurdity before the eyes of the world.

Now three kinds of capital investment can be distinguished. Firstly, accumulated sums of money can be invested in productive capital, which will lead to an economic cycle in which goods are produced and sold. (Because the process is itself productive, this use of capital is clearly likewise productive.) Secondly, accumulated sums of money can be used in a manner which is quite legitimate, although not productive, that is, for consumption. This may be either private or public, the latter including for example the building of schools, manufacture of armaments, administrative offices, etc. This is a normal process of decapitalisation of accumulated potential capital by its employment in consumption. Thirdly, there are the various forms of application of capital which are factitious in the sense that they do not relate to a necessary function of the real economic organism. An example is speculative dealings on the Stock Exchange. What is happening here is that accumulated funds are being used to turn a profit on buying and selling, with a time interval between.

Still more removed from the real needs of the economy is the type of foreign exchange speculation which we have been describing. The profits on such transactions are essentially parasitical, in that they extract value from the economy without performing any real service in return. This is reflected in the losses of other speculators from whom the profit-making speculator have gained. This sort of thing was the cause of the Herstatt Bank collapse in 1974. This should really be a warning against the continuance of an economic system which bases itself on the belief that selfishness can be geared to satisfy human needs. The investment of capital in such forms contradicts fundamentally the whole economic principle of using the minimum of resources to achieve a given effect. Capital which could be used productively is instead diverted into applications which do nothing for the real economy. Thus, productive opportunities are passed over. Moreover, in addition, the circulation of money is, as we have seen, put into disequilibrium.

Finally, it should be noted that the tactics of the oil-producing countries fall under the category of capital investment we have been discussing, since these countries use their monopoly position to raise prices to the maximum extent possible, thus driving their customers into inflation.

As a result, the oil-producing nations accumulate funds which do not correspond to an equivalently valued economic service but only to the naturally bestowed raw materials—which do not have the same value. The money sums thus accruing cry out, of course, to be used in some way. Various possibilities exist. First of all, such funds are used to make investments in currencies which appear to be stable. Then the oil-producing countries together began to develop a more sophisticated approach, and consortia were formed with Western banks, in order to provide advice on the management of these funds. According to one of these bank consortia, the total funds involved already totalled fifty thousand million dollars in 1974 and were expected to reach six hundred thousand million dollars by 1985. Roughly a third of this has been allocated to the oil-producing nations themselves, and other allocations include the support of less well-endowed Arab states and the developing countries in general.

However, the larger part of these funds will be found as investments in the international money and capital markets. Some commentators in the West have seen a danger in this, however. For example, the *Düsseldorfer Handelsblatt* of 10 September 1974 felt there was a distinct possibility that the extortionate oil-rich sheikhs and rulers would start buying up entire Western industries and even countries. However there may be some merit in applying the thousands of millions of oil dollars in productive investment in the same economies that they have exported inflation to, by means of excessive prices. The investment of accumulated monopoly profits is not the same thing as currency speculation, when inflationary money is put to the best possible economic use in new productive plant. This is a normal economic aim, and not speculative at all. As was remarked in the September 1974 issue of *Neue Politik*, it would be senseless to increase the burden on Western countries still further by adding the payment of interest thereto.

APPENDIX 4
ASSOCIATIVE POSSESSION IN AGRICULTURE

Establishing a new system of possession in agriculture

Food, clothing and housing are the most basic or essential components of demand; that is why human existence on earth is based upon the economics of the land.

Moreover, the fundamental human urge is towards self-realisation, and if mankind is ever to achieve this for all, we must find a just way of sharing the riches of the earth and the land itself.

Throughout history, the land has occupied the central place in economic relationships. But towards the end of the middle ages, it began to be deeply influenced by the development of a new factor in economic life, the impulse which began with the development of trade at that time.

The guiding factor in trade is of course the market. Around the 15th century, the market began to grow in importance under the combined effects of new ideas, and of the production of a mass of new goods. Agriculture was drawn into this new market economy, and so came under the rules of the market. Now it is apparent that an economic system based on the market principle cannot be right for agriculture. In fact it makes difficulties for it. The industrial market economy is arranged in such a way that it is only suitable for a rationally structured economic mechanism. It is not equal to the essentially organic nature of agriculture. Increasingly the growing problems of agricultural markets, brought about by this inherent unsuitability, have led to government intervention, to avoid socio-economic catastrophe. However, it is evident that the convulsions caused in agriculture by the impact of the anti-organic and mechanistic market economy cannot be cured by government action. Indeed, the means by which agriculture is now maintained by government funds has gone beyond what is rational; what is now happening is that massive donations in the form of financial help and tax allowances have now to be made to keep agriculture going at all.

The market-orientated economy, based on trade and industry, is simply not in a position to bring agricultural activity into a rational or balanced relationship with demand; this can be seen in the thoughtless and bankrupt policy adopted for agricultural products. While this policy is intended to help agriculture, it in fact enjoins partial over-production, which governments then have to support. Storage is, of course, a costly matter. Sometimes sales at low prices have been made, for example of butter to the Soviet Union, these low prices having at least reduced storage costs

Much has been said about how this is a perversion of the market, and has in any case failed in its aim of establishing a workable system for agricultural products. The farmers are allowed to go on working, and of course using up their means of production, to the point of over-production, when the costs involved in absorbing this over-production could be used to give direct support. The whole business is opposed to real self-reliance in agriculture.

Fundamental reform of the economic system requires the insight that real economic efficiency can only be achieved when agriculture is put on a basis corresponding to the distinctive requirements of its own logic, which will involve the construction of a special economic super-structure for agriculture. Once it is seen how the peculiar conditions of agriculture call for a special approach, once it is grasped what action is necessary to set free the potentialities of agriculture, and how this action requires an organic and indeed humanistic approach, it will then be understood what a profound shift in the economic centre of gravity is involved. The collaborative spirit needed may best be seen by looking at the structure of landownership. To establish a proper relationship of possession which will correspond to the logic of agriculture, a special structure is needed. Under this structure, the management of agriculture will need to work on three distinct levels.

The various aspects of possession and ownership

Some clarification of terminology is first necessary. Colloquial usage about ownership is confused, and we have to be precise about what it is and what it involves.

In old German law, the relationship of a person with an object, particularly with the land, was represented by the term "Gewere". This originally signified the *possession* or *holding* of a piece of land. It constituted a form of legal induction into possession, by which the legal result of this induction was gained, on the one hand, the personal rights of possession, and on the other hand the object possessed, viz., house and land. The essence of "Gewere" was usufruct, the right of use.

To this concept, around the 13th century, the term "ownership" came to be applied. This came to mean full dominion over a thing with the right to use it for profit, to dispose of its substance as thought fit. Thus, possession came to be enveloped in ownership, although jurists constantly endeavoured to separate the two. We must see the two things not so much legalistically, as from a humanistic point of view.

Possession denotes the control of an object and the ability to dispose of it, whether this situation is legally secured or not. This is a surface relationship, and neutral in character. As regards *ownership*, it should be understood as a particular form of the possession relationship between people and things.

We must differentiate between:
—the un-individualised *organic* possession relationship
—the highly individualised and concentrated desire to exercise possession in the form of private ownership
—the form of relationship to things which a trustee might feel, in which he must take care of, and use things productively, but in a way which involves responsibility to others in the community, a way which is not related to the "trustee" as an individual with his own interests.

1. *Organic possession*: the typical form of this was the original agricultural tribal working group, in which soil, plants, animals and people formed a living whole in the shape of an organism which was at once both physical and social. The member of the tribe is also a member of this organism. Possession relationships for each member are like the relationships between cells in the body, or in some instances like the relationships between organs. This type of economic unit is permeated by living forces, which act ecologically and so in a way which transcends individuality—the people and the things they "own" constituting a living union. This is not unlike the animal communities—not unlike the birds who possess their mutually built nests in the same way.

2. *Individualist ownership*: this is found in the personalised possession relationships of individual persons to objects. The urge of

the modern individual, insulated from his fellows by comparison with the tribal member, is to possess, to make himself master of the objects of the material world. This drive has applied with particular force to the land. To satisfy the basic drive involved, the acts of possession are required to be invested with the full power of disposal. This is the whole basis of private ownership. This has, of course, been given social recognition by the establishment of its legal form. In seeking and experiencing the physical power of disposal over an object—or over a contractually acquired right—it becomes an extension of the individual's personality. This becomes consolidated, the thing owned fusing with the self, so that the individual gives the object such a valuation as to identify with it.

The individualistic principle leads to the urge to "keep up with the Joneses" and to acquire more and more possessions. When this drive is realised through the means of private ownership, it runs counter to to the proper principle underlying all law, namely real justice, since it affects adversely the fair division of wealth in the community. What is still more serious, it tends to disrupt the organic unity of society, to the degree that individuals live in isolation from the community and identify themselves almost exclusively with the things they own. It is, of course, as a reaction against the negative aspects of private ownership that the notion of common ownership has developed—but by this is usually meant the acquisition of private property by the state.

3. *"Trustee" ownership*. Humanity is capable of something more than the lower drives concerned purely with self. It is a fact that people can be, and are, seized by ideas and desire to pursue them for their own sake. This is a natural expression of something fundamental in our nature. These aims involve such characteristics as altruism and awareness of responsibility to others.

A form of possession arising from such characteristics exists, and can be seen as possession in which the self as such is scarcely relevant. This form joins the possession relationship with these drives. Now such can in fact be the foundation of a new type of ownership, which would be based on co-operation in the community. Now any form of ownership which is feasible can of course be given legal form, and while this may be a matter of secondary importance, some legal right must always be established if there is to be usufruct in material objects with social consent.

This form of the possession relationship is both the most advanced and also the most intensely felt. It is closely connected with the most advanced form of human development as a whole. Goethe's poem, "Die Geheimnisse" ("The Secrets") may be cited here:

> Doch wenn ein Mann von allen Lebensproben
> die sauerste besteht, sich selbst bezwingt,
> dann kann man ihn mit Freuden andern zeigen,
> und sagen: das ist er, das ist sein Eigen!
>
> (But when a man comes through the bitterest
> of all life's tests, by mastering himself,
> then one may joyfully point him out to others.
> and say, "That's him. What he has is his own."

Agriculture at three levels

The three different levels to which agriculture relates were mentioned above. By these three levels, man's very physical existence is related to the soil. It is necessary to realise the way in which agriculture must in turn relate to the land on which it operates. These three levels are:

1. The physical level—the earth itself.
2. The social level—working together.
3. The level of ideas—the influence of the universe of thought.

All human activities take place on these three levels. Now the way in which these three levels interact needs further analysis, as follows:

1. *The physical level*: physical objects are physically acquired. (This is in fact a form of the Roman legal concept of *occupatio*.) By the processes of nutrition, food is assimilated into the body. Thus what the earth has produced becomes a constituent part of man himself. Now the earth is subjected to ownership in other ways, since the land, its resources and its fruits are the subject of personal ownership relations, which may be secured by legal—that is social—sanctions.

2. *The social level*: in relationship with one another, men establish communities. When two or more are gathered together, a third thing is created, which is in some way beyond individuality. This is reinforced by the interaction with the physical level, the earth. When men work the earth together, they are bound to each other and to it in the process. This naturally brings about some fusion, of a very specific and organic kind, of human effort with the natural productivity of the earth, varying of course in its nature and extent with the geographic and climatic conditions. Now there is nothing in this complex of inter-

actions which presupposes an ownership relationship, as such. The actual basis which would necessitate it is lacking.

3. *The level of ideas:** in this level, we are involved with the most profound aspects of the cosmos. Maybe people will rise to awareness of this fact through religious outlook, or this interconnection may be working purely at a subconscious level. The onward development of human thought is essentially healthy, inspiring indeed, capable of bringing about harmonisation, and of providing the main point of reference for individuals in working out their destinies. But there can be no such thing as a narrow relationship of possession at this level, one cannot "own" an idea, nor can governments enact any legal form of securing the use of an idea to one individual. Once we perceive this deep all-pervasive interconnection on this level, we will see how meaningless our notions of land-ownership are.

Through each of these three levels, the content of the relationship between men and the earth is specified by the very forces of life itself. Collaboration in agriculture, and varying degrees of awareness of the impact upon agriculture of the world of thought combine to ensure this. None of these relationships, however, specify any need for private ownership of the land in the individualistic, possessive sense. Such ownership is not necessary nor can it be made necessary by society. Use of the land is in reality independent of the matter of ownership. As regards terminology, even such words as usufruct, or "trustee" ownership may imply too much of the individualistic form, and perhaps we should seek some such expression as existed in the old German term "Eigen".† What is important is to grasp the close relationship of man, earth and thought, in which present concepts of "self" play little part. In ancient times, the earth was tilled, and livestock herded, in this spirit. It is necessary for modern thought to regain this sense of relationship, if the resources of the earth are to be conserved and used wisely. The importance of this development can be seen by a brief examination of some historical facts.

The more deeply one delves into history, the more the original

---

*An essential aspect of Wilken's ideas is, of course, the connection between all spheres of human thought, religious, artistic, scientific, etc, which are seen as an interacting whole—Editor, English edn.

†No immediately obvious English term has suggested itself, but the point of terminology is indeed important if misunderstanding is to be avoided—Editor, English edn.

tribal/clan structure, with its organic relationship with the land, can be seen to be linked with religion. We have late examples of such a communal attitude in the examples of the Jugoslav house community, and the Russian *Mir*, which derived from the old Russian peasant communities. The word "Mir" has three meanings: first, the social organisation of the peasantry, closely connected with the soil—this organisation being responsible for the joint working of the land belonging to it. Secondly, it means, "Peace", that is, the ideal conditions for people living in a socio-legal relationship with one another. Thirdly, the word means, "World"—the heavenly universe, and the earth and its peoples, ruled over by God, both aspects being joined in the one concept.

The relationship between tribal man and the land was similar in the old German *Hof*, although it was much more strongly individualised, whether in tribe, clan or individual family, The Edda cantos relate how the Hof was endowed with the spirit of the gods. The Hof was the place of worship—which is the derivation of the word, just as in Gothic it was called "Gudhus"—house of God. This demonstrates the association of tribal ties, religious feelings and tribal group owner-ship. The change from man's original feeling of envelopment in a cosmic unity to our present conceptions of individualised personal ownership has been very slow. Gradually the legal institution of private ownership of land developed. As the concept evolved that the means of production were capital which produced profit, this notion of capital broadened out from the new industrial economy to include agriculture. The various controls which prevented this movement were removed. On the introduction of capitalistic attitudes into the agricultural sphere, the structure of peasant society was weakened, and the old relationship with the land was superseded by business-economic thinking of a type originating in America, wherein calculation came to be exclusively in terms of prices, costs and profits. Thus it was that the organic link between the land and the people working on it came to be severed. The land is seen as if it were an industrial means of production, to be exploited with labour and with the application of chemicals.

In 1933 a law was passed in Germany which sought to revive the traditional concept of the Hof, but which also had other implications. This law created a form of peasant ownership, of which the main points were as follows: the Hof became inalienable, and could not be sold, nor could money be borrowed on its security. Distraints on the Hof and speculation were both in this way prevented. On death, the Hof could only be passed undivided. Only property other than the Hof could be divided in the will. There was provision to give agricultural training to the brothers and sisters of the heir, who were entitled to residence on the Hof if they needed it, and were not in debt.

There are aspects of these rules which might be copied, in so far as they remove the land from commercial speculation, even though the motives of those concerned with the law involved an anti-Christian attempt to revive the irrational notion of the Blutgruppenseele, the so-called group-soul based on blood, or ancestry. (The holder of the Hof had to have German citizenship, and German or other racially-acceptable ancestry.)

Moreover, compared with the old German traditional Hof, the Hof of 1933 operated only on two of the three levels. There was no connection with the world of ideas. This limitation to the two remaining levels was in conformity with the Nazi conception of race. On the social level, the family unit—in which German ancestry was essential—was the cell-form of the race. The materialism of National Socialism, peculiarly evil in its form, is, of course, complementary to the materialism of communism. Both are equally anti-Christian. Their clear purpose was to provide a materialistic substitute for the religious component of the world of ideas. Thus, the Nazi Hof was incomplete, and lacked the natural relationship with all three levels. It was thus a headless torso, compared with the needed form. It is the triple relationship which provides the cement necessary to establish a genuine working community, linked with the natural forces of the earth, correctly structured at the social level, and having that vital contact with the universe of human thought which contains all the inspiration that is needed to guide the enterprise. Early man knew this, but both in the Nazi Hof, and in the modern capitalistic agriculture, which also has a tendency to work only on two levels, the knowledge has been lost. It is, of course, awareness of and exposure to the world of ideas which strengthens the understanding of the organic nature of the soil. Lack of awareness constitutes an estrangement of the deepest significance, and the bearing this has on the weakening of the family will not be lost.

Towards a new arrangement for the agricultural economy

We have analysed the way in which agriculture must be seen on three levels, if it is to be organic and social in structure, and if it is to be in touch with and helped by the world of ideas. Now this poses the question, how—given the social needs of our time—a reformation of the relationship between men and the land is to be constituted. In particular, in considering whether there can be such a thing as ownership of the land, it is important to start with this threefold set of relationships, if we are to find a way in which the wealth of the land can be properly made use of. To reiterate these relationships, they concern the living productive forces of the earth, the social relationships moulded in jointly working the earth, and the contribution of the world of ideas, the last-named being highest of the three relationships, one that once was conceived in religious terms, and that now needs the fullest and most comprehensively philosophical approach possible. With this in mind, let us proceed to analyse in what way ownership of the land can be justified.

1. Now the usufruct of the land, whether for agriculture or industry, does not depend on the user being personal owner of the land. This is quite easily seen in practice, when the land is made available to users through various types of tenure—fee, lease, copyhold, etc. The right of usufruct can be conceived as being a sort of *control* under trust rather than as full trustee ownership (see above). Any concept of ownership tends to carry with it a connotation of fixity, more so than the form of control which is needed, which is much more limited in scope. We can say, in relation to usufruct in the land, that ownership as such is of no value, it adds nothing.

2. The material ownership of the land by *group* tenure had historical importance in bygone days. It formed the basis of the political and social system, as can be seen in the development of nation-states. During medieval times, government rested on the principle of the ownership of all land being vested in the feudal sovereign. Thus, for example, Charlemagne was the owner of all land in all his various territories. Some lands he administered directly through ministers, some was leased to feudal overlords. These overlords formed their holdings into the basic units of feudal society, without having any actual ownership of the land. With the passing of the feudal system and the rise of individualism, they of course became owners of their lands, a development connected with the formation of nation-states. Their serfs in turn became peasants, and in the nineteenth century, peasants started to be owners of their farms. Similarly, urban land came to be privately owned, under the market economy.

Now when political power is founded on land ownership, the

corollary is that land ownership founded on dominating the product of the land is the basis of a corresponding economic power. In modern democratic states, the political power of the big landowners has tended to weaken. But on the other hand, the development of increasingly massive concentrations of power in the industrialised economic system is associated with other forms of real estate ownership. The basic dogma of the free market economy is freedom to trade anything in money terms, and this has made it possible to capitalise the land. However the money sums which result from this kind of capitalisation are in fact non-economic, and not in any way productive. That is because no productive activity results; all that has happened is that the land involved has become a commodity. But in becoming a tradeable object it is thereby estranged from its nature. Now this commercialisation of the land through the legal institution of private property is a very recent development in human history. It followed in fact from the desire of the newly-awakened individualist personality to procure a physical expression of his valuation of himself, via the appropriation of material goods. As a result, the entire surface of the globe became legally divided into innumerable units of ownership. Similarly, on the political level, the whole earth became occupied by nation states, as the supreme form of landownership complexes. These states are independent and in a posture of opposition to one another.

No longer is political power wielded by feudal monarchs who were the ultimate owners of all land. The establishment of the democratic nation state put power nominally in the hands of the people as a whole, but in practice into the hands of an élite, whose power was underpinned by the police and the army. In this situation, ownership of the land is removed from the political sphere and commercialised. However, there has been a tendency for individualised land ownership to be transmuted into state ownership. A survey has shown that in Western Germany, the state's holdings of land increased from 22.6% in 1937 to 28.2% in 1973. (Broadly 65% of the land was in private possession in 1973.)

One particular social injustice must result from the individualisation of land ownership—namely, that only a proportion of the total population can enjoy such a form of ownership. At the same time, the opportunity is opened up for misusing the land by capitalising it, which means money without the personal effort involved in useful work. Moreover, this helps the creation of multinational economic power complexes. This is why the legal institution of land ownership is inimical to the best interests of the people, not to mention the fact that it is without productive value, and so quite unnecessary.

3. Looking at it from the standpoint of the world of ideas, it is not possible ultimately to separate out ethical aspects from our consideration of the totality of human social and economic relationships with the land. This is because the aim of all these relationships is to perform services which are mutually useful. Now ethically there is no reason whatever to have the institution of individual ownership of the land, for no ethical precept can be found which could require such a rigid and entirely closed system to be applied to the surface of the earth. This applies whether ownership is by individuals or by groups. It is only when we have lost the sense of the interrelationship of all ideas, including ethical ideas, that we could permit such an institution, let alone restrain criticism of it. It cannot be in conformity with any impulse of conscience, still less the spirit of Christianity. One could indeed relate the exploitation of the land for such selfish purposes to the force of atheism.

Now the social classes who are deprived of ownership naturally see no way of changing this apart from socialising the land. By this, they mean nationalisation, which however brings the land into subjection to political interests.

What this all means is that there is neither rational nor ethical content to the notion of individual landownership. It is because of this that such ownership has no productive function, and can only be a misleading economic form. Individualised ownership can, of course, properly apply in the case of consumable goods produced by the land, but this cannot extend to the substance of the land itself. Human thought cannot admit fixed irrationalities into any system of ideas able to claim itself as a valid reflection of fundamental or universal truths. The world of ideas must indeed reflect a cosmic system or order, in which ownership is, as already mentioned, irrelevant, because the essence of ideas is to be useful, to be available to all who want them, except to those who would pervert or misuse them.

The private ownership of land opens the door to greedy speculation, and works against the natural order of things. In this connection, Novalis, who had such insight, said: "Nature is the enemy of perpetual ownership, and destroys—according to fixed laws—all signs of it. It is to humanity as a whole that the earth belongs, and all ownership rights must lapse within a prescribed period. Nature will not be the exclusive possession of a single individual. If attempts are made to own it, nature turns into a poison, which banishes peace and becomes a cause of temptation, of all-embracing covetousness, with all the endless cares and lusts which result."

The group right of usufruct in agricultural land

Material ownership of land is neither necessary nor desirable, nor is it even effective. This has been shown in relation to three levels of awareness. Hence the concept "ownership" which has become rigid, should be avoided altogether as the basis for legal forms of usufruct in the land. For example, if we wish to have a new form of land use, which can be withdrawn, it will not be dispossession to withdraw it, because under our new form, there will be no ownership rights to take away —and dispossession as a term is only meaningful in relation to the concept of legal ownership. What we need is a legal form by which we can give the right to use a piece of land to particular people, and this form must be clear and well-established, and must only give a right to use. This is the key thing we now need, socially speaking, to define such a law. This will require considerable discussion on the part of all concerned, to arrive at legal forms which accommodate mutually the natural title of each and every person to a share in the land. In other words, a truly social land system will be one of stewardship, indeed of self-stewardship. This way there would be no division of the surface of the soil into ownership units. Instead of land ownership we would have a limited right of usufruct for each unit; perhaps the holders of these rights could be called "usufruct owners".

The times are ripe for this concept of mutual stewardship, which in replacing private ownership would also exclude dealings in land, either by private individuals or by governments. The concept of exclusive social stewardship naturally excludes the present land system, based in materialism, with its concomitant physical ownership by individuals.

This system would not substantially affect the position of the holders of small plots used for homes and for gardens. They would continue to be legal *possessors*, though not legal *owners*. They would have the usufruct for these purposes. They would not be able to turn the plots into money capital; the plots would not be saleable commodities. They would not be able to mortgage or bequeath the land as such, though in case of need, the buildings standing on the land could be sold, transferred or pledged. Their rights of usufruct, and of possession, would still be legally secured in the same way as the old ownership rights would previously have been, but there would be no more of the old antisocial conversion into factitious capital [See Chapter 3, section 2.—Editor, English edition.]

The following table shows some figures for West Germany. These will give some idea of the values involved in agriculture. Now close on two-thirds of the land is in the hands of farmers or peasants. In 1970 the total capitalised value of agriculture amounted to 127 thousand million Deutsche Marks. This total breaks down as follows:

LAND USE IN GERMANY
(thousand million marks)

1.	Land:	23.4	
2.	Permanent tillage:	1.4	24.8
3.	Agricultural buildings:	31.5	
4.	Dwellings:	18.1	49.6
5.	Machinery & equipment:	20.6	
6.	Livestock:	16.8	37.4
7.	Current Assets:		14.9
			126.7

Now the farming unit of land, legally established as usufruct, would not be saleable nor bequeathable. This would, under certain conditions, apply also to farm buildings and equipment. This is because the soil provides the basis for an agricultural working unit which is essentially organic. The two are not to be separated. They are related by three lines of forces, to the three levels: there is the agricultural entity formed by the living relationship with the productive forces of the soil; the socially formed working group; and the continuously evolving forces at work in the world of ideas, once religious in form. now to be seen in broader scope. The force of these ideas is the essential ingredient in welding the working group into a truly effective community, understanding the full implications of its own actions.

Such a working organism, with its key threefold relationships, will take the form of a legally recognised working group having stewardship of the land. The groups might possibly be organised on a village basis. These would, of course, be different from the racial or family groups advocated by the Nazis! The groups would be freely entered into by free individuals.

It would be important to ensure objectivity in the matter of forming the units, and defining the responsibilities of usufruct. Legal arbitrators will be necessary to help here. The meetings that form the groups must obviously strive to arrive at rational, humane and just arrangements.

Thus, the new arrangements would be self-generated and socially creative, offering fulfilment for individuals to develop themselves, and in particular giving scope to young people wanting individual responsibility and social involvement. Now it has to be recognised that resistance to this self-generating approach may come from people who are unwilling to take trouble, and content to leave it to governments to resolve social issues. Personal responsibility is an effort, of course, and some people may want to save themselves this effort. This is where the doctrine of remote political common ownership of nationalisation has been so thoughtless, in creating a generalised and depersonalised form which however contains within itself the same principles as the private property system it seeks to replace. This form secularises, as it were, the old religious form of ownership of early times. Now there are many signs that the state is becoming overloaded with problems, which pass to it because the market economy is unable to solve them. Therefore, every responsibility which can be taken on by individuals acting in the common interest helps to relieve this overloading and this may perhaps prove the spur to prople shaking off this widespread indolence. That is in fact the only way in which conditions can be prevented from sinking into a nadir of apathy, the only way in which the correct actions can be taken.

APPENDIX 5
SUEZ AND THE OWNERSHIP OF MONEY CAPITAL

The following statement was published at the time by the author, with the purpose of demonstrating that the lifespan of investment capital should be limited.

The Suez Canal, a major waterway for international shipping, was owned by an international company since its construction in 1869. During the period since the end of the Second World War, the world watched the chain of events which led to the take-over of the Canal by the Egyptian government. While the shareholders were promised repayment of their capital, their rights as owners passed to the state.

This affected the economic interests of most seafaring countries. The Canal had become the most important oil route in the world; by 1955, 69 million tons of oil per year were passing through it, from the Middle East to the West. In nationalising this means of transport, a single nation-state acquired complete power over something of international importance. The matter became a major issue in power politics. Up to the expropriation, the Canal had played a key role in English foreign policy, because of their ownership of it.

The way in which England came to own it, and the ensuing political problems, have been dealt with by the writer before, on a theoretical level, which however has proved to be close to the mark. Two fundamental questions are raised. Should capital facilities of economic significance be allowed to come under political control? And what has happened to the ownership of the means of production—in this case, the canal installations—particularly as regards their money capital equivalent?

Those who hold that the administration of economic assets should —to prevent abuse—be kept separate from political life, will recognise that bringing the ownership of the Canal into politics is counter-productive, economically speaking. The Egyptian expropriation has replaced one political ownership by another, and so broadened the antagonism between East and West into a wider conflict. Below is reproduced the writer's analysis of the political side of this problem.

There remains the question of the *economic* ownership of the Canal. Can the former shareholders still be considered as its legal owners, based on the rights established in 1869? Should they rightfully continue to run the Canal? According to the traditional viewpoint, they are undoubtedly still the owners. Now the shares are held internationally, with England as the largest shareholder; and under the international agreements concerning the running of the Canal, the shareholders' rights are limited to secure the free use of the Canal. However, the fundamental question is this: does the ownership of the capital go on for ever? Is its life-span unlimited—even though the physical installations cannot last indefinitely? Let us look at the facts in the light of this question.

The Canal was completed in 1869. The building costs totalled 430 million gold francs; 200 million francs came through the shares, and the rest was borrowed. Net profits—income less depreciation and provision for replacements—were divided as follows: 71% went to the shareholders, 15% to the Egyptian state, 10% to the founders (165 of whom had been given free shares) and 4% to the administration and employees. As in the early years no profit resulted, the share capital was paid interest at 5%. After that increasing dividends were paid—as shown in the following table:

SUEZ CANAL DIVIDENDS

Year	Dividend	Peak share quotation (500 French francs)
1870	5.0%	380
1879	5.6%	770
1889	17.2%	2450
1899	21.6%	3830
1911	33.0%	5450

Here we have an important example. The shortening of transport routes which was the result of the technical achievement of the Canal, generated cost savings. These savings are of course precisely what is meant by the formation of free capital. The other side of the coin is the profits accruing to the Canal Company as a result of its monopoly position and the pricing policy pursued.

After the First World War came a period of monetary disorder. The value of gold started to fluctuate, depreciation being caused by over-production. By 1955 the franc had fallen by about 200%. But through the decades following 1914, the share capital of the Canal Company was maintained at its original value. The nominal capital was only 200 million francs, but this came to be worth 40 thousand million francs. Dividends increased, by 3800% up to 1955. This means that on a share with a nominal value of 250 francs, 9500 francs were paid out at the currency value then existing. Taking into account the reduction in the purchasing power of the franc by 200%, this means that the dividend was 19%. Such is the measure of the extent to which the shareholders were able annually to profit from the world economy. However, on looking closer, it can be seen that the money value of capital based on a particular point in time is in fact totally deceptive, and out of all relation with true values.

The myth of corporate permanence

It has always been seen as the characteristic of a company that it is permanent. Wherein does this permanence lie? Certainly not in the physical capital—the fixed and current assets, or means of production. Sooner or later these wear out and are written off. Originally the shareholders supplied the money capital with which to buy these assets. As soon as they were paid for, this money capital disappeared into circulation. But the claims of those who provided the money capital did not disappear. Now if they had given the money merely as a loan, they could claim repayment, but shareholders do not have this right. They are considered to be the owners of the enterprise, because they have financed it—but not because they run it. They do not have an absolute ownership however, in the sense that they do not have an absolute right of disposal over the property, nor, significantly, are they actively *responsible* as owners; their ownership is *financial*, limited to the right of usufruct. What this amounts to is the right to share in dividends, and certain administrative controls. Only in the case of a liquidation is there some sort of capital repayment—and a liquidation is not a natural end for an organisation considered to be permanent. This permanence is legally enshrined in the concept of the company being a legal person, independent of any change in membership, and of the continual process of renewal of plant. The machinery wears out;

the members of the board change; shareholders sell or bequeath their shares; but the legal person which the company is goes on indefinitely, and with it the rights of the shareholders, in particular the right to dividends. The share capital could not be share capital without the concept of legal personality. Now, beyond a certain point, the dividend rights turn into what is in effect an annuity. The permanence of the company brings about permanence of the ownership of the money capital, and so generates this permanent payment of a sort of rent. When the analysis of the facts shows that share capital cannot indefinitely receive this sort of payment, the question is raised, whether we have not made a fundamental error in endowing the limited share company with this characteristic. How can it reflect economic or social reality?

A penny deposited at compound interest at the time of the birth of Christ would by now have been "worth" a quantity of gold greater in volume than the earth itself! One could see in this example the suggestion that money capital cannot function in this way without there being some limit. The question is what this limit should be; the answer is, to take economic and social aspects into account.

The life-cycle of economic enterprises

Let us take a practical example. A company is set up with a share capital of ten million. This is used to buy the plant, buildings, machines and patents. Working capital is borrowed from the bank. The 10 million's worth of plant is worn out in the process of use, some parts more quickly than others. Some wears out in 5 to 10 years, some lasts 20 to 30 years. Accounting provision is made for this wearing out, and depreciation is included as a cost in product pricing, in order to compensate the company. As plant is worn out and written off, it can be replaced by the element of depreciation recovered in revenues.

This cycle of death and rebirth does not have any counterpart on the money capital side. The shares remain unchanged in quantity, and are indeed separated from actual economic events. Their claims continue. There is, however, a deeper logic or insight into economic processes, and this logic requires that the money capital should phase out as the means of production purchased with it wear out. This is simple enough as a line of argument, but it is hard to put into effect, since it conflicts with established notions. But if an argument is in fact based on economic reality, then it must be workable. To find out how, let us look more closely at a particular aspect of the life of a company.

In the example presented above, we took a static model. The company does not expand; after twenty years it is in the same state as at its foundation. All organic structures are however subject to growth and decay. How this works out may be complicated by various circumstances. A company which finds itself stagnating or deteriorating may perhaps find a new impulse in some modernisation or reorganisation. This will depend on the creativity of the leading personalities in the company. If regenerative impulses are lacking, then the company dies, slowly perhaps, as with the using up of its original equipment, it ceases to be economic, and has in the end to be liquidated. Of course, continuous growth may not be requisite in small businesses—agriculture, handicrafts or retail, say. Growth processes in small businesses appear to be carried out slowly and a little at a time, perhaps when the growth of a small town stimulates the addition of new retailers or workshops. But the law of the necessity of growth asserts itself in full vigour in large businesses, whether in industry or commerce, and this now accounts for most economic development.

Economic growth requires the introduction of new means of production which in turn necessitates money capital. On the other hand, growth brings about a continuing process of capital formation, bringing about an accumulation of money capital. This I call the formation of free capital. This accumulation is over and above the replacement of worn-out capital, of course. It is basically due to technological progress. Now when to a technological innovation is added the ability to create a monopoly, a further source of accumulation is opened up. This was precisely the case with the Suez Canal, the use of which cut journeys, and therefore costs. For a period, the savings thereby generated constituted formation of free capital—so long as they gradually become reflected in progressive reductions of the product price. This normally occurs under the pressure of competition; but in the case of the Suez Canal, there was no competition. Hence the Canal was and is a monopoly. For this reason, it was possible to perpetuate the accumulation of capital, and, while the Canal tariffs did in time come down a little, they never fell to the extent that this accumulation stopped. On the contrary, the pricing policies adopted ensured that profits continued to accrue to the shareholders. This went far beyond normal dividend payments; in addition was paid out what were really capital sums, and this went on for nearly three generations. One can understand Nasser's desire to secure this source of income to his state, as a continuing means of formation of capital for his far-ranging economic plans.

Two aspects of the Suez Canal example, then, require to be noted. First, the absence of any limit on the claims made for share capital; secondly, the way in which price policies generated large amounts of continuing capital formation, due to the monopolistic nature of the Canal. This is quite unlike the normal cycle of an enterprise after a technological development. The abnormality is illustrated by various facts. The Canal was completed in 1869. About twenty years later it had to be widened and deepened, and this was carried out between 1887 and 1898. The cost of this work amounted to 203 million francs, a little more in fact that the share capital; and this was paid for by self-financing. The deepening and widening was really equivalent to a completely new plant, in factory terms. The old "plant" completely disappeared. The originators of the project must by now have been dead; De Lesseps died in 1896, and with him the various statesmen who had made various nation-states shareholders. (The states continued to exist as institutions, of course, but this is beside the point—the life-span of money capital is what is at issue.) In accordance with the life-cycle of the company itself, the share capital at the time of the renewal of the plant should have been redeemed—which could easily have been done, considering the level of profit payments.

From this point of view, the shareholders should not really have been owners of the Canal at all after the turn of the century, on the basis that the plant financed by them had been completely renewed, by depreciation and by capital formation and thus no longer existed. The extensive self-financing reserves, from which the reconstruction had been paid for, should have been used for repayment of the share capital. For the reconstruction, normal financing procedures could have been followed, either in the form of loans or new shares. That would have been in accordance with the economic realities to which I refer. The unsoundness of the whole set-up is seen when one considers that the original capital has been paid back to the shareholders eight times over. This results in a more seriously wrong deployment of assets than any rational socio-economic system can in the long run cope with.

If the life of share capital were instead limited to say 20 to 25 years, at the end of which period it had to be repaid or redeemed, this would neither affect the technique of share financing, nor—if presented properly—deter subscribers. It would of course put a constraint on the activities of speculators.

The redemption of share ownership

It is often said nowadays that shares issues are really only a special form of loan. Compared with the private entrepreneur who is the unlimited owner of his capital, the shareholder appears as a lender with limited ownership rights, and other rights have to be ceded or left to the company management. It is not the individual shareholder, but the shareholders' meeting, which has the right to take certain initiatives. The shareholders' meeting elects the board of directors, but the management is selected by the directors themselves. The shareholders have nothing to do with the preparation of the balance sheet and accounts. Only large shareholders can bring influence to bear on the working of the company and the distribution of profits. For the typical shareholder, his ownership rights are consolidated into his claim on profits. However, this claim is limited by the interests of the company as a whole. In order to make the company more secure, depreciation provisions may be generous, in order to establish self-financing reserves. Also, of course, the state intervenes to take tax before the shareholders' dividends are arrived at. A further part of the profit may be taxed as capital gains. This is the realistic position as regards shareholders' rights in the company.

Of course, these limited rights gain in importance when large industrial units come under a single control. A concentrated share majority can dominate the general meeting, and by this domination particular policies are pursued, for example through elections to the board. By contrast with loan capital, share capital has a life of its own. It becomes the object of speculation, and various interests struggle so as to gain influence and control. It is a means, therefore, for introducing conflict into industry; this can include political conflict when, as in the case of the Suez Canal, governments become shareholders. None of this is possible in the case of loans. Stock exchange speculation, and the development of concentrations of industrial power by means of holding companies, has brought about a sort of cancerous growth, so far vainly resisted, in the capitalist market economy. To a large extent the Great Depression of 1929 was brought about by the breakdown of unsound controlling interests. Much of this would have been avoided, or mitigated, had the life of share capital been limited. This was needed both for social reasons and to bring financing arrangements into line with the underlying dynamic. When plant wears out, a parallel process must take place on the side of the money-capital arrangements; the original capital must also "wear out".

The "financial" life of share capital could be limited to a period of 20 to 25 years—equivalent to the typical life span of productive plant, within which period it is depreciated to zero. The amounts accruing would serve to redeem investment capital, whether in the form of loans or shares. Socially, the shareholder is thus seen as the justified possessor of part of the value of the plant he has financed—until such time as that plant is worn out. To go on receiving created value after this point puts him in the position of receiving an annuity, and socially he then is seen as being unjustifiably rewarded from the exertions of others. Naturally, this will be thought of as a radical departure, when for so long we have been accustomed to the principle of shares with no redemption date. However, this kind of approach could have the social effect of defeating misuse of power by large groups.

A reform of shareholders' rights must therefore start with the limitation of the life of the share capital, which would thus come closer to a straightforward loan. This means that the shareholders' participation would be liquidated, together with the original physical capital —though not necessarily with the company itself. If the natural life-span of the company coincides, however, its liquidation will automatically have taken place. If the enterprise is dynamic, then naturally the company continues when the share capital has been repaid. It may go on in various ways: by loans, by a new issue of shares, or by self-financing. Possibly at the time of repayment, some of the original plant will still have some use left in it, and new plant has not yet been installed; in which case the company is continuing on the basis of a stock of usable means of production. It is now worth more than its initial share capital; the value of the physical capital is greater than the nominal capital was. This will be the case when—as with the Suez Canal—the original share subscription covered only a part of the capital and the rest was covered by loans. Now, assuming that from depreciation or capital formation these loans have been repaid, a new question arises. To whom does the company now belong?

The answer is that it does not belong to anyone in particular, and can only be administered as in trust. This need involve no difficulty. For example, Volkswagen had no legal owner until 1956, and was during that time well run. A company whose share capital has been liquidated belongs to no one from the point of view of disposability. Now responsible ownership of the usufruct in trust can come into its own.

When share capital has been thus liquidated, some body or organ is required, to direct and administer the company. This body should not be governmental, but should be a purely economic structure. So long as the Suez Canal Company has shareholders, they will control pricing, utilisation of capital, etc. However, from the economic standpoint, the Canal is supported not by states but by shipping companies. Governments only come into it in so far as warships make use of it. The main aim of the Canal was never political. A management structure is what is needed to enable it to fulfil its economic purpose, and this structure will naturally work with all the employees who will have become the owners of the usufruct. This administration will come to terms with canal users; since the institution is now based on purely economic relationships, there will be no need of legally drafted regulations for its use or for terms of payment.

As actually happened, the Egyptian government was able to enforce its political control, and in so doing undertook the above duties. However, the Canal Company could still be liquidated in the way I suggest, and it could then become an example of the new forms of ownership. The management, the owners of the usufruct, the canal users and the Egyptian government would all have to participate in the negotiations for the disposal of the assets. In effect, a form of constitution would need to be drafted, which would include provisions under Egyptian law for limiting the possibility of transfer of the canal assets. The result would be co-operative self-administration of the Canal, which would be insulated from political or non-economic pressures.

Thus the Suez Canal could be managed by this form of organisation which enshrines co-operation between economic and political users of the Canal, with the administration taking the responsibilities of ownership, and with the personnel in the position of enjoying the usufruct, in the form of their remuneration.

Now the participation of the staff in the administration of the capital of the enterprise depends on the stage of development achieved socially. In the market economy it may not be likely to happen.

Certainly, the organisation must not be an isolated, still less a closed body; its running must be open. In this way, all affected by its work will have the opportunity to comment on aspects that affect them; thus, control will become participative. This will embrace all the various sectors of the economy which as producers, merchants or consumers are involved in the flow of goods through the Canal. For instance, all prices of all goods passing through the Canal are affected by the management and its price policies. Gradually, the control thereby exercised would be able to eliminate undesirable aspects. Run in such a way, the Canal could never be the site of a concentration of power. Economic rationality would in the end prevail.

It is in this way that private capital enterprises, based on self-seeking, can become self-managed economic units based on mutuality. Above all, the influence of chauvinism can be excluded, making a genuine world economy possible; after all, the Suez Canal is not a national but an international economic concern.

Various questions arise in relation to the proposal that the life span of a share company be limited. It might be argued that shares lose their meaning, becoming simply a means of disposing of profits and losses. It could also be claimed that the shareholder would wish to have some personal participation in the company as the result of his investment. This would cease at the time of redemption, but this is after a long period. The payment would be based on the nominal value, that is, the amount originally subscribed, and naturally would be adjusted for the effects of inflation. There would be little difficulty in practice as the new pattern of ownership evolved naturally. What is being proposed is a third way, neither individualistic nor collectivistic, both these forms being based in fact on the same materialistic conceptions. This third way will be genuine mutual participation.

Section 5 of Chapter 8 should be consulted for details of the ways in which redemption of shares may be carried out. This particular case concerns one specific procedure, affecting only the capital function of the share, since the value of the share is not confiscated. It is explained in the text that superannuated productive capital may be dispersed into purchasing power. It could also be converted in some form of common or co-ownership. It is not a matter to dogmatise about here. Much will depend on the level of social development reached by those directly involved. It will be for them to decide to what extent to retain the concept of shareholding, as it gradually comes to be understood how this form has in fact distorted the economy.

APPENDIX 6
FUNDING THE GEISTESLEBEN

As seen in Chapter 8, the *Geistesleben* can be funded from three sources:

1. Individual incomes
2. Free capital formation
3. Superannuated capital

As regards the first, it could be thought reasonable that parents—or perhaps all married people—should contribute towards the education of their children by the *Geistesleben*. Fundamentally, the parents have the ultimate responsibility for their children. Now this responsibility can be shared with the community at large. However, it can be seen that the complete transfer of responsibility to a remote state authority weakens the development of the much-needed ability to take responsibility, and also is conducive to purely self-orientated utilisation of the free service. A similar situation prevails with the deduction of social security contributions at source: the sense of responsibility is blunted. Effective social arrangements need to be individualised, so that they, in fact, develop responsibility. The factual situation is that social arrangements need to have reciprocity—so that there is full awareness of social commitments.

Once the nature of the *Geistesleben* is grasped, then the needs of the people working in it will be seen as having to be met. This can only be done by donations from those in the economy, as a social equalisation which would have to be kept in mind. This might be done on a company basis by giving a proportion of the added value. Some of the new-style companies have moved in this direction.

Fundamentally, this may be done either by donations, or by legally settled endowments. Obviously, such donations imply a measure of sacrifice on the part of the worker.

However, it may be made in a more impersonal form if allocated out of free capital. Strictly speaking, this is quite just, since the *Geistesleben* is the source of this capital. Moreover, it is already financed from this source, only via the roundabout means of state taxation. As already mentioned, the state appropriates a significant proportion of free capital both through corporation tax and through the high rates of tax on large incomes. All this, of course, goes into the general pool of government revenue and all state expenditure has to be financed thereby. Under this system the tax from particular sources cannot be related to particular purposes, although this would be a sensible thing to do. This point is examined more fully in my *Die Reform des Steuerwesens*, Frieburg 1968.

An indication of the extent to which the government appropriates free capital can be gleaned from German official statistics. In 1972 it was calculated that a group of over eight hundred important companies had realised a profit before tax of 13.5 thousand million marks, of which 8 thousand million were taken in tax. These figures can only be indicative, because parts of free capital find their way into income tax on individuals, which, in the same year, came to nearly 73 thousand million marks; the proportion of free capital in this cannot be calculated.

Before dealing with the more tricky question of how the *Geistesleben* can be financed from time-expired capital, we must be clear about the exact form in which the transfer of economic values to it will take place. This presupposes a socially developed and self-administering economic system, run on an associative basis. This would enable the development of company structures which would facilitate such transfers. This involves two quite radical assumptions. First of all, both the *Geistesleben* and the economy must be autonomously established. The self-administering *Geistesleben* will need to be run by self-contained bodies in the various fields of work, educational, religious, sporting, research etc.

Secondly, the economy must understand and be convinced about the reasons for the finance of the *Geistesleben*. This conviction will be easier when the ownership of free capital is neutralised.

The practical details of the administration of free capital involve various problems. particularly in relation to capital which is time-expired. This is dealt with further in section 5 of Chapter 8.

Notes

Editor's Note

The principle obstacle in putting Folkert Wilken's ideas into the English language has been the gap between German and English thought. One might indeed think, from the difficulties encountered, that this gap is now widening still further. The general reader may not wish to be brought up against these difficulties, but he should at least be warned that in areas of the ground covered wherein he encounters more than usual difficulty in following the line of thought, the fault may well lie more in the translation than in Wilken's original. Fortunately, Wilken's approach is "iterative"; that is to say, propositions which are barely outlined in early parts of the book are referred to in greater depth at a later stage, so that the difficulty will usually be found to disappear as progress is made.

This divergence in thought dates probably from the time of Goethe and Hegel. Indeed, it is no accident that wholly satisfactory translations of Goethe and Hegel are still rather thin on the ground. The same difficulty dogged Marx, albeit to a lesser extent. It is with the personality of Rudolf Steiner, still largely unknown in England, except among a small devoted group of disciples, that the difficulty becomes peculiarly sharp. Steiner's German terms are quite clear, in that language, and his writings present no difficulty to the German reader except perhaps for the remarkable concentration of his thought. Yet, although many of Steiner's most important works have been re-translated in an effort to make them easier for the English reader to understand, it would seem to be a fair assessment that his key ideas are only seen through a glass darkly in England, though they may have made more headway in America. This is particularly important in understanding Wilken. For Wilken's *Capital* is without doubt the most substantial work of economics yet to emerge from a Steinerist point of view. While Steiner made some interesting comments on political economy, his primary aim was to expound his scheme for society as a whole. Wilken however has tested—on a monumental scale—the Steinerist scheme and indeed added to it, fleshed it out, purely from the point of view of economics.

To the non-Steinerist reader, to whom this edition is largely addressed, the primary point to be grasped is that to Wilken the economy is not a mechanism, nor a set of autonomous interacting mechanisms. It is an *organism*. Economic processes are in his view essentially organic. Just as the system of the lungs will differ from the system of the stomach, and both from the system of blood circulation, so Wilken sees no reason to suppose that systems which are appropriate to one part of the organism will be equally appropriate in others. Thus, for Wilken, the market system is of much more limited value than any classical Western economist would readily accept. At the same time, Marxist economists might criticise Wilken as being too market-oriented. In fact, in the controversy between Western and Marxist economists, Wilken might best be seen as being on an altogether different plane.

This is because in analysing the competing alternatives of capitalism and communism, he focuses attention on the *motivation* of the main protagonists in each system. Moreover, his theory of motivation is deeply thought out at sociological and philosophical levels. It will not seem entirely unfamiliar to followers of, say, Maslow, but at the same time, Wilken is probably unique in the way in which this theory of motivation is shown to have economic consequences, via the social/legal system which he analyses as being based on the consequences of masses of humanity experiencing wave-forms of motivation at the same time, for example during the Renaissance.

In posing communism as a reaction to capitalism, Wilken's approach is deeply Hegelian, deeply dialectical. Marx made the famous claim that he had turned Hegel on his head to expose the rational kernel. Wilken could justly say that he has turned Marx on his head. He has seen that capitalism is a *thesis*, and therefore communism its *antithesis;* the inexorable consequence of this will be readily apparent to those familiar with Hegelian, or Marxist, dialectic—namely that there has to be a *synthesis* which will incorporate and supersede both thesis and antithesis. It is for this reason that Wilken finds it necessary, as he says in his preface, to make his analysis "in the belief that economics must be *rebuilt*, from the bottom up." It is precisely at this point that the principal difficulties in translation have been encountered.

Virtually every point in Wilken's closely reasoned analysis is an attempt to work towards this synthesis—an attempt both to incorporate and to supersede both capitalism and communism. In German, the presentation of such a viewpoint is facilitated by the use of the German verb *aufheben* or its noun form *Aufhebung*. As Hegel was the first to perceive, this word has two alternative and rather opposite meanings, an accident which he used deliberately in expounding his system of philosophy. The word literally means "raise up", but it has come to have the meanings of "abolish, cancel, annul" on the one hand, and "preserve" on the other. Hence Hegel deliberately used this word to indicate a synthesis of opposites, as part of his theory of dialectical movement. Unfortunately there is no English word which happily combines these opposing meanings in the same way, and much difficulty in translation results.

Wilken then sees capitalism and communism as ideas for the running of society which on the one hand had to be attempted, but which on the other hand have now decisively proved themselves to be inadequate. Only by a dialectical synthesis can a forward-looking society be evolved. Hence it is that Wilken himself said, in a letter to Ernest Bader (without whose efforts this translation would never have seen the light of day): "I am not so much interested that the book should be read as a passive activity but that it should act as a spur for the realisation of what needs to be done." This book is therefore aimed at those who wish to participate in making a new society different from both capitalism and communism. What will this new society look like?

Essentially, it will follow Steiner's ideal of a society in which the three component organs of the social organism would be separately organised. These three organs are, in German, the *Geistesleben*, the *Rechtsleben* and the *Wirtschaftsleben*. Unfortunately again we have considerable difficulty in finding an English term. It is precisely for parallel reasons that the English language has tended to adopt the term *Zeitgeist* for "spirit of the times". The German word *Geist*, etymologically identical with the English "ghost" as in "Holy Ghost", lacks any modern English equivalent. There are indeed those who regret the modern usage of "Holy Spirit" in place of "Holy Ghost", precisely because the only apparently available word—"spirit"—has totally wrong associations or overtones. *Geist* has as wide a range of meanings as it is possible to conceive—it could mean "mental" or "intellectual" or "spiritual" in the religious sense, or "cultural" in the anthropological sense—yet to use any one of these mutually exclusive terms wholly distorts and destroys the real meaning of the term. Thus *Geistesleben* means the entire intellectual, cultural, artistic, religious, mental, ideological, technological, educational life. In the text, various devices, of varying degrees of clumsiness, have been employed for this key concept—key because it is in the *Geistesleben* that capital finds its true source. Occasionally, however, it has been necessary to use the German terms, just as one might have to use the term *Zeitgeist* in an English analysis of literature or manners. The other two terms are somewhat easier to put into English, though it should be borne in mind that *leben*—literally "living"—implies something much more *alive* and changing than the English word "system" which springs all too readily to mind. *Wirtschaftsleben* may be easily put as "economic activity"; while for *Rechtsleben* one can only offer "juridical system", conscious that it is much more mechanistic in tone than is at all desirable. However, as long as it is seen that all social activity must be capable of being classified under one of these three heads, the main idea will be grasped well enough.

The importance of these terms for Wilken's analysis of capital has already been hinted at. Capital, in his view, is like a river which flows from the *Geistesleben* into the *Wirtschafstleben*, before permeating every aspect of the latter. It is moreover necessary now for the *Rechtsleben* to evolve new forms of company organisation which reflect the economic fact that capital, originating in the *Geistesleben*, cannot truly *belong* to any one individual or group of individuals, but must be treated as social property in trust. The idea of trusteeship is essential to Wilken's ideas on the management of capital, and here we are lucky in possessing an English term which seems to convey better what is needed than the German *funktionell*. To me, at least, the concept of being "functional" does not convey the essential idea as clearly as being "in trust".

One other difficulty needs to be mentioned—that of translating Steiner's *Hauptgezetz* or "General Principle" into English. This has often been translated as meaning that everyone should *give away* what he produces to others, presumably in the hope that they will give him something in return. This translation seems to me quite foreign to Steiner's highly practical turn of mind—particularly if contrasted with his ideas for the *contractual* sharing of added value. It has therefore been put as meaning that social welfare or health is increased the more there is *reciprocity* in work.

Lastly, it should be pointed out that this book contains no more than a passing reference to his theory of value. This is dealt with in other works of his, so far, regrettably, untranslated. Briefly, Wilken believes, following Steiner, that human work cannot properly be assigned a value, in the sense understood by either Marx or Western economists. Commodities have a value once produced, but this is a separate issue. This has important consequences, as does Wilken's theory of the origin of capital in the *Geistesleben*, for the critique of Marx's theory of exploitation. It is in fact on this critique that the logic of Wilken's rejection of the communist *antithesis* must hinge. This is dealt with in Chapter V, possible one of the most important chapters in the book.

It would not be proper to close this short note without acknowledging the help of many who have given freely of their time in order to help me wrestle with the often abstruse points arising in editing this translation for publication. Among these, I must mention Dermot O Flynn of the Department of Finance, in his private capacity, Willi Kobe-Kaegi of Zurich, Angelika Hekker of Solingen, Ron Jarman of the Steiner centre in Sussex, Emerson College, Christopher Budd, author of *Prelude in Economics*, Bill Anderton of *Soluna*, and my colleagues in An Grianán—Anne Poniard, Annette Doran, Celestine Rowland and Pat Farrell.

Professor Wilken himself, although he was in his early nineties, gave every possible help, more than we had any right to expect considering the difficulties lay not in any quality of his thought but in the fact that the grain of English runs at an angle to that of German. He died only last year, happy, I believe, to have his last two books out in print.

Only a few days ago, Ernest Bader went to join him. Without that mighty man's energy and drive, which lasted up to the day on which he went to bed to fall peacefully asleep, this book would be nowhere. Ernest has so many memorials, but many of us who worked with him on this believe there would be few dearer to his heart than this book. Unfortunately he did not live to see it in print, but only a few days before I had been privileged to show him the final proofs, which he received with characteristically boyish glee.

David Green
Athenry
February 1982

Glossary

Anteil: a German word meaning "part". Steiner uses it to denote a part of the human psyche orientated to or in sympathy with the world beyond this one.

Anthroposophy: the science of the human spirit, founded by Rudolf Steiner.

Antithesis: a concept of major importance. In the Hegelian logic, followed by Marx, the movement of all processes is from a proposed thesis, to its dialectical opposite, the antithesis, thence by a process of conflict to the *Aufhebung*, (q.v.), or synthesis. Thus, capitalism may be seen as a thesis, socialism as its antithesis, and the new social order which Wilken foresees, the *Aufhebung* of the conflict between the two.

Appropriation: the process by which free capital, being unclaimed, comes into the hands of the entrepreneurial class.

Artificial capital: titles to ownership of capital, which while traded in the capitalistic system, do not in actual fact represent, in Wilken's view, part of the real—or socially necessary—process of capital utilisation.

Association: a special group set up for each industry in which the various producers and users will plan production and investment.

Aufhebung: as this German word meant both "raising" and "superseding", Hegel used it to indicate the difficult and laborious process of synthesising, or working into a balanced and harmonious whole, the dialectical opposites of thesis and antithesis. The German word has been used to stress the fact that this process is much more difficult of realisation than the English word "synthesis" tends to suggest.

Bourgeoisie: though often thought in English to have a pejorative sense, this word is used in quite a detached way to indicate the social class that owns capital and carries out the entrepreneurial function in capitalistic society.

Capital formation: the process by which value sums, perhaps in the form of money, combine with the creative forces of the *Geist* to produce the central function of the economic organism, capital.

Capital stock: the total of the whole capital of an enterprise at any given moment, that is after the initial investment, but before it is totally used up.

Capitalistic: this somewhat Germanic form of the adjective has been deliberately chosen to stress the difference in approach between Wilken's analysis of capitalism and that of Marx. Essentially, Wilken sees capital as a necessary and continuing category in the economic system of the future, and his critique of the capitalistic system focuses on its one-sided (q.v.) procedures for controlling the use of capital.

Common ownership: although this phrase is often used in left-wing politics as a synonym for nationalisation, in Wilken's system it relates to the new form of organically-developed company, in which the ability to take a detached responsibility for the use of capital is the key feature.

Competition: Wilken uses this term mainly for capitalistic competition, in contrast with the more constructive and progressive form of emulation (q.v.).

Constant capital: the Marxist term to include all the capital advanced to purchase other commodities, of whatever nature, except for the purchase of wage-labour, or strictly, of labour-power (q.v.). Constant capital thus includes both material purchases and the acquired means of production. Marx calls it constant because in his system it is not seen as generating any increase in value, the entire increase in value being held to result from the application of labour-power to dead matter—the purchase of such labour-power being given the connotation of variable capital (q.v.).

Consumer money: in the future economic system, Wilken foresees the development of different types of money for different purposes, so that inflation will be prevented by controlling the quantity of money available for each category of economic activity, a separate money system being developed for capital purposes.

Critique: in the dialectical system, the necessary step from thesis to antithesis and from antithesis to *Aufhebung* is taken by means of a critical analysis of the faults or one-sidedness of the preceding stage.

Decapitalisation: the process by which assets no longer required for capital purposes are put to other uses.

Economic rationality: the sum total of the needs, and the consequences for the organisation of production of these needs, in the need-orientated economy (q.v.) of the future.

Emulation: the normal and inevitable process by which each individual or company will measure its own achievements against the achievements of others—in contradistinction to the competitive behaviour found in capitalism, which contains a corrosive element of aggression and the attempt to eliminate competition.

Factitious capital: capital which under the conventions of capitalistic thinking is considered to be capital, but which does not in fact relate to any real or socially necessary capital function.

Free capital: the part of added value which derives from the creative activies of the *Geist* in making technological and organisational improvements which result in economies in the utilisation of labour. As this free product cannot in justice belong to any one individual or group, the private appropriation of this value quantity is at the root of the distortions and one-sidedness of ᴛhe capitalistic system, and a causal factor in the generation of both inflation and unemployment.

Functionally-centralised state: in the Steinerist analysis, the present form of government in which all functions of administration ultimately or directly come under the control of the one state structure. This is in contradistinction to the threefold state in which the functions of the economy, and of the *Geistesleben* (q.v.), are separated away from the state proper and become totally autonomous and self-determining.

Geist: this word has often been translated as "spirit" but in fact is much more comprehensive, including activities far beyond the meaning usually understood by the English word "spiritual". It embraces all conscious activities of a creative or analytical kind, including not only religious but artistic, scientific, educational, medical, and professional activities of every conceivable kind. It is not unlike the coverage given by Marxists to the term "consciousness". The German word has been employed, because of the lack of any equally wide-ranging English substitute, and because to vary the translation according to the context quite shattered the unity of Wilken's thought. It is hoped that this usage will transplant into the English language in the same way that the term "Gestalt" has done in psychology, or "leit-motiv" in music.

Geist capital: the quintessential capital which is a creation of the mind, in contradistinction to the money or physical forms subsequently taken.

Geistesleben: the total ensemble of all mental, spiritual, artistic, educational, scientific, technological, medical and other professional activities—which ensemble forms one of the members of the social organism (q.v.).

Historical materialism: a Marxist name for the Marxist philosophy.

Impulse: a term in the psychology of Steiner, relating to a deep inner motivational drive. The "Christ-impulse" for example is seen as being an emanation from within, in the manner of a slowly but steadily growing source of light.

Income formation: the process by which a portion of added value is allocated and distributed to all those collaborating in the economic process.

Labour-power: a Marxist term denoting the ability of the worker to work, which is hired out to the entrepreneur under the wage system (q.v.).

Law of the tendency of the falling rate of profit: Marx's key theoretical prediction on which he based his belief that capitalism would in the end collapse because of its inner contradictions. This would happen because profit could only derive from variable capital (q.v.) but the effect of technological development was steadily to tend to reduce the proportion of variable capital to constant capital—from which no profit could, under the Marxist system, possibly be derived.

Life span of money: Steiner foresaw that in the future economy, money would be issued with an expiry date, and this as an essential means whereby inflation would eventually be brought under control.

Mind of matter: the function of matter itself to think, albeit in a totally materialistic way.

Need-orientated economy: the economy of the future, in which the guiding principle will be to meet ascertained needs, rather than to make a profit.

Negation: the conflict relationship between the stages of the dialectical process, as seen by both Hegel and Marx. That is, the antithesis "negates" or contradicts the thesis; and is in turn itself negated by the eventual *Aufhebung*. Though Hegel was as conservative as Marx was revolutionary, Marx could not have developed his system without Hegel's logical system, as Marx himself generously admitted in the preface to Volume I of his "Capital".

Occupatio: the Latin word used in Roman law to indicate the appropriation of unclaimed objects—and hence used by Wilken to characterise the appropriation of free capital (q.v.).

One-sided: in the dialectical process, both thesis and antithesis (q.v.) are one-sided and imbalanced. It is in the *Aufhebung* (q.v.) that this opposing conflict of one-sided forces is reconciled and transcended,

in a new situation which contains and supersedes both. The important
point to realise, particularly in Chapter 5 of this book, is that since the
dialectical process is held to be inevitable, both one-sided stages of the
process are necessary transitions, without which no progress could be
made. Thus, there had to be both capitalism and socialism, although
both are equally one-sided and unsatisfactory.

Personality development: the Steinerist analysis is that humanity is still
undergoing a process of development of the human individuality, which
is as yet not fully achieved, and which once achieved, will bring about
the future economic and social system.

Physical capital: the material objects, machinery and equipment, in
which the *Geist* capital becomes incorporated after investment.

Plant: the plant, or works, is contrasted with the essentially social
form of the enterprise, which relates the purely technical function of
the productive equipment to its social purpose.

Possession: the actual control for the purpose of utilisation, as distinct
from the social form of ownership in itself.

Primary incomes: incomes formed in the economic system proper, as
distinct from the secondary incomes paid to those working in the
Geistesleben and in the *Rechtsleben.*

Privatisation: the private utilisation for private purposes of the social
capital.

Proletariat: the "estate" as Marx put it, which having no interest in
exploiting others—except the farmers, perhaps—would liberate society.

Producer money: in the future economy, the money reserved for
capital purposes, and kept totally separate from consumer money
(q.v.).

Pseudo-markets: markets for shares, for labour and for land, in which
trading activities do not, in Wilken's analysis, relate to a real function
of the rational economy.

Purchase capital: in Wilken's early work, he defined this broadly, so
that it was coterminous with Marx's constant capital (q.v.); but, e.g. on
page 231, he also uses it to mean more narrowly the capital advanced to
purchase materials and components—roughly what is understood by the
term "inputs" in the calculation of value added tax.

Rechtsleben: the state in its proper functions of justice and security.

Reciprocity: the performing of services for one another in society.

Re-commercialisation: the re-sale on a pseudo-market of a capital asset
hitherto at work. This is seen as harmful, because it can only happen
in circumstances which are not properly analysed and decided upon,

and which therefore constitute a source of economic maladjustment.

Setting capital to work: this phrase should be understood as implying the using up of capital in its deployment.

Social organism: the ensemble made up—just as a biological organism is made up—of separate systems, specifically of the three systems, which ought to become self-determining, and will in time, namely the economy, the *Rechtsleben* and the *Geistesleben.*

Stagnant capital: capital made static and fruitless by being diverted from the natural flow of the stream of capital from source to using up.

Steiner's main social law: the law propounded by Rudolf Steiner to the effect that social welfare would be the greater, the greater the extent of reciprocity (q.v.) in economic life.

Surplus value: in the Marxist system, the excess of added value over what is needed for simple subsistence.

Variable capital: in the Marxist system, the term used for wage capital or work capital (q.v.). Marx called this variable because it was used to purchase labour-power, the price of which tended to be the cost of subsistence for the labourer. As the labourer could produce more —much more—than his subsistence, the result was a surplus value which represented the exploitation of the labourer, who was in fact deemed to be the only real creator, or perhaps the only legitimate owner, of all the added value.

Work capital: the capital advanced to provide the incomes of those working in the company concerned. Wilken, in a letter to the editor, says that work capital must not be seen—as the Marxists would see it —as buying a commodity. On the contrary, its purpose is to "invest" money into the circulation system, so that what is produced can in fact be bought, taking the economy as a whole. Wilken does not see the purchase of labour-power as being the purchase of a commodity, as does Marx. Following Steiner, he sees the whole existence of the labour market as being a consequence of the wrong treatment of labour, as if it were a commodity when it is no such thing. This point is crucial to understanding Wilken's critique of Marx. Although at first glance, work capital appears to be coextensive with Marx's variable capital (q.v.), it is hardly synonymous with the Marxist concept. On the contrary, it is the point of departure for a completely new approach to the whole question of labour economics and is, for example, related to Steiner's advocacy of the contractual sharing of added value, which would, of course, abolish the wage system altogether. This concept should be very carefully distinguished from "working capital" which also see; in particular for an explanation of the reason why it seemed unavoidable for the English translation to use two such similar terms. (They are not similar in the original German.)

Working capital: the total of capital advanced for both purchase and work capital. With some misgivings, the conventional English term for this category has been adopted, in spite of its similarity to the term "work capital", from which it should be carefully distinguished. (The option of calling "work capital" "wage capital" was also rejected, since the whole point of Wilken's analysis is to look forward to a time when the wage system as known today will have disappeared; moreover, he is at pains to point out that work capital includes not only wages but all other company incomes.)

Bibliography

The literature of economics in general and of specialist studies in particular—on the market economy, competition and growth—has become too voluminous to be reviewable here. Even the literature on new-style companies and the economic future has become quite considerable. Here, therefore, are indicated only a few titles which should prove thought-provoking and instructive. The bibliography to my book *The Liberation of Work* (English edition, London, 1969) may also be consulted.

General Economics

J.S. Mill, *The Principles of Political Economy* 1848: new edition by University of Toronto Press. (A standard work of classical economics.)

Friedrich List, *Das nationale System der politischen Ökonomie* Jena 1910. (An analysis of economic events in the German tradition.)

Karl Marx, *Capital* (three volumes) Lawrence and Wishart, London, Vol. I 1965, Vol. II 1956, Vol. III 1959.

Max Weber *The Protestant Ethic and the Spirit of Capitalism* London, 1948.

Edgar Salin, *Politische Ökonomie* Tübingen 1967.

Joseph Schumpeter, *Theory of Economic Development*, English edition 1961.

—— *Wesen und Hauptinhalt der theoretischen Nationalökonomie* Berlin 1970.

H. von Stackelberg *Grundzüge der theoretischen Volkswirtschaftlehre* Tübingen 1951.

W. Eucken *Grundlagen der Nationalökonomie* Berlin 1965.

Paul A. Samuelson *Economics* McGraw-Hill, 11th edn.

Rudolf Steiner *World Economy* London 1949.

—— *Nationalökonomisches Seminar* Dornach 1974. (An unpublished translation of this is available from the Rudolf Steiner Library in London.)

Folkert Wilken *Die Metamorphosen der Wirtschaft* Jena 1931.

Problems of the Market Economy

Herbert Gross *Das Geistkapital* Düsseldorf 1971.

Michael Tolksdorf *Ruinöser Wettbewerb* Berlin 1971.

E. Ott *Wachstumzyklen* Berlin 1973.

Démètre Zarlaris *Subventionen in der Bundesrepublik Deutschland 1951* Berlin 1971.

Bernhard Gahlen *Einführung in die Wachstumtheorie* Tübingen 1973.

Hans Rimbert Hemmer *Strukturprobleme des Wirtschaftswachstums* Freiburg 1972.

J.K. Galbraith *The New Industrial State* Houghton Mifflin.

Folkert Wilken *New Forms of Organisation in Industry* Varanasi (India) 1962.

—— *The Liberation of Work* London 1969.

Formation of Multinationals

Robert Liefmann *Cartels, Concerns and Trusts* 1977.

Graham Bannock *The Juggernauts* Penguin 1973.

Benn B. Seligman *The Potentates, Business and Businessmen in American History*.

Economic Reform

E.F. Schumacher *Small is Beautiful* Abacus Books 1974.

Erik Boettscher *Theorie und Praxis der Kooperation* Tübingen 1972.

W. Krelle, J. Schunck, J. Siebke *Überbetriebeliche Ertragsbeteiligung der Arbeitnehmer* Tübingen 1968.

Geissler, Arnulf, Fricke and Wolfgang *Demokratisierung der Wirtschaft* Hamburg 1973.

Emil Küng *Wohlstand und Wohlfahrt* Tübingen 1972.

—— *Wirtschaft und Gerechtigkeit* Tübingen 1967.

Ota Sik *The Third Way* Wildwood House 1976.

Wilfried Heidt *Der dritte Weg* Achberg 1973.

Hans Erhard Lauer *Aggression und Repression* Achberg 1973.

Wilhelm Schmundt *Revolution und Evolution* Achberg 1973.

Folkert Wilken *Selbsgestaltung der Wirtschaft* Freiburg 1949.

Rudolf Steiner *Toward Social Renewal* London 1977.

—— *Geisteswissenschaft und soziale Frage* Dornach

—— *The Social Question as a Matter of Consciousness* (Unpublished typescript available from Rudolf Steiner Library.)

—— *Threefold Order as Body Social* (Unpublished typescript, no longer directly available, but may exist in appropriate libraries.)

——*Inner Aspects of the Social Question* Rudolf Steiner Press, London.

—— *The Christ-Impulse and the Development of Ego-Consciousness,* Rudolf Steiner Press, London.

H.G. Schweppenhäuser *Das soziale Rätsel* Institut für soziale Gegenwartsfragen e.V., Berlin.

M.U. Rapold *Demokratie und Wirtschaftsordnung* Zürich 1960.

Rudolf Kreutzer *Meine Ziele* Munich 1967.

Fred Blum *Work and Community: the Scott Bader Commonwealth and the Quest for a New Social Order.*

Index